BREAKING

UPDATED EDITION

Beth Moore

LifeWay Press®
Nashville, Tennessee

Published by LifeWay Press®
© Copyright 1999. Living Proof Ministries, Inc.
Updated 2009
Second printing August 2010

ISBN 1415868026
Item 005222032

Dewey Decimal classification: 248.843
Subject heading: WOMEN-RELIGIOUS LIFE \ BIBLE.O.T. ISAIAH-STUDY AND TEACHING

Unless otherwise noted, Scripture quotations are from the Holy Bible, New International
Version, copyright © 1973, 1978, 1984 by International Bible Society. Scripture quotations
identified NASB are from the New American Standard Bible. © The Lockman Foundation, 1960,
1962, 1963, 1968, 1971, 1972, 1973, 1975, 1977. Used by permission. Scripture quotations
identified NKJV are from the New King James Version. Copyright © 1979, 1980, 1982, Thomas
Nelson, Inc. Publishers. Used by permission. Scripture quotations identified KJV are from the
King James Version. References marked *Strongs* are from *Strong's Exhaustive Concordance of the
Bible* © 1988 Hendricks Publishers.

Art Direction and Design: Jon Rodda. Design, collage illustration and hand-lettering: Juicebox
Designs. Cover Photography: David Bailey. Other photos: Getty Images: pages 8, 56, 126, 172;
iStockphoto: pages 102, 150, 194; Veer: pages 32, 78, 218. Persons pictured are models and
images are for illustrative purposes only.

To order additional copies of this resource: write LifeWay Church Resources Customer
Service; One LifeWay Plaza; Nashville, TN 37234-0113; fax (615) 251-5933; phone toll free
(800) 458-2772; order online at *www.lifeway.com;* e-mail *orderentry@lifeway.com;* or visit the
LifeWay Christian Store serving you.

Printed in the United States of America

Leadership and Adult Publishing
LifeWay Church Resources
One LifeWay Plaza
Nashville, TN 37234-0175

CONTENTS

*To my beloved staff at
Living Proof Ministries (aka The Village)
Without your trustworthy and tireless partnership,
I could not devote the majority of my time to
writing Bible studies. Thank you for sharing my
vision for God's people to get into His Word and
break free! You've inspired me, taught me, laughed
with me and cried with me. You are my very best
friends in the whole wide world.
I love you so much,
Beth Moore*

About the Author

Beth Moore has written best-selling Bible studies on the Patriarchs, Esther, David, Moses, Paul, Isaiah, Daniel, John, and Jesus. *Breaking Free, Praying God's Word*, and *When Godly People Do Ungodly Things* have all focused on the battle Satan is waging against Christians. *Believing God, Loving Well*, and *Living Beyond Yourself* have focused on how Christians can live triumphantly in today's world. *Stepping Up* explores worship and invites us to reach a new level of relationship and intimacy with God.

Beth has a passion for Christ, a passion for Bible study, and a passion to see Christians living the lives Christ intended. God bless you as you join Beth and explore the new and updated version of *Breaking Free: The Journey, the Stories.*

Introduction

I once believed only the spiritually lost were captives. God pried open my comfortably closed mind from the inside out with my life as the object lesson. I had no idea I was in captivity until God began to set me free.

As a small child I received Christ as Savior. I never missed a church service or church-related event. If anyone told me Christians could be in bondage, I'd have argued with all the volume a person can muster with a yoke of slavery strangling her. I was the worst kind of captive, a prisoner unaware. The kind of prisoner most vulnerable to her fellow cell mates.

Perhaps you're also unconvinced that Christians can live in bondage. Don't take my word for it. Take God's: "It is for freedom that Christ has set us free. Stand firm, then, and do not let yourselves be burdened again by a yoke of slavery" (Gal. 5:1). This liberty plea was directed not at the world but to the church. To genuine believers.

If you've joined me in previous Bible studies, you'll notice several differences. I will be asking you to join me in Scripture memorization this time. The Word of God, our book of truth, is the key to unlocking the gates of our prisons. Begin by memorizing Galatians 5:1. Tape it to your mirror or refrigerator, or take it in the car with you; but say it, say it, say it until the truth is engraved on your soul.

The following statement will be our definition of captivity throughout our study: **A Christian is held captive by anything that hinders the abundant and effective Spirit-filled life God planned for her.**

Our themes will come from Isaiah, a book about the captivity of God's children, the faithfulness of God, and the road to freedom. Week 1 will overview the Book of Isaiah through the lives of the kings who ruled during the prophet's ministry. These kings exemplify many of the obstacles to freedom with which we must deal. Then beginning with week two we will seek to apply the formula for freedom to our lives.

Each week contains 5 lessons requiring 30-45 minutes to complete. If you spend this kind of time in the Word of God, He will change your life. I urge you not to miss a single lesson. Get completely involved, picturing yourself as an eyewitness to the events you study. Ask God daily what He wants to say to you.

Each day will include one Principal Question, marked with an asterisk. Discussing the answers to these questions weekly in small group will help ensure each person's basic understanding of the material.

In addition to these 5 content-oriented questions, you will find a Personal Discussion Question in each lesson identified by this color of print. These learning activities help group members personally apply the material by relating the events to their own lives. The weekly group discussion will consist of 5 Principal Questions and 5 Personal Discussion Questions.

No one will be expected to share personal experiences with the group. Sharing is voluntary, and we hope no one will share anything causing herself or others harm. Please answer the questions whether or not you choose to share them in small group.

Each daily lesson begins with a Scripture called Today's Treasure representing the theme of the lesson. Each lesson will invite your full participation through Bible reading and various interactive exercises. Don't simply read my journey. This is your journey. Your full participation will enable you to make liberty in Christ a reality in your life. The letters and exerpts in the book are genuine, from past students, but the photos are models, not pictures of those students.

I primarily use the *New International Version* of the Bible in *Breaking Free*. If you do not own one, you will still be able to answer virtually every question without significant confusion. I have used several resources for study of Greek and Hebrew words. Definitions taken from *The Complete Word Study Dictionary: New Testament* and *The Complete Word Study Dictionary: Old Testament* (Chattanooga, TN: AMG Publishers), are enclosed in quotation marks with no reference. I have also used *Strong's Exhaustive Concordance of the Bible*. Words taken from Strong's are enclosed in quotation marks with the word Strong's in parentheses.

I'm so glad you're along on this trip. I believe it will be one of the most important journeys you or I have ever made. God is good to let us travel together.

BREAKING *Free*

session one viewer guide

Introductory Session

Isaiah 61:1-3 shapes the heart of our study and states the gracious intent of our God. Before we take this process forward, we'll trace it backward and capture a fascinating parallel for freedom drawn in Isaiah 9:4.

Turn to Judges 6:1-6. A few things we need to know about yokes and how they can be shattered based on the example of "_____ _____."

1. The blessed *people of God* can live under *great oppression*

   The goal of the oppressor is to make us …

   - *Unproductive* (vv. 3-4)—Hebrew *shahat*: *ruin … corrupt … lose … spill … waste.*" In the KJV terminology, the oppressors *destroyed* the *increase* ~~too possible~~ (Strong's Exhaustive Concordance.)

   - *Impoverished* (v. 6)—Hebrew *dalal*: "bring *low dry up* be *empty*, not be *equal Jail*, be impoverished." (Strong's Exhaustive Concordance)

2. If we don't seek *Freedom*, we will seek *Shelter* (v. 2 and glance ahead to v. 11).

Consider a little history on the relationship between the Israelites and the Midianites …

Read Judges 6:7-17.

John 15:8

Judges 6:11

Strongholds lead to isolation.
We hang with people that we want to be our shields.
People that shelter us also ~~protect~~ betray us.

3. God stands to get much glory from making _Mighty Warrior_ out of
   the _least likely_. _Warriors_

Read Judges 6:17-23.

Learn how to use the word of God to release
Strong holds.

4. Whatever we may end up setting _on_ the _altar_ will be _wholly_
   received by God.

5. The purpose of this journey is _not to kill us_ but to _bring_
   _us_ to the full measure of _real lyg;_ He promised us (v. 23).

Review
Isaiah
61: 1-3

* You have permission to make copies of the viewer guides.

Untying the Cords of the Yoke

He is a God who breaks strongholds.

I knew that God could set me free from my insecurity but had lived all of my life comfortable in my chains. I understood that He wanted to deal with the insecurity in my life, so I asked Him to take my shaking hand and walk me to the other side, to freedom. And He did. It's a cliché but so true— I felt like a completely different person. I see things so differently now. The world of truth outside the walls of that prison of lies is so unbelievable!

I completely laid down my life to the Lord.

Day 1
The Reign of Uzziah

Welcome to *Breaking Free*. The themes will flow from Isaiah. No book has more to say about captivity and freedom. In weeks 2 and 3 we will consider five primary benefits of our relationship with God and five obstacles that keep us from those benefits.

Since we often see ourselves best through the examples of others, this week we will begin by getting to know the kings who reigned during Isaiah's ministry. Sometimes we see traces of ourselves in them, but we will also develop a much greater appreciation of the prophet's wonderful themes as we view them against the backdrop of his day. Each day we will examine the reign of a different king who ruled Judah in Isaiah's day. We will receive important insight into the spiritual state of God's people and discover why their choices made captivity inevitable.

Isaiah 1:1 lists the four kings who reigned over Judah during Isaiah's life. Find their names in the list below and order their reigns 1, 2, 3, 4.

____ Hezekiah ____ David ____ Josiah ____ Uzziah
____ Ahaz ____ Jotham ____ Saul ____ Ahab

Before we turn to the first king, let's consider a few facts about Isaiah—God's primary spokesperson to the people of Judah during this historical period. Isaiah ministered as a prophet in and around Jerusalem in the time when Israel was a divided kingdom. After King Solomon's death in 931 B.C., the formerly united Kingdom of Israel divided to the north and the south. The Southern Kingdom took on the name Judah. The Northern Kingdom continued to be called Israel.

Isaiah primarily served the Southern Kingdom of Judah, the location of Jerusalem, the holy city. The prophets Hosea and Micah were his contemporaries. Isaiah's name means *The Lord Saves,* and the word *salvation* is used in his book 27 times—twice as many as the other Old Testament books of the prophets combined. The prophet Isaiah was married, and I think you might be blessed by the title he gave his wife in Isaiah 8:3.

What did Isaiah call his wife?

Can you imagine them being introduced as the prophet Isaiah and his beloved wife, the prophetess? I like Isaiah already, don't you? He and the Mrs. had two sons: Shear-Jashub and Maher-Shalal-Hash-Baz. I would have nicknamed them Jash and Hash to save time. I doubt that he did. Under normal circumstances he may have had a playful side, but these were not funny times. At a speaking engagement someone said to me, "I've heard you before. You used to be funnier." I grinned and retorted, "Life used to be funnier." I'm sure life used to be funnier for Isaiah too. Nothing is humorous about God's impending judgment.

Today's Treasure
"After Uzziah became powerful, his pride led to his downfall."
2 Chronicles 26:16

God moved me for a true place of humility.

Isaiah was obviously well-educated. He was probably born in Jerusalem of a family related to the royal house of Judah. God inspired him to write the longest book in the Bible written by a single author. Isaiah's ministry extended approximately 40 years, bridging 740 B.C. to at least 701 B.C. As we study each king's reign, keep in mind that before the prophecies of physical captivity were fulfilled, evidences of an internal captivity already appeared. As you study this week, look for benefits God intended for His people and obstacles to those benefits.

Isaiah's calling came, not coincidentally, right after the death of King Uzziah. To understand Isaiah, we'll launch our history lesson with a brief examination of Uzziah's reign. Please read 2 Chronicles 26:1-15; then complete the following:

The name *Uzziah* means "the Lord is my strength." In what ways does this passage suggest much of his reign was a reflection of his name?

In the margin, describe why you think Uzziah would have been a hero to a boy like Isaiah.

Did you note that Uzziah became king when only 16? The Southern Kingdom enjoyed great prosperity and protection under his reign. Although his father, Amaziah, foolishly caused the city of Jerusalem to be vulnerable (2 Chron. 25:18-23), Uzziah faithfully fortified it and raised up an army to defend it.

Isaiah's parents and grandparents must have spoken often of the close call under Amaziah's reign. They would have proclaimed the heroics of King Uzziah who saved the day, strengthening Jerusalem's ramparts once again.

The Southern Kingdom must have seemed secure, practically invulnerable to captivity. Now read 2 Chronicles 26:16-23 and complete the following:

What primary sin proved the downfall of Uzziah (v. 16)? _____

What about 2 Chronicles 26:5,15 hints that Uzziah also might have allowed the obstacle of prayerlessness to roll between himself and God?

Uzziah had more power than any other individual in the Southern Kingdom. Virtually the only authority withheld from him was the authority given to the priests of God to serve in the temple.

In the margin describe why you think Uzziah presumed this forbidden role and why the confrontation by the priests took such courage.

Just picture the scene with me. We have no idea what possessed Uzziah to suddenly grasp such a sacred task, but we certainly can assume he knew better. According to verse 5, Zechariah "instructed him in the fear of God." We can also assume that power motivated him far more than worship.

Whatever moved him to action, Uzziah rose from his throne and headed out the palace doors. He marched through town, through the temple gates, and across the courtyard. Bystanders watched and whispered. He probably took a utensil and gathered coals off the altar of sacrifice to burn the incense, then headed arrogantly into the holy place. By this time, he had the undivided attention of 81 stunned priests who summoned the courage to follow him in for a confrontation. They were not motivated by turfism but reverence for the One who had appointed them. Uzziah had not offended the priests. He had offended God.

Consider Uzziah's reaction when confronted by the priest. How do you know he hadn't just made a mistake in judgment?
☐ his pride led to his downfall   ☐ he was unfaithful to the Lord
☐ he became angry when corrected   ☐ all of the above

Parts of the Bible really make me grin. The occasional understatements get a laugh out of me almost every time. Read 2 Chronicles 26:20 one more time. I love the part that says, "Indeed, he himself was eager to leave." Yes, I suppose he was. I wonder if he got a glimpse of himself in the mirrored laver on the way out.

The rest of the story is not amusing at all. In fact, our egos could probably stand a few moments of sobering meditation on 2 Chronicles 26:21-23.

Based on all we've learned by Uzziah's example today, in the margin describe why you think God hates pride so much (Prov. 8:13).

God's hatred of pride doesn't mean He wants you to feel bad about yourself. In fact, putting ourselves down represents another twisted form of pride. God hates pride because it dethrones Him and puts ourselves at the center of our universe. I believe God's hatred of pride expresses His love. Pride slights Him, but it destroys us.

Uzziah had been a good man. An excellent king. A wonderful provider. A courageous warrior. Even a visionary and an entrepreneur (v. 15). Yet when his life was over and his body rested in the grave, all people could say was, "He had leprosy." How like our human natures—both in our tendency toward pride when we are blessed with success and in our tendency to judge someone's entire life by a brief season of failure. Pride, in itself, can lead to captivity (Jer. 13:15-17). We certainly see that it led to a real and tangible captivity in Uzziah's life.

As we close today, let's take a moment to think about a very real issue in our Christian lives. God wants very much to prosper us. I'm not thinking in terms of monetary prosperity. I'm just thinking of His desire to give us victory and successes in our efforts. He probably does not enjoy humbling us any more than we enjoy being humbled, but pride is so crippling to the believer that He often has little choice.

In the margin write your thoughts on how a person can avoid falling to the temptation of pride when he or she meets with success. Conclude by giving prayerful consideration to the example we've seen today.

Day 2
The Reign of Jotham and the Call of Isaiah

Today's Treasure

"In the year that King Uzziah died, I saw the LORD *seated on a throne, high and exalted, and the train of his robe filled the temple."* **ISAIAH 6:1**

Did you notice this week's title? We direct our efforts this week to untying the cords of the yoke. This yoke bound God's people to the captivity the prophet Isaiah foretold. We have two goals for this unit: (1) to deepen understanding of themes from the Book of Isaiah and (2) to learn more about captivity and freedom from the successes and failures of God's people.

Our method of reaching this goal is to analyze each king who reigned during Isaiah's lifetime and ministry. Yesterday we read the tragic last chapter of King Uzziah's life. The pride that captivated him internally finally captivated him externally, and he died in seclusion after a very prosperous reign. Remember, Uzziah reigned in Jerusalem 52 years, so he was the only king Isaiah had known. Uzziah must have had a tremendous impact on Isaiah. To meet the second king affecting Isaiah's ministry, today's reading will overlap yesterday's slightly. Please read 2 Chronicles 26:21–27:9. Then complete the following:

 How was Jotham similar to his father, and how was he different?

similar

different

Verse 6 tells us "Jotham grew powerful because he walked steadfastly before the LORD his God." In the margin describe why you think Jotham might not have fallen into the same trap of pride that his father did.

Though great wisdom rests in learning from the mistakes of others, we don't always learn so easily, do we? Especially when the example happens to be a parent!

What was the spiritual state of the people under Jotham's reign?
☐ corrupt   ☐ reverent   ☐ fearful   ☐ repentant

We will center our thoughts on two events in the reign of Jotham: Isaiah's call and the corrupt practices of the people. Read Isaiah 6:1-8 slowly and aloud. We want to look at Isaiah's call to see what we can learn about the kings who reigned during his lifetime. Keep our task in mind as you complete the following:

If you could describe God with just one word based on Isaiah's vision, what would it be?

Isaiah's vision of God caused a sudden awareness of what specific sin?
☐ idolatry ☐ adultery ☐ pride
☐ unclean lips ☐ impure thoughts

As overwhelming as the vision must have been, why do you think Isaiah so readily responded to the call? Respond in the margin.

Isaiah grew up under the reign of the mighty King Uzziah and no doubt idolized him as a young boy. Imagine the future prophet with his friends, squeezing through the crowds gathered in the marketplace when the victorious King Uzziah returned in pomp and splendor after the crumbling of the walls of Gath.

Imagine the excitement that permeated the tiny homes in Jerusalem when the watchman on the wall announced the coming of the ambassador of Ammon, bringing tribute to King Uzziah. As the little boys played war, they would have fought over who got to play the part of King Uzziah. Now he had the audacity to die and leave them hero-less. Perfect timing. "In the year that King Uzziah died, I saw the Lord."

In no way do I want to minimize the pain and tremendous challenge of losing a very important hero-figure. The experience can seem earth-shattering; and if we were loyal enough to the old, it can leave us bitter toward the new.

Have you ever lost a hero? ☒ Yes ☐ No
If so, who was it and why was he or she such a hero to you? *Fair -*

Gentleman

I could never express the challenge of facing the passing of a hero like the anointed tongue of the late Oswald Chambers. These words are so important to me, I practically have them memorized. Read and meditate.

> Our soul's history with God is frequently the history of the "passing of the hero." Over and over again God has to remove our friends in order to bring Himself in their place, and that is where we faint and fail and get discouraged. Take it personally: In the year that the one who stood to me for all that God was, died—I gave up everything? I became ill? I got disheartened? Or—I saw the Lord?
>
> It must be God first, God second, and God third, until the life is faced steadily with God and no one else is of any account whatever. "In all the world there is none but thee, my God, there is none but thee." Keep paying the price. Let God see that you are willing to live up to the vision.[1]

Oswald Chambers was not suggesting those who are devoted to God are those who do not care for others. We are to love one another, share each other's burdens, and actively encourage one another as the body of Christ. We are to reach out to the lost and care for the downtrodden.

So what do you think Chambers meant when he wrote "until the life is faced steadily with God and no one else is of any account whatever"?

I believe Isaiah idolized King Uzziah. When he pictured a throne, he most likely pictured Uzziah, not the King of all creation, sitting on it. He, as well as most of his fellow patriots, did not look on King Uzziah as a simple instrument in the mighty hand of God. They saw a mighty man who, at the most, used God as an instrument for victory.

I love to watch the playoffs of most any sport. Something about naming a team or a player as the best excites me. I always watch the interviews afterward and sit smugly satisfied when the winners thank God for the victory. Yet I must confess I don't grab the next morning's newspaper to read about God. It's the star player. Although the star may thank God, it's not God who gets the ring. The team doesn't retire God's number. They don't boast about His statistics. And we wouldn't expect them to. The point is—the players become the heroes. At best, some may mention God as their means to their heroic end. I believe this scenario was true of King Uzziah. He may have sought God in advance for strength and victory and he may have thanked God when He delivered, but the king didn't go out of his way to resist heroics. Finally, he believed his own press. Big mistake.

I see an important point emerge from his example. A wide gulf lies between thanking God for our wonderful victories and pointing people to God as the One and only Sovereign victorious. People crave a human worth worshiping. We are wise not to try to deliver. Uzziah accidentally left poor Jotham hopeless to measure up in the minds of many. I believe Isaiah was one of them.

Notice Isaiah 6:1 does not say, "In the year Jotham became king, I saw the Lord." Not the existence of something new but the removal of something old opened Isaiah's eyes to the kingship of God. At no time is our vision more capable of seeing God in His rightful place than when the focus of our former attentions has been removed from our sight. Sadly, however, the removal of our earthly king could be to no avail. Like the people of Isaiah's day, we can choose to be everseeing, but never perceiving.

Can you think of a time when you allowed God to change your focus from someone else to Him? In the margin describe the circumstances.

Now let's turn our attention to what Isaiah saw when God called him. The light of His glory not only shined on the throne room of God but it also fell on the carnal man before Him. The more Isaiah saw God, the clearer he saw himself. He was

People crave a human worth worshiping. We are wise not to deliver.

undone (v. 5, KJV), *ruined* (NIV). The word means "to be destroyed ... a violent end." He had just heard the sound of the angels roaring, "Holy, holy, holy is the LORD Almighty!" If when the angels spoke, the door posts and thresholds shook, what in the world would happen when he opened unclean lips and tried to speak? In his opinion, he was as good as dead. All he could do was confess his sin.

This was Isaiah's brilliant moment. No other response fit. For unclean lips to join in praising the holiness of God would have been as unthinkable as King Uzziah burning incense in the temple. Isaiah was probably just as corrupt in mind, mouth, and practice as the people surrounding him. To make a point, God often calls the unworthy, present company included. I don't believe He called Isaiah because he was a man of character, like Noah. I suspect He may have called him because he was just as sinful as the rest of them. Who better to speak to the sins of the people than one who has also sinned and turned to God?

Reread 2 Chronicles 27:2. This verse takes the spiritual temperature of the people of Isaiah's community. The mercury hardly shows. Their leader, Jotham, walked steadfastly before the Lord. He did not enter the temple of the Lord like his father. Yet the people continued their corrupt practices. Why? Probably because of a little tidbit of information appearing in 2 Kings 15:32-35.

What did Jotham fail to do?
☐ remove the high places ☐ restore the temple ☐ fortify Jerusalem

The high places were sites elevated on hilltops and dedicated to worship of pagan gods.[2] Alarming, isn't it? The thought of the people of God building shrines to other gods is almost unthinkable, yet they did it over and over. God warned His people constantly not to take on the practices of the Canaanite pagans. He told them He would not share His glory with another and that such practices would surely lead them into captivity.

Jotham sought God faithfully and walked steadfastly before Him, but he refused to demand respect for the one and only God. Jotham was boss. He could have destroyed the high places, but he obviously feared the people more than he feared God. Jotham conquered nations, but he refused to rule his own people. He chose to overlook a terribly grievous sin.

Is it any wonder God called a man by the name of Isaiah out of the midst of the people? He was one of them, yet a cut above. Educated. Opinionated. Of probable means. Like the rest of us, Isaiah probably tended to act like whomever he spent his time with. Then one day, "he saw the Lord seated on a throne, high and exalted."

That's the only way we'll ever truly see the Lord. He cannot be less than who He is. That day God cleansed the lips of Isaiah to speak some of the most poetic expressions that ever kissed a scroll. For indeed, out of the overflow of a changed heart the mouth most beautifully speaks. May we voluntarily dethrone every Uzziah and every Jotham in our lives and put them in their rightful places. Only then are we free to see the Lord seated on a throne, high and lifted up, as we journey to our destination.

God lifted me.

How does God want you to respond to what He showed you today?

Day 3
The Reign of Ahaz

In the lives of Uzziah and his son Jotham we have seen huge obstacles of *pride* and an unwillingness to stand against *idolatry*. We also saw a continuous suggestion of *unbelief*, because they were warned over and over about the consequences of their defiance. As we continue our study of the kings in Isaiah's day, note that the same obstacles they faced confront us as we seek to enjoy the benefits of salvation.

God chose the nation of Israel as a people to experience His benefits, but they resisted His blessings. God's people spurned the benefits of their covenant relationship with God. Yet He remained faithful. Though they suffered the consequences of their actions, God never deserted His people. He always had a plan for their deliverance. Today as we peer into the life of the third king, keep in mind the term *Judah* represents the Southern Kingdom and *Israel* represents the Northern Kingdom. In today's reading you will see them at war against each another. Read 2 Chronicles 28:1-15 and complete the questions that follow. Verse 1 refers to David as the father of Ahaz. Actually, Jotham was the father of Ahaz, but he was born in the lineage of the great King David.

Based on verses 1-4, identify Ahaz's evil practices. Check all that apply.
☐ He made cast idols for worshiping the Baals.
☐ He worshiped the Babylonian god Tammuz.
☐ He burned his sons in the fire as sacrifices.
☐ He offered sacrifices and burned incense at the high places.
☐ He walked in the ways of the kings of Israel.

How did God show His disfavor to King Ahaz and the nation of Judah according to verse 5? Choose one.
☐ He struck the people with diseases.
☐ He dried up the water.
☐ He allowed them to be defeated in battle.
☐ He shortened the reign of Ahaz.

The Lord was angry with the Southern Kingdom, but He also became upset with the Northern Kingdom.

In the margin describe what the Northern Kingdom did to displease God according to Oded, the prophet who served Israel (vv. 9-11).

Review verses 13-15. Like the leaders of Ephraim (the Northern Kingdom of Israel), a reminder of our own guilt should have a tremendous impact on how we treat others who are also "guilty."

The soldiers didn't just set the captives free. What else did they do?

Clearly God never wanted His people to be taken prisoner by their enemies nor did He desire to see them take *others* captive. Especially their own countrymen!

With all my heart I believe God hates meanness for meanness' sake. God never heaps more chastisement on His children than necessary for their benefit and return to obedience. The Northern Kingdom was enjoying being avengers more than victors. Victory can surface the contents of a heart faster than a sprinter can leave the starting blocks. Which do we tend to enjoy most: God-given victory or our foe's defeat? Our attitude can be the litmus test. Does victory humble us and bring us to our knees in thanksgiving to God, or does victory make us proud and arrogant toward those less victorious?

In this case, the soldiers responded rightly to the admonition of their leaders. If only Ahaz, the king of Judah, had also seen the error of his ways. Read 2 Chronicles 28:16-27, and complete the following:

King Ahaz sent to the _____ for help (v. 16).
If the Lord humbled Judah because of the unfaithfulness of Ahaz, what should he have done instead of seeking help from a heathen king?

We might be tempted to think Ahaz felt God would no longer hear him if he cried out to Him. Wrong. Read the events and dialogue that took place at this same time, according to Isaiah 7:1-13.

How did King Ahaz reveal stunning foolishness in these verses?

In your opinion, did Ahaz have a greater problem with unbelief, pride, idolatry, prayerlessness, or legalism? Why? Respond in the margin.

Ahaz had the perfect opportunity to receive God's merciful help, but he refused, preferring to ask the king of Assyria instead. The foolishness of his decision seems so clear to us, yet often God yearns for us to ask His help; instead, we also look for the aid of human agents.

Why do you think we make this kind of choice at times?

Jesus has set me free!

Reread Isaiah 7:13. Why is God so patient according to 2 Peter 3:9?

We can hardly comprehend how God can be so merciful. He was willing to hear the repentant cry of a king who had personally worshiped idols and had even sacrificed his own son in the fire! Does this example not prove God can forgive any sin if true repentance occurs? Please do not miss the fact that Ahaz had "offered sacrifices and burned incense at the high places." Look back at 2 Kings 15:32-35.

✳ **Why were high places accessible to a young and impressionable Ahaz?**

The atrocity Jotham chose to ignore was the one that snared his own son. Because of the ever-increasing nature of wickedness (Rom. 6:19), Ahaz descended from sacrificing offerings at the high places to personally casting idols, to sacrificing his own child. Yet God would have forgiven him if he had come to repentance.

Do you find the prospect of God's forgiveness of Ahaz hard to believe? Glance forward two generations (2 Chron. 33:1-20) to Manasseh, grandson of Ahaz. We are momentarily looking into the future to make a point regarding God's mercy.

What hints do you see that Manasseh's wickedness may have surpassed even that of Ahaz? Respond in the margin.

Compare 2 Chronicles 33:10 and 11. How do these Scriptures suggest Manasseh might have been able to avoid being taken prisoner?

We might say that Manasseh "hit rock bottom" in verse 11. How might this terrible descent have been considered a "blessing in disguise"?

Some of us would never have looked up had we not hit bottom. We often don't recognize our captivity until the enemy has a hook through our noses! I hope we're going to learn to thank God for the times misery led to liberty, but we're also going to try to learn how to recognize a foreign yoke prior to receiving the hook!

Our momentary hopscotch into the future has offered us a vivid picture of God's mercy to a horribly wicked king. Second Chronicles 33:13 says when Manasseh prayed, "The LORD was moved by his entreaty and listened to his plea." Manasseh ended up repenting of his actions, ridding the nation of the foreign gods and idol altars, and instructing the people to serve the Lord. He has a unique distinction of being possibly the worst and one of the best kings of Israel. Note that when Manasseh reigned the Northern Kingdom had been destroyed, so the term *Israel* once again referred to Judah. How's that for confusing?

Now let's return to Ahaz. God would have extended the same mercy to him if only he had prayed and shown his repentance through godly actions. According to Isaiah 7, God invited Ahaz to reach out to Him and ask for a sign.

Why do you think God wanted Ahaz rather than Isaiah to ask for the sign? After all, Isaiah was the prophet God had assigned to Judah.

God is the glorious initiator of reconciliation. Isaiah could not bridge the gap that separated Ahaz from the God of his fathers. God extended His hand of mercy to carry the wayward king across the chasm, but Ahaz would not grab hold.

Ahaz was in captivity long before his people were. He was the saddest kind of captive, one who refused to be free on God's terms—the only terms that exist for authentic freedom.

What excuse did Ahaz give for not asking God for a sign in Isaiah 7:12?

Ahaz referred to the command in Deuteronomy 6:16. This is the same man who had broken several of the Ten Commandments in staggering ways. What a time for legalism! If God had given Ahaz permission to ask for a sign, He obviously would not have been *tested* and offended by the request! God is the One who establishes His laws, and He can override with a higher law anytime He pleases.

"Do not test the Lord *your God as you did at Massah."*
Deuteronomy 6:16

No wonder the people of God were on their way to captivity! Their king was captive to sin and refused to be loosed. I fear that in the same way many Christian leaders have led their flocks to places of captivity rather than liberty because they themselves were in bondage. I've known the terrible burden of leadership when I was still tied in the knots of painful bonds. I also know the joy of leadership as a freed woman and it is worth anything. *Christ* is worth anything.

Some years ago, a fine pastor unknowingly worked himself into the bondage of fear through a lengthy, uninterrupted study of spiritual warfare. He became very unbalanced in his teaching, only preaching on Satan, the powers of darkness, and warfare. Ultimately he began practicing exorcisms on Sundays in the time frame that once was used for an invitation to receive Christ. Needless to say, his congregation also became unbalanced and fell captive to fear. This leader had been chosen to glorify God and at one time his ministry radiated with Christ, but eventually only the enemy was "glorified."

How does God want you to respond to what He showed you today?

Hopefully, far greater numbers of leaders are faithfully leading their flocks in paths of freedom. The point is clear: If we are leaders of any kind, we have an even greater responsibility to make liberty in Christ a reality in life. Not only is the quality of our Christian lives at great risk, but also the quality of those lives following us are at risk. As leaders we're tempted to answer, "But we're only human too!" The apostle Paul penned a wonderful statement that stands as the rebuttal to the plea that Christians are nothing more than feeble humanity.

As you conclude today, in the margin paraphrase 2 Corinthians 4:7.

We don't want to be like Ahaz in any conceivable way. God's will for our lives is freedom in Christ. No matter what kind of gulf seems to stand between authentic liberty and us, God is extending His hand. He has given us the power of the Holy Spirit to help us grab on for dear life.

Day 4
The Reign of Hezekiah

Today's Treasure

"Then Isaiah said to Hezekiah, 'Hear the word of the LORD Almighty: The time will surely come when everything in your palace, and all that your fathers have stored up until this day, will be carried off to Babylon. Nothing will be left, says the LORD.'" **Isaiah 39:5-6**

Today's lesson will be a pleasant respite in many ways after our disconcerting look at King Ahaz, whose actions were shocking even in comparison to pagan dynasties. How disturbing to realize he was the king of Judah. Titles and heritage mean nothing if the king of the chosen nation has no heart for God.

Today we consider a remarkable phenomenon—one that is highly improbable without God. We will study the righteous son of an unrighteous father. Scripture has more to say about this particular king than we have time and space to contemplate, and yet I want you to know as much as possible for our purposes. Expect lots of reading today, but I think you will find it interesting. Begin by reading 2 Chronicles 29:1-11,29-30; 30:1-15; 31:1,20-21.

✳ Why do you think Hezekiah turned out so differently from his father?

Hezekiah's grandfather, Jotham, also had been a good and righteous king. What did Hezekiah do, however, that Jotham failed to do? Compare 2 Kings 15:35 and 2 Chronicles 31:1.

As you can see, Hezekiah was a godly king who wholeheartedly sought both reformation and restoration. He sought to restore Israel to her godly identity. She had a divided heart and had ceased fulfilling her God-given purpose. Hezekiah's defiance of his father's rule and his tireless attempt to usher the nation to her former relationship with God showed both guts and grit.

I wonder when Hezekiah's attitudes and philosophies began to depart from his father's. Is it possible he resented losing a brother on a pagan altar and distrusted any father who could do such a thing? Notice we read no insult directed personally toward Ahaz, but we need not wonder if Hezekiah had strong feelings about his father's reign because his own seemed opposite in every way.

Now let's continue our reading about this intriguing Old Testament figure. Read 2 Chronicles 32:1-23.

The Southern Kingdom easily could have gone into captivity during the invasion of Judah by Sennacherib (king of Assyria). Verse 22 intimates that God was honored by how Hezekiah handled the attack of a mighty enemy.

What kind of tactics would you say Sennacherib used against Hezekiah and the Southern Kingdom of Judah? Check all that apply.
☐ He used fear and intimidation.
☐ He attempted to overwhelm them with force.
☐ He tried to undermine their faith.
☐ He sought to cause them to distrust God.

Please don't miss an important point: According to 2 Chronicles 32:1, we can be faithful to God and centered in His will and still be attacked by the enemy. Sometimes our enemy attacks the weak and wandering believers because they are easy prey. Other times he attacks competent, fully surrendered servants of God for the challenge and the possible contagious effect of a fall.

> We can be faithful to God and still be attacked by the enemy.

     Let's not be fooled into thinking we can somehow avoid all Satan's attempts to take us captive. We are wise never to consider ourselves invulnerable, so that we stay alert and aware at all times. Satan cannot force us to go where he leads, but he can certainly choose a scenic route for a lure.

From the tone of 2 Chronicles 32:20, Hezekiah and Isaiah were obviously frightened, but what did they do with their fears?

Sometimes faith is the absence of fear. Other times faith may be choosing to believe God even when your heart is melting with fear. Perhaps, then, faith is tested by what we do with fear, not whether or not we have it. Hezekiah may have considered Sennacherib's attack to be the most frightening experience of his life … until he was hit with a different kind of fear, a far more personal kind. The saga of Hezekiah continues. Read all of Isaiah 38.

What are some fairly typical or expected things Hezekiah felt and thought after he found out he was going to die?

What did Hezekiah vow to do because he had suffered such anguish of the soul? Choose one.

☐ help the oppressed ☐ walk humbly all his years
☐ offer a sacrifice to God ☐ praise God

Did you note that God healed Hezekiah through medical treatment? Obviously God did not build a wall between faith and using medicine.

My heart breaks every time I see a grown man cry. Being blessed with the emotions of a woman, I can cry over greeting card commercials. I'm not ashamed of it. I rather like it. Many men are so different, though. I guess I am particularly touched when men cry because I realize how moved most must be before they resort to tears. My heart tenders at the thought of Hezekiah, the mighty king of Judah, turning his face to the wall to cry so no one but God could see him.

I remember when Michael, our son for seven years, used to cry. The older he got, the more he hid his face when the tears started to roll. The more personal the matter, the more he did not want anyone to see him cry. Nothing could have hit Hezekiah more personally. He wasn't fighting this present battle for Judah's sake. This time he was on his own. The royal counsel couldn't help. The king's army couldn't fight it off. Somehow death has a way of stripping us of all status, power, and privilege, doesn't it? We're on our own with God … and we want to know Him before we get there.

God was also obviously touched by Hezekiah's tears and pleas. He extended his life for 15 years and gave him a remarkable sign by reversing the movement of the sun's shadow, causing time to go backward for a moment as a symbol.

No sooner had Hezekiah recovered than he started making "knowing" statements, as if his close encounter with death came with an automatic doctorate. He said things like, "In your love you kept me from the pit of destruction," as if the death or decision to spare one of God's own has anything to do with love. He cannot love us any more or any less than He does this moment. His healing has nothing to do with loving one person more than another. Hezekiah also assumed God gave him 15 more years because only those living on this earth can praise Him (v. 19). All these years I've figured my best abilities to praise God would come with my death and until then I was severely limited. Neither of these statements by Hezekiah was the biggy, though. Someone should have stuffed that fig poultice in his mouth before he was able to utter, "I will walk humbly all my years because of this anguish of my soul." You're about to find out why. We have two last segments to read. First, read 2 Chronicles 32:24-33.

Where did Hezekiah temporarily go wrong?

Each of us has a crippling tendency to forget what God has done for us. For a while, we're humbled. Then, if we don't guard our hearts and minds, we begin to think God is so good to us because we have done something right.

I RECEIVED CHRIST AS A LITTLE GIRL BUT DID NOT LIVE AS A FREE CHILD OF GOD.

Truly God is compassionate. But He hears the cries of the just and the unjust, the righteous and the unrighteous. We never will be able to figure out why God responds differently to the cries He hears; but we trust He is always good, always right, and always loving. I believe Hezekiah may have decided his life was spared more on the basis of merit than mercy. One last reading … and it's a sobering one. Let's find out where pride raised its ugly head. Read Isaiah 39:1-8.

To whom did Hezekiah show his treasures?

What does the constant repetition of the word *his* in verse 2 suggest?

Hezekiah's actions typify someone rubbing shoulders with an enemy. Babylon would be the nation to take Judah into captivity. Because he was so anxious to show off his treasures, all of which belonged to God, he foolishly led the enemy into far too much familiarity. Hezekiah let down his guard and enjoyed the approval of the godless.

How do we also tend to flaunt our treasures to the godless, enjoying their favor and approval?

> Hezekiah let down his guard and enjoyed the approval of the godless.

At some point after his uprising of pride, Hezekiah repented according to 2 Chronicles 32:26, but we are wise not to miss his stunning response after Isaiah foretold the captivity of Judah in Isaiah 39:8.

Why wasn't Hezekiah devastated over Judah's coming captivity?

I believe we do not think about nor pray enough for our descendants—our children, grandchildren, and their children. Our actions, both good and bad, will have consequences after we are absent from this earth. While we are enjoying the bliss of heaven and the mercy of God's grace, our grandchildren still could be reaping painful consequences of situations we've sown. Or, on the other hand, they could be enjoying the benefits of faithful lives lived by great-grandparents whom they may never have known.

I won't soon forget Hezekiah. His life is a blatant reminder that no one is immune to foolish actions fueled by pride. We may be afraid to ask God on a daily basis to keep us humble because we know humility will involve discomfort. We may have to suffer some embarrassment, even some failure. I ask this of myself as much as I ask it of you: Why are we not far more frightened of what pride can do? Pride can cost us—and probably those after us.

Several years ago I began developing the habit of confessing and repenting of pride daily, even if I may not have been aware of its presence. I asked God to show me where it was raising up its head or sneaking up on me. So often God will show me little bits of pride that, if left to grow, could be devastating. Let me share a recent example.

I decided the time had come to purchase a new Bible. My other one looked like someone had accidentally put it in the dishwasher and turned the dial to "pot scrubber." Let me assure you that no bookstore employee likes to help me buy a new Bible. To me it's like choosing a mate! I pull out at least 20 different Bibles and by the time I've inspected all of them, the whole shelf looks like it's been through an automatic car wash. I finally decided on one.

A new Bible takes some "breaking in" so the pages turn readily. I told my coworkers that I was going to keep the new one at work until I could get accustomed to it and still take my old one on speaking engagements for a while. As the words came out of my mouth, the Holy Spirit seemed to whisper in my ear, "Sounds like pride to Me." He was right. I didn't want to have to struggle to find Scriptures in front of a group. I felt sick to my stomach. That moment I put up my old Bible. I've flip-flopped my way through the new one ever since.

Did you notice in our study this week that the godly kings seemed to struggle with issues of pride more than the ungodly kings? How can you personally apply this point and guard against it in your own life?

You've worked so hard with me today. I know we've read an abundance of Scripture, but I think I've learned something "for keeps" and I hope you have too. Please allow me to conclude with one last point.

How does God want you to respond to what He showed you today?

By the time the Babylonian prince sent envoys to Hezekiah, the Northern Kingdom (still called Israel) was already in captivity to Assyria. I sense a strong message in Hezekiah's failure to be on his guard with the heathen prince's advances. You see, he considered Assyria to be the threat so he didn't consider Babylon to be a problem. He was so cautious with one foe that he didn't see the other one coming. He thought captivity could only come one way. Big mistake. Eighty years later, the kingdom of Judah would be overtaken by the mighty Babylonians.

God taught me a shocking lesson a few years ago. I had guarded myself diligently regarding men. Little did I know that an unstable woman who struggled with homosexuality would become obsessed with me. I was prepared for the advances of men; I was totally unprepared for the advance of a woman.

Beloved, we have much to learn. Ignorance is not our friend. God used my experience to help me discern not only well-hidden instability in people who approach me at times but also to be on guard in relationships with women as well as men. May God use this Bible study powerfully in each of our lives so that we will know how to protect ourselves from every direction.

Day 5
The Reign of Christ

We began our study by getting to know the kings who reigned in Isaiah's lifetime. In chapters 1–35, Isaiah preached about the rebellion of God's people and the threat of the Assyrians against Judah and Jerusalem. The Northern Kingdom was taken captive by Assyria in 722 B.C. In chapters 36–39, Isaiah recorded Assyria's defeat by the Southern Kingdom as King Hezekiah rightly responded to Sennacherib's attack. Isaiah also recorded the illness of Hezekiah—his bout with pride and the future rise of Babylon.

We've learned something important from our study of Judah's kings. Not even the best were sufficient. Not even the most honorable were holy. Not even the most humble were immune to pride. No earthly leader is incapable of misleading. Sometimes leaders' saddest detours are made trying to gain approval from fickle followers. Many leaders battle areas of personal and internal captivity. If our liberty in Christ is going to be a reality in life, we are going to have to learn to walk in the freedom of Christ, independent of everyone else we know. In our quest for freedom, we don't just need a leader. Someone could lead us to freedom and we could still return to captivity.

We need more than a leader on our road to freedom. We need someone to stick around and empower us to remain free. We need a Savior—One who keeps on saving. Many people only think of salvation as their initial invitation for Christ to forgive them and come into their lives. Although we need to be *saved* from eternal separation from God only once, Christ continues His saving work in us for the rest of our lives.

Can you think of a few potential disasters from which Christ saved you since your initial experience of salvation?

Chapters 36–39 precede a new theme in Isaiah. In chapters 40–66, God inspired Isaiah to prophesy about the time when the captivity would approach an end; Israel would be comforted by God and restored to her appointed purpose. I love the way God worded the prophetic turning point in the Book of Isaiah after He declared her grievous sins and chastisements in the first half of the book.

Write Isaiah 40:1 in the space below.

Today's Treasure

"The Spirit of the Sovereign LORD is on me, because the LORD has anointed me to preach good news to the poor. He has sent me to bind up the brokenhearted, to proclaim freedom for the captives and release from darkness for the prisoners." **ISAIAH 61:1**

Isn't that a wonderful verse? The next verse begins with the words, "Speak tenderly to Jerusalem." Oh, how I thank God for tender words He has spoken to me after I have been chastened for sin. Many of them have come from the Book of Isaiah.

We will learn volumes from both, but we stand to receive much healing from God's words of comfort. Sometimes I wonder why He continues to be so faithful. Yes, He is faithful to chastise or how would we otherwise learn from our rebellion? But He is also so compassionate in His comfort. Like Israel and Judah, much of our own captivity is caused by failure to remove obstacles of unbelief, pride, idolatry, prayerlessness, and Spirit-quenching legalism; yet God still woos us to a spacious place free of earthly bonds.

Please consider the following statement carefully because it is the crucial connector between the Book of Isaiah and our study of freedom: God chose the Book of Isaiah, a treatise on captivity, to record some of the most remarkable prophecies about Christ in the entire Old Testament. In a book through which God prophesied the horrors of a foreign yoke, He introduced the Deliverer.

In some instances, God fulfilled prophecies temporarily through a human agent like Cyrus while ultimately fulfilling them in Christ. In the segment of Scripture that provides the foundation for this study, we see undeniable proof that these Scriptures are fulfilled in the Messiah, Jesus Christ. Give utmost attention to Isaiah 61:1-4. Read these verses aloud if possible. Let's draw several important points from these wonderful Scriptures.

1. God hears the cry of the oppressed. God even hears the cries of those who have been oppressed as a result of sin and rebellion. We must never cease believing God cares about those in physical, emotional, mental, or spiritual prisons. Everything that concerns us is God's domain. God issued Isaiah 61:1-4 as a response to the captivity He foresaw as He looked down on rebellious Judah.

Let's take a look at a much earlier instance when God looked down on the slavery of His people. I want you to see that part of God's consistent character is wooing the captive to freedom. Read Exodus 3:7. Notice that God initiated the saving relationship between the people and the Liberator.

What impact was slavery having on the Israelites? Were they
☐ suffering?   ☐ turning to sin?   ☐ forgetting God?

What did God hear?
☐ their complaints   ☐ their groanings   ☐ their cries

When we are suffering because of captivity (or for any other reason), we must learn to cry out! Yes, of course, God sees our suffering and cares deeply for us, but acknowledging the slavery is a crucial starting place toward authentic freedom.

In Exodus 3:7, the King James Version says: "I know their sorrows." The Hebrew word for *know* suggests a deeply intimate relationship and perception. God is intimately acquainted with the sorrows and suffering that result from slavery of any kind. He also has a remedy. He is the meeter of our needs.

God chose Isaiah to record some of the most remarkable prophecies about Christ.

Whether the Israelites fell victim to their taskmasters as in Exodus or walked into slavery because of disobedience and idolatry as in the Book of Isaiah, God had deliverance in mind for them. As long as the sun comes up in the morning, God will keep offering to deliver His children. As Psalm 102:17-18 says, "He will respond to the prayer of the destitute; he will not despise their plea. Let this be written for a future generation, that a people not yet created may praise the LORD." We are one of those future generations suffering from captivity.

For every captive, God sent a Deliverer. God's liberating words in Isaiah 61:1-4 concerning the One who was sent to proclaim freedom for the captives apply just as surely to us as they did to the Israelites as they faced Babylonian captivity. They will continue to apply as long as God looks down from the height of His sanctuary, views the earth, and hears the groaning of the prisoner.

2. God fulfills Isaiah 61:1-4 in Christ alone. Luke 4:14-21 records the beginning of Jesus' ministry in Galilee. He quoted Isaiah 61 as His personal charter. Look at the context of Luke 4:14-21.

What had Christ just been through according to Luke 4:1-13?

How are we told He returned to Galilee in Luke 4:14?
☐ by way of the sea ☐ in the power of the Spirit ☐ weak and famished

How encouraging to know that because the Spirit of God dwells in us, we too can come out of temptation more empowered by the Spirit than ever! Let's take a look at the fulfillment of Isaiah 61:1-4 in Christ. Notice both Isaiah 61:1 and Luke 4:14 tell us that Christ Jesus, the Deliverer sent by God, would be empowered by the Spirit of God. Through our study, we are going to see how important the Holy Spirit is to making freedom in Christ a reality in life.

Second Corinthians 3:17 will become a vital truth to us. It tells us that "where the Spirit of the Lord is, there is _____."

Christ sets us free by the power of His Spirit; then He maintains our freedom as we learn to live from day to day in the power of His free Spirit. According to Isaiah 61 and Luke 4, only Christ was appointed by God to offer this kind of freedom.

Luke 4:16 tells us that Christ customarily came to the synagogue in His hometown on the Sabbath. With a fresh anointing, commission, and compassion, Christ stood before His audience and unrolled the scroll to the most glorious job description ever given. Can you imagine Him reading the eternal words of His Father? Words that had waited centuries for their fulfillment! There before the audience stood their hometown boy—the Lord wrapped in flesh—the fullness of the Godhead bodily (Col. 2:9, KJV). He read the words describing Himself, rolled up the scroll, sat down, waited until every eye was on Him, and said, "Today this Scripture is fulfilled in your hearing." Hallelujah!

The Word says, "All spoke well of him and were amazed." I am touched again by the realization that speaking well of Christ and even being amazed by His works or words does not equal belief.

3. Christ's ministry is a ministry of the heart. God sent Christ in the fullness and power of His Spirit to bring the heart under the freeing authority of God's Word. Look back at Jesus' job description in Isaiah 61:1-4.

List all the ministries God anointed His glorious Ambassador to fulfill.

Christ came forth to "bind up the brokenhearted, to proclaim freedom for the captives and release from darkness for the prisoners … to comfort all who mourn … to bestow on them a crown of beauty instead of ashes … a garment of praise instead of a spirit of despair" (Isa. 61:1-3). Anyone who takes the heart out of the gospel frankly doesn't have a lot left. Jeremiah 17:9 tells us "the heart is deceitful above all things." Therefore, nothing needs the infiltration of God's truth more than the heart. We will find freedom to the degree our hearts accept, rely, and respond to the truth of God's Word.

At this point in your relationship with God, which of the following statements best describes you?
☐ I am completely comfortable with prioritizing the heart.
☐ I tend to wonder what is wrong with people who become emotional during Bible study or worship.
☐ I am more comfortable with intellectual Bible lessons and sermons.
☐ I have surrendered to God full access to my heart.

Let Isaiah 61 and Luke 4 stand as proof to you that setting captives free is an absolute priority to Christ, and the involvement of the heart is a necessity. Based on 2 Peter 3:9, His first priority is setting captives free from the bondage of eternal destruction, but saved people can still be in bondage (Gal. 5:1).

What do you think of when you think of Christians who remain captives to some area of bondage?

When I think of bondage, I most often imagine yokes that come from some area of childhood trauma or victimization. Why? Because the yoke formed in my childhood has been the biggest area of captivity I personally have had to combat. I make this point because most of us unknowingly limit our perceptions of captivity to those bonds we've personally witnessed or experienced. For this study to be most effective, let's receive the challenge to expand our thinking about captivity.

When I realized God was calling me to write this study, I asked the group of women I teach to broaden my horizon in terms of areas of captivity believers can face. I asked any of them who had been set free from an area of bondage to consider sharing with me two pieces of information through a letter:

- the specific area of captivity they faced
- the specific ways and lengths of time God employed to set them free

I'm not sure anything could have prepared me for their responses. I have permission from some of them to use excerpts from their letters at appropriate times in this study. Although they will remain unnamed, you know women just like them. These respondents are bright, educated Christian women. They serve faithfully in their churches. Many sing in the choir. They come from all economic backgrounds. For fear of judgment many of them have never told anyone but a godly counselor what they battled.

I heard painful testimonies of bondage to lust and a pattern of falling into sexual sin. I tearfully read about struggles with homosexuality and a fear of men because of childhood abuse. Some spoke about a previous inability to love people fully, including their own husbands and children. One wrote me about the victory God had given her over a compulsion to steal. Another had been freed from habitual dishonesty.

A friend I never would have suspected wrote me about her freedom from the bitterness flowing from physical abuse she endured as a child. My heart broke for one woman who described how deep insecurity had stolen friendships, church work, and a contented marriage from her. I've heard from many who were held captive by a critical and judgmental heart toward people. Others had wrestled terribly with anger toward God. Doubt. Discouragement. Loneliness. A chronic lack of satisfaction.

Please keep in mind that these letters were only from those who had found freedom in Christ. Imagine how many are still struggling! Believer,

- Christ came to set the captive free—no matter what kind of yoke may be binding them.
- He came to bind up the brokenhearted—no matter what broke the heart.
- He came to open the eyes of the blind—no matter what may have veiled their vision.

How does God want you to respond to what He showed you today?

1. Oswald Chambers, *My Utmost For His Highest* (Westwood, NJ: Barbour and Company, Inc., 1935), 195.
2. Trent C. Butler et al., eds., *Holman Bible Dictionary* (Nashville: Holman Bible Publishers, 1991), 645.

BREAKING Free

session two viewer guide

Few books of the Bible are more fascinating or more prophetically baffling than the Book of Isaiah. Not coincidentally, the name of the prophet—and subsequently the book—means "The _Lord saves_ or "The _Lord is Savior_." It is a hotbed of messianic prophecies, several of which are grouped in sizeable segments we'll read today.

Segment One
Isaiah 9:1-7 prophesies _Christ's Birth_

Segment Two
Isaiah 61:1-3 prophesies _Christ's Ministry_

• See Luke 4:14-21. Christ takes complete _ownership_ over the job description given in Isaiah 61:1-3.

• Compare Luke 8:40-48. In verse 44 the word translated "edge" (*Kraspedon*) is "used for the _tassles_ the Israelites wore on the _4 corners_ of their _garments_ (*Word Bible Commentary*) According to the New International Commentary of the New Testament, "This is the story of her resolution to _cross the border_ of legitimate behavior to gain _access to divine power_."

Segment Three
Isaiah 52:13–53:12 prophesies _Christ's Suffering_

We will read the entire portion, and then discuss several key elements, particularly those with the greatest bearing on our present journey:

- 52:13—The Hebrew words translated " _raised + lifted up_ "
are used as a pair four times in Isaiah and nowhere else (see 6:1; 57:15). They
are highly significant here because they refer to _God Alone_.

- Three kinds of suffering this prophetic poem predicts:
    1. _Physical_
    Beaten
    Physical Pain
    Pierced
    2. _Mental_
    Rejected   _Sorrow_
    Disrespected
    Opressed
    3. _Spiritual_

- The highly intentional repetition of terms in Isaiah 53:3-4:
    Verse 3: "A man of _____, one who knows _____."
    (*New International Commentary on the New Testament*)

    Verse 4: "But surely it was _____ _____ he carried, _____ _____
    he bore." (*New International Commentary on the New Testament*)

- The great paradox: that _____ can flow from a _____.

* You have permission to make copies of the viewer guides.

Week 2

That You
May Know

I always viewed myself as a big spot
on a white dress — a spot that everyone
saw and pointed at in disgust. I thought
everyone was beautiful in God's sight
but me. At a wedding, I watched in awe
as the stunning bride walked down the
aisle. God whispered to my heart,
"That's how I see you." I can't begin
to tell you how free I am! I no longer
feel dirty or spotted with guilt. I am a
true child of God — without spot
or blemish.

Day One
To Know God and Believe Him

Isaiah's glorious thesis on captives set free describes God's benefits this way: "Since ancient times no one has heard, no ear has perceived, no eye has seen any God besides you, who acts on behalf of those who wait for him" (Isa. 64:4).

Circle what Paul added in 1 Corinthians 2:9 to Isaiah's description.

no eye has seen   no ear has heard   no mind has conceived

God wants to do for you what your eyes have never seen, your ears have never heard, and your mind has never conceived. But just as the Babylonians held the children of Israel captive, areas of captivity can keep us from living out the reality of Isaiah 64:4 and 1 Corinthians 2:9. Take a moment to reread our definition of captivity: "A Christian is held captive by anything that hinders the abundant and effective Spirit-filled life God planned for her."

One of the most effective ways to detect captivity is to measure whether we are enjoying the benefits God intends for every child of God. This week we will ask ourselves: *Am I experiencing the benefits of my covenant relationship with God through Christ, or do the benefits I read in Scripture seem more like warm, fuzzy thoughts?* Just as the Israelites were in bondage, a foreign yoke may keep us from realizing five primary benefits God plans for His children to enjoy.

We will study these benefits "that you may know" what is yours (Isa. 43:10) and be able to recognize what may be missing. The absence of any one benefit will become a very helpful indicator of captivity. According to the Book of Isaiah, God has graciously extended the following benefits to His children.

1. To know God and believe Him
2. To glorify God
3. To find satisfaction in God
4. To experience God's peace
5. To enjoy God's presence

These five benefits and their scriptural references will serve as a road map to lead you home when you've been carried away captive. The remainder of today's lesson will be a general consideration of the first benefit; then we will study Benefits 2 through 5 on each of the subsequent days of this unit. For Benefit 1 "To know God and believe Him," read Isaiah 43:10-13 and answer the following questions.

Why have we been "chosen" (v. 10)? Check any reasons that apply.
☐ so we may know God
☐ so we may be happy
☐ so we may find God
☐ so we may be prosperous
☐ so we may believe God
☐ so we may understand He is God

Today's Treasure
"'You are my witnesses,' declares the LORD, 'and my servant whom I have chosen, so that you may know and believe me and understand that I am he.'" **ISAIAH 43:10**

A Christian is held captive by anything that hinders the abundant and effective Spirit-filled life God planned for her.

✳ According to these verses, in the margin describe the One you have been chosen to know, believe, and understand to be God.

In Isaiah 43:10, the Hebrew word for *know* is *yadha*. The term reflected a personal level of familiarity and often depicted the relationship of a husband and wife. One of your chief purposes is to know God intimately and with reverent familiarity.

Have you received Christ as your personal Savior? ☐ Yes ☐ No
If not, I urge you to do so, because Christ is the only entrance to the freedom trail. Paraphrase John 8:36 in the space below:

One of the most beautiful elements of salvation is its simplicity. Christ has already done all the work on the cross. All you must do is …
   1. acknowledge you are a sinner and cannot save yourself.
   2. acknowledge that Christ is the Son of God and only He can save you.
   3. believe His crucifixion paid for your sins and His death was in your behalf.
   4. give Him your life and ask Him to be your Savior and Lord.

If you already know Christ, how long have you been a Christian?

How would you characterize your relationship with God?
☐ distant   ☐ somewhat close and personal   ☐ close and personal

If you said close and personal, what characteristics of your relationship reflect a degree of familiarity? If not, what causes you to feel distant?

If you enjoy a close relationship with God, this study is an opportunity to deepen your relationship. I deeply desire for you to say when you turn the last page, "I thought I knew Him and loved Him when I first began." If you can't characterize your relationship as *close* and *familiar,* don't despair! As we allow God to penetrate our hearts, mend them, change them, or simply make them more like His own, we will also have many priceless opportunities to get in tune with His heart.

God not only desires for us to know Him, He also wants us to believe Him! The Hebrew word for *believe* in Isaiah 43:10 is *aman*, which means "to be firm, to be enduring, to trust." Our level of trust is a monumental issue in the life of every believer. Many variables in our lives affect our willingness to trust God. A loss or betrayal can deeply mark our level of trust. A broken heart never mended by the true Healer handicaps us terribly when we're challenged to trust.

Trusting an invisible God does not come naturally to any believer. A trust relationship grows only by stepping out in faith and making the choice to trust. This step sometimes seems more than we can take, but God is anxious to help us overcome our unbelief. The ability to believe God develops most often through pure experience. "I found Him faithful yesterday. He will not be unfaithful today."

Positive

How would you best characterize your level of trust at the present?

☐ tentative   ☐ conditional   ☐ strong   Negative
☐ fading   ☐ deep   ☐ comfortable
☐ unconditional ☐ almost nonexistent ☐ growing

In the margin describe experiences that have had both a positive and negative impact on your present level of trust.

Have you recognized any symptoms of captivity? ☐ Yes ☐ No

What is Benefit 1? _____

If we feel hindered in knowing God and believing Him, something is holding us back. Now don't get your "guilt juices" flowing and decide you've done everything wrong! Rejoice that Christ wants to set us completely free to know Him and believe Him. Part of the process will be acknowledging that something is holding us back and learning to identify what it may be.

I learned what Jesus is all about.

Conclude by writing our definition of captivity (accentuated in today's study) in the space below so you can begin to commit it to memory.

You must have a personal relationship + Believe in him. Trust!

Write a brief prayer making yourself fully available to God; thank Him for being satisfied with nothing less than what "no eye has seen, no ear has heard, and no mind has conceived."

How does God want you to respond to what He showed you today?

John 3:16

I am immeasurably thankful for your willingness to join me on this freedom trail. I am praying for you daily.

Day 2
To Glorify God

Today's Treasure

"Everyone who is called by my name, whom I created for my glory, whom I formed and made." **ISAIAH 43:7**

One of our goals in *Breaking Free* is to identify our personal hindrances to abundant life. On day 1 we recognized the absence of any of the primary benefits of being a child of God may indicate an area of captivity. Based on the Book of Isaiah, we established a checklist of five benefits God intends for every one of us but that remain virtual theories—in part or whole—for those held in areas of bondage.

Based on your recollection of day 1, check the five primary benefits we are free to enjoy as children of God. Review for any you missed.
- ☐ experience daily victory
- ☐ experience God's peace
- ☐ display patience during tribulation
- ☐ find fulfillment in serving God
- ☐ find God's healing
- ☐ enjoy God's presence
- ☐ know God and believe Him
- ☐ find satisfaction in God
- ☐ overcome the evil one
- ☐ glorify God

Drawing from your memory as much as possible, what is our definition of captivity?

Something that hinders.

In day 1 we briefly discussed Benefit 1: To know God and believe Him. You may have realized that you are hindered in your desire to know God and are hesitant to believe Him. My prayer is that God will gloriously liberate you to pursue and trust Him by the time we turn the last page of our Bible study. Today we examine Benefit 2: To glorify God.

According to Isaiah 43:7, why did God create us?
- ☐ for fellowship with Him
- ☐ for His glory
- ☐ for the honor of His name
- ☐ for His world renown

Without looking any further, what do you think God means by "my glory"?

The more I study God's glory, the more I see it is almost indefinable. We will look at several Scriptures and learn the Hebrew and Greek meanings. However, keep in mind that God's glory far exceeds anything we can comprehend in human terms. His glory is everything we're about to learn and infinitely more.

Consider each of the following Scriptures carefully and note anything you learn about God's glory:

Isaiah 6:3

Numbers 20:6

2 Chronicles 5:13-14

Psalm 19:1

Psalm 29:9

Isaiah 42:8

[handwritten margin note: Glory: The way he makes himself known & recognizable]

God's glory not only reflects Him but it is part of who He is! In each of these Old Testament references, the Hebrew word for *glory* is *kavodh* meaning "weight, honor, esteem." The word *kavodh* comes from another Hebrew term that can greatly increase our comprehension. The word *kavedh* means to "be renowned … to show oneself great or mighty." In other words, God's glory is the way He makes Himself known or shows Himself mighty. God wants to reveal Himself to humans. Each way He accomplishes this divine task is His glory. God's glory is how He shows who He is.

God's glory is the way He makes Himself recognizable.

Consider the following New Testament uses of glory and note what they add to your understanding.

John 1:14

John 2:11

Hebrews 1:3

2 Peter 1:3

[handwritten margin note: Isaiah 64:4 43:7]

The Greek word for *glory* in these New Testament references (*doxa*) is "the true apprehension of God or things. The glory of God must mean His unchanging essence. Giving glory to God is ascribing to him His full recognition …The glory of God is what He is essentially." *Doxa* comes from another wonderful word, *dokeo* meaning "to … think or suppose." God's glory is the way He makes Himself recognizable.

Read Isaiah 43:7 once more. Based on what we've learned from our Scriptures and definitions, what do you think being created for God's glory means now? Respond in the margin.

I believe being created for God's glory means two marvelous truths to those who are called by His name:
- God wants to make Himself recognizable *to* us.
- God wants to make Himself recognizable *through* us.

How do you interpret 1 Corinthians 10:31 based on what we've learned?

God desires to be recognizable in us in all we do! A life that glorifies God is a life that reveals God. If you're like me, you're probably overwhelmed by the enormous responsibility of such a calling. We're imperfect creatures! How do we help others recognize something about God just from watching our lives and knowing us?

Consider another portion of the definition of *doxa* that relates the term to human beings: "the glory of created things including man is what they are meant by God to be, though not yet perfectly attained." The following Scriptures will help us sort out God's glory in relationship to those who are called by His name:

What do we learn about God's glory in Romans 3:23?

Now read Colossians 1:24-27. What is the mystery God used the apostle Paul to make known according to verse 27?
- ☐ our salvation
- ☐ Christ in you
- ☐ the acceptance of the Gentiles
- ☐ Jesus is God

Paul announced the mystery that Christ Himself dwells in every believer. Christ in us! Romans 8:9 tells us that "if anyone does not have the Spirit of Christ, he does not belong to Christ." The moment we received Christ as our Savior, the Holy Spirit of Christ took up residence in our inner being.

Do you see the key? We have no hope whatsoever of God being recognizable in us if the Spirit of Christ does not dwell in us. If we are not occupied by the Holy Spirit, we have nothing of God in us for Him to show. Christ is a human being's only "hope of glory"! Do you see what I mean? "Christ in you, the hope of glory."

We glorify God to the degree that we externalize the internal presence of the living Christ. A life that glorifies God is not something we suddenly attain.

Read 2 Corinthians 3:17-18. What does verse 18 say about God's work in you?

I hope you didn't miss that God is changing us into Christ's "likeness with ever-increasing glory." The KJV says "from glory to glory"! You see, people living out the reality of liberation in Christ (Gal. 5:1; 2 Cor. 3:17) progress in an "ever-increasing

I lift my hands, bow down, and worship Him.

glory." As they grow in spiritual maturity, the Spirit of Christ becomes increasingly recognizable in them. So when Christ is not recognizable in a redeemed life, we want to identify and allow God to treat that area of captivity.

We were created for the purpose of giving God's invisible character a glimpse of visibility. If we grasped the eternal implications of such a destiny, we would want to do anything possible to make sure all hindrances were removed. Remember the definition of *doxa* as it relates to human beings?—"What they are meant by God to be." Now reflect once again on the words of Isaiah 43:7: "Everyone who is called by my name … I created for my glory." Allow me to attempt to summarize what we've learned:

- We were created for God's glory.
- We have no hope of God's glory without the indwelling Spirit of Christ who comes at our salvation.
- We fulfill what we were "meant to be" when God is "recognizable" in our lifestyle.

A life that glorifies God or makes Him recognizable is a process that progresses with time and maturity. You may be wondering how a person could recognize whether or not his or her life was glorifying God. The following Scriptures and statements may be helpful in determining whether or not Benefit 2 is a present reality in our lives.

Please don't be dismayed if you feel you are not already living a life that glorifies God! Remember, He never sheds light on our weaknesses or shortcomings for the sake of condemnation. Romans 8:1 assures us "there is now no condemnation for those who are in Christ Jesus." God makes us aware of hindrances so He can set us free!

Mark each statement with *T* for true, *F* for false, or *P* for making progress.

_____ My most important consideration in every undertaking is whether or not God could be glorified (1 Cor. 10:31).

_____ I do not seek my own glory (John 8:50,54).

_____ My sincere hope in my service to others is that they will somehow see God in me (1 Pet. 4:10-11).

_____ When I am going through hardships, I turn to God and try to cooperate with Him so He can use them for my good and for His glory (1 Pet. 4:12-13).

_____ I am sometimes able to accomplish things or withstand things only through the power of God (2 Cor. 4:7).

Don't worry! Most people probably wouldn't be able to fill in every space above with a confident "T"! None of us consistently glorify God in everything we say and do, but we can experience genuine liberation in Christ. God wants to do more in us than we've ever heard, seen, or imagined (1 Cor. 2:9).

God protects us from pride by keeping us somewhat unaware of the degree to which we are effectively glorifying Him. However, when we are able to respond to the statements above with an affirmative answer of "True" or "Making Progress,"

God is being glorified! You can count on it! Just be sure to turn around and give Him the glory!

How does God want you to respond to what He showed you today?

Today's lesson may have been difficult for you. You may feel like you have a long way to go before you are fulfilling His purpose in creating you (Isa. 43:7). Instead, I hope you see the magnificent potential He planned for you to fulfill. On the other hand, you may be able to celebrate some progress you're making in the pursuit of a God-glorifying life. No matter what God has exposed to you today, you can relish the wonderful words of Christ that pertain to you.

What did Christ say has come to Him through those who believe in Him (John 17:9-10)? ☐ mercy ☐ atonement ☐ grace ☐ glory

In this context, Christ used the word *glory* to indicate wealth and riches He had received. No matter where you are on this journey to the glorifying, liberated life in Christ, you are His treasure. He does not want to take from you. He wants to give to you and free you from any hindrance to the abundant and effective Spirit-filled life He died to give you.

Please conclude today's lesson with a brief prayer about the God-glorifying life. Learning to dialogue with God in very personal ways is a crucial part of the freedom process. Share with Him your sincere response to today's lesson.

Day 3
To Find Satisfaction in God

Today's Treasure
"Why spend money on what is not bread, and your labor on what does not satisfy? Listen, listen to me, and eat what is good, and your soul will delight in the richest of fare." **ISAIAH 55:2**

Today we consider Benefit 3: To find satisfaction in God. As we approach this benefit, recall John 8:32. We are journeying toward the liberated life in Christ.

According to John 8:32, what will Christ continually use as the means to our destination?

Not only is God's truth an absolute necessity in our progress toward complete freedom, but our truthfulness is also a necessity. Psalm 51:6 says God desires "truth in the inner parts." Our present journey will amount to many hours of wasted time if we do not allow God's truth to penetrate the inmost places in our lives and bring out our own truthfulness in response. A combination of two vehicles—God's truth and our truthfulness—will drive us to our desired destination. Honesty with God is an absolute requirement to keep moving on this journey.

I mention the importance of honesty because I may be about to get more honest than some of us can stand. I ask you to hear me out and consider what I have to say. Many Christians are not satisfied with Jesus. You may nod or you may gasp; but no matter your response, I believe you have probably experienced exactly what I mean.

Before you call me a heretic, let me set the record straight: Jesus is absolutely satisfying. In fact, He is the only means by which anyone can find true satisfaction. However, I believe a person can receive Christ as Savior, serve Him for decades, and meet Him face-to-face in glory without ever experiencing satisfaction in Him on this earth. If you have indeed discovered genuine satisfaction in Christ, I am going to assume that—like me—you are so zealous for others to find Him satisfying, you will gladly participate in this lesson anyway.

The Bible uses the word *soul* in a number of ways. One way is to refer to the nonmaterial part of us. When I speak of soul hunger, I mean our need of spiritual satisfaction. Few people find this subject comfortable, but it's time to let the truth break the locks off the closets of our secret dissatisfaction. First let's each attempt to word our own definition of satisfaction.

What do you think being satisfied with something means?

Now allow me to ask you a question I hope you'll answer honestly before God but not on paper: Is your soul, your spirit, your own inmost place, the real you, entirely satisfied with Christ? As we meditate on our answers, let's consider the biblical meaning of satisfaction through several Old Testament Scriptures.

What does God seem to be offering in Isaiah 55:1-2?

In the margin restate His question in verse 2 in your own words.

What kind of satisfaction is God emphasizing in these verses?
☐ physical   ☐ emotional
☐ spiritual   ☐ mental

The Hebrew word for *satisfy* in Isaiah 55:2 is *sob'ah* meaning "to have enough, be full ... sufficiently." God was asking, "Why do you work so hard for things that are never enough, can never fill you up, and are endlessly insufficient?"

Can you think of anything you've worked hard to attain that ultimately failed to bring about the satisfaction you were expecting? ☐ Yes ☐ No

Benefit 1
To know God and believe Him

Benefit 2
To glorify God

Is your soul (entirely) satisfied with Christ?

41

We've each been disappointed by something we expected to bring great satisfaction. Let's look at another fitting reference to satisfaction. Read Jeremiah 31:23-25.

In verse 23, when did God say He would refresh the weary and satisfy the faint?

In Jeremiah 31:25 the Hebrew word for *satisfy* is *male,* meaning "to fill, accomplish, the filling of something that was empty … the act of replenishment as well as the experience of satiation." The word for *faint* is *da'ab* meaning "to pine" (*Strong's*). We can easily be led into captivity by seeking other answers to needs and desires only God is equipped to meet. How often do we "pine" for something we can't even identify? Perhaps we've each experienced a longing that we tried our best to ignore.

A crucial part of liberation in Christ means allowing Him to fill our empty places. Satisfaction in Christ can be a reality. I know from experience, and I want everyone to know how complete He can make us feel. I'm not talking about a life full of activities. I'm talking about a soul full of Jesus.

The filling only Christ can give does not automatically accompany our salvation. I was in my early 30's before I understood the huge difference between salvation from sin and satisfaction of the soul. Salvation secures our lives for all eternity. Soul satisfaction ensures abundant life on earth. God often teaches us spiritual truths by paralleling physical realities. We can learn several truths about satisfied souls by drawing a parallel between the soul and the physical body. I know this seems simplistic, but humor me for a moment as I ask you the following two questions.

How do you know you are hungry? Describe the sensation of hunger.

How do you know when you are thirsty? Describe it.

Continue to humor me here. What do you usually do when you're hungry or thirsty? When you are thirsty, you don't want a bag of popcorn. You want a tall glass of water! When you're hungry, you seek what will meet your need. If you ignore your physical needs long enough, not only will you be miserable but you will soon be ill. You can easily recognize the signals the body gives, but great wisdom lies in learning to discern your spirit's signals. Psalm 63 offers insight into the satisfied soul. Read Psalm 63:1-8.

Why do you think this writer had such a hunger and thirst for God?

> Not a life full of activities but a soul full of Jesus.

What was the writer's expectation after he confessed his thirst for God and earnestly sought Him (see v. 5)?

How would you rate the kind of satisfaction the writer was accustomed to finding when he earnestly sought God?
- ☐ like water to the thirsty soul
- ☐ very adequate
- ☐ like the richest food to the hungry
- ☐ miraculous
- ☐ barely sufficient

The most obvious symptom of a soul in need of God's satisfaction is a sense of inner emptiness. The awareness of a "hollow place" somewhere deep inside. The constant inability to be satisfied.

Can you think of a time in your life when you knew you should be satisfied but you weren't? Describe how you felt.

The soul can also manifest physical symptoms. I think of it this way: Just like my stomach growls when I'm hungry for physical food, my spirit tends to growl when I'm in need of spiritual food. When a checker at the grocery store seems overtly irritable or grouchy, I sometimes grin and think to myself, *I bet her kids woke her before she had a chance to have her quiet time!* I can certainly assure you that my personality is distinctively different when I haven't had the time I need with the Lord. My soul can do some pretty fierce growling!

How about you? Does your hungry soul ever manifest physical symptoms? ☐ Yes ☐ No If so, what are they?

☐ irritability	☐ selfish ambitions	☐ anger
☐ impure thoughts	☐ envy	☐ resentment
☐ eruptions of lust	☐ other _____	

When a soul is thirsty for the Living Water (John 4), it can also manifest a physical symptom. Just like my mouth gets dry when I am thirsty, my spiritual mouth tends to get dry when I need the satisfying refreshment only God can bring. The following Scriptures suggest a few of the signs that go along with a mouth wet with God's Living Water.

For once in my life, I am free and God is my pilot

Based on these verses, what might be the manifestations of a thirst recently satisfied with God?

Psalm 71:8

Psalm 119:172

Isaiah 50:4

What are a few ways in which a dry spirit might manifest itself?

Our final point is very important. We can positively assume that our soul is hungry and thirsty for God if we have not partaken of any spiritual food or drink in a long while. Souls accustomed to food are more likely to have a highly developed appetite. Take a look at Psalm 63 again. David was accustomed to beholding the power and glory of God. He was so acquainted with God's love, he considered it "better than life." Therefore, he missed God's refreshment when he didn't have it.

I think we have the same tendency. The more we've been satisfied by God's love, His Word, and His presence, the more we will yearn for it. On the other hand, we can spend so much time away from the Lord and His spiritual food and drink that we may no longer feel hungry or thirsty. I know from personal experience that if you fail to partake of the spiritual food and drink of God for a while, you are hungry and thirsty for His satisfaction whether or not you know it! Return to the Bread of Life and the Living Water! "Taste and see that the Lord is good" (Ps. 34:8).

God can satisfy your yearning soul. Satisfying your innermost places with Jesus is a benefit of the glorious covenant relationship you have with God in Christ. Over the weeks to come, we will begin to discern things that are holding us back from experiencing the satisfying life.

How does God want you to respond to what He showed you today?

Conclude today's lesson by recording the insights you learn about Benefit 3 (to find satisfaction in God) from the following Scriptures:

Psalm 103:1-2,5

Philippians 4:19

Revelation 3:20

Open the door, Beloved! He waits to satisfy your hungry soul.

Day 4
To Experience God's Peace

Are you beginning to see a need for greater freedom in Christ? I am praying for you. If you grant God complete access to your heart, mind, and soul, then as you turn the last page you will be "free" to love Him in ways you never dreamed.

This Bible study is going to lead you to freeing Scriptures and demand from you a level of cooperation God will honor. A harvest of fruitfulness is coming. Today Benefit 4: To experience God's peace. I can't overemphasize the importance of peace as a real and practical benefit of our covenant relationship with God. His peace should not be an infrequent surprise but the ongoing rule of our lives.

According to 2 Thessalonians 3:16, how often and in how many areas of life does God desire to give you peace?

Peace can be possible in any situation, but we cannot simply produce it on demand. In fact, we cannot produce it at all. It is "fruit of the Spirit" (Gal. 5:22). We have Christ's peace. It has already been given to us if we have received Christ. We just don't always know how to activate it. Today we're going to discover the key to experiencing the practical reality of God's peace. Then throughout the course of our journey, we're going to work on becoming more free to turn the key.

The Book of Isaiah uses the word *peace* 26 times. God continually promised peace when His captives returned wholeheartedly to the Lord. Let's begin to uncover the key to experiencing the peace Christ left as our inheritance.

Identify what each of the following passages teaches you about peace; watch for hints of a common denominator between many of them.

Isaiah 9:6-7

Isaiah 26:3

Isaiah 32:17

Isaiah 53:5

Isaiah 54:10

Isaiah 57:2

Isaiah 60:17

Today's Treasure
"If only you had paid attention to my commands, your peace would have been like a river, your righteousness like the waves of the sea." ISAIAH 48:18

Benefit 1
To know God and believe Him

Benefit 2
To glorify God

Benefit 3
To find satisfaction in God

Christ & Righteousness
Peace accompanies authority

45

Did you see any hints of a common denominator tying several of these Scriptures together? ☐ Yes ☐ No If so, what was it?

Isaiah 9:6-7 perfectly portrays the key to peace, "He will be called … Prince of Peace. Of the increase of his government and peace there will be no end." Beloved, let God write this principle on your heart forever: The key to peace is authority. When we allow the Prince of Peace to govern our lives, peace either immediately or ultimately results. Peace accompanies authority.

In the margin describe a time when you know you experienced the peace of God transcending your understanding.

Can you also say, as I can, that you have had an absence of peace in much less difficult circumstances? Have you ever wondered what the difference was? Peace comes in situations completely surrendered to the sovereign authority of Christ. Sometimes when we finally give up trying to discover all the answers to the "why's" in our lives and decide to trust a sovereign God, unexpected peace washes over us like a summer rain. We sometimes lack peace in far less strenuous circumstances because we are not as desperate or likely to turn them over to God.

I finally had to turn some of the hurts of my childhood over to God's sovereign authority because I realized they would consume me like an invasive cancer. When at last I allowed Him to govern everything concerning my past, not only did the Prince give me His peace, He actually brought good from something horrible and unfair. If you have not yet bowed the knee to God's authority over areas of your past, my friend, something is holding you captive.

Christ desperately wants His people to experience His peace. Perhaps you would be blessed to know how much. Several Greek words are translated into the English words *crying* or *weeping* in the New Testament. Each Greek word represents different degrees of externalized grief. The Greek word *klaio* is the strongest word used in the New Testament for *grief*. It means "to weep, wail, lament, implying not only the shedding of tears, but also every external expression of grief." Christ wept on several occasions, but on only one occasion is His grief described with the word *klaio*.

Read Luke 19:41-42. Why did Jesus show such extreme grief?

You must believe, bend the knee, and learn how to receive.

I believe Christ still grieves when He sees hearts in unnecessary turmoil. You can have the peace of Christ, believer, no matter what your circumstances; but you must believe, bend the knee, and learn how to receive.

Some of us will submit to God's authority in troublesome areas almost immediately. For others, surrendering to Christ seems harder. We will hopefully discover reasons why we are so reluctant to submit to God's authority. We must also remember that bending the knee is ultimately a matter of pure obedience.

You may never feel like giving your circumstance, hurt, or loss to Him; but you can choose to submit to His authority out of belief and obedience rather than emotion. Obedience is the mark of authentic surrender to God's authority in any matter.

When I finally bent the knee to the Prince of Peace over hurts in my childhood, I realized He was directing me to forgive the person who hurt me. God did not insist on my forgiving for the sake of my perpetrator but for the sake of peace in my life. Once I began to surrender to Him in this painful area, He began to give me a supernatural ability to forgive. A segment of Scripture in Isaiah beautifully reveals the relationship of obedience, God's authority, and peace. God has a right to all authority because of who He is.

Read Isaiah 48:17-18. By what names is God called in verse 17?
☐ Anointed One ☐ Holy One ☐ Redeemer
☐ Savior ☐ Lord ☐ Prince
☐ God ☐ Son of Righteousness

Allow me to reverse the order God mentioned Himself by name and share my outlook on His right to complete authority:

> He is God, the Creator of the heavens and the earth, the Supreme author of all existence. He reigns over all and in Him all things exist. He is Lord, the Master and Owner of all living creatures. He is the covenant Maker and the covenant Keeper. He delights in humanity, His prize creation, and woos us to the riches of relationship. He is Holy. As Lord, He will never ask anything of us that is not right, good, and open to the light. He is perfect and undefiled. Lastly, He is Redeemer, the One who bought us from sin's slave master so we could experience abundant life. He bought us to set us free.

"What, then, shall we say in response to this? If God is for us, who can be against us?" (Rom. 8:31). Now let's consider the following question:

According to Isaiah 48:18, what would happen if we paid attention to God's commands? Check any that apply.
☐ We would get what we asked.
☐ Our righteousness would be like the waves of the sea.
☐ We would have peace like a river.
☐ We would prosper and have good health.

Consider the following descriptions as you imagine peace like a river.

A river is a moving stream of water. God's Word doesn't say we'll have peace like a pond. Some imagine peaceful people as boring and a breath from death. We think we'd rather forego peace and have an exciting life. Beloved, few bodies of water are more exciting than rivers! When was the last time you saw white-water rapids? We can have active, exciting lives without suffering through a life of turmoil.

God did not insist on my forgiving for the sake of my perpetrator but for the sake of peace in my life.

When God used the analogy of a river, He described a peace that can be retained while life twists, turns, and rolls over boulders. Let's resist picturing peaceful people as expressionless monks. To have peace like a river is to have security and tranquility of heart and mind while meeting many bumps and unexpected turns on life's journey through change. Peace is submission to a trustworthy Authority, not resignation from all activity. Remember, however, any activity that cannot be brought under the umbrella of God's authority will prove to be a source of turmoil and exhaustion.

Can you describe a time when you experienced peace accompanied by a busy schedule that would have caused chaos had you not been in God's will? ☐ Yes ☐ No   If so, briefly describe that time.

A river is a body of fresh water fed by springs or tributary streams. I've found that I can't retain a spirit of peace in the present by relying on a relationship from the past. Peace comes from an active, ongoing, and obedient relationship with the Prince of Peace. He wants to feed us with the Living Water of His Holy Spirit and a steady stream of His Word until we have peace like a river. This and other Bible studies are examples of ways God desires to feed a peaceful river in your soul.

What are a few other ways you can give God the opportunity to keep a spring of fresh water welling up within you? Respond in the margin.

A river begins and ends with a body of water. Every river has an upland source and an ultimate outlet or mouth. Rivers are fully dependent and are always connected to other bodies of water. Likewise, peace like a river flows from a continuous connection with the upland Source, Jesus Christ, and a timely reminder that this life will ultimately spill into a glorious eternal life. This life is not our destination, hallelujah! We who know Christ personally move continually over rocks and sometimes cliffs, through narrow places and wide valleys to a heavenly destination. Until then, abiding in Christ (John 15:4) is the key to staying deliberately connected with our upland Source.

Take pleasure in knowing that God inspired His Word with great care and precision. He chose every word purposely. When He said we could have peace like a river in Isaiah 48:18, He wasn't drawing a loose analogy. He meant it. What does it take? Paying attention to God's commands (by obedience) through the power of the Holy Spirit within us. Why should we obey? Because God is incapable of making mistakes with our lives. Isaiah 48:17 tells us He teaches us only what is best for us. He directs us only in the way we should go. Obedience to God's authority not only brings peace like a river but righteousness like the waves of the sea. Not righteous perfection. Righteous consistency.

Can you think of any ways righteousness itself brings peace?

How does God want you to respond to what He showed you today?

You see, God's way is the safe way. The right way. And the only peaceful way in a chaotic world. Beloved, I hope you've discovered today that peace is not beyond your reach. It's not a goal to one day meet. You can begin a life of authentic peace today. Right now. The path to peace is paved with knee-prints. Bend the knee to His trustworthy authority. Surrender every part of your life and every concern of your heart to the all-powerful, all-sufficient, all-knowing Creator of heaven and earth. "Let the peace of Christ rule in your hearts" (Col. 3:15).

Conclude today's lesson by sharing any new insight into Benefit 4 you have received: To experience God's peace ...

Day 5
To Enjoy God's Presence

We've already considered four wonderful God-given rights or benefits: (1) To know God and believe Him, (2) to glorify God, (3) to find satisfaction in God, and (4) to experience God's peace. Benefit 5 is: To enjoy God's presence. The five benefits intertwine, but I hope you can also see each of them as distinctive.

I doubt any believer feels God's wonderful presence every second of every day. Sometimes we're challenged to simply believe He's with us because He has promised (Heb. 13:5). That's faith.

God has given us many assurances of His abiding presence. Let's draw our first attentions to the assurance of God's presence in Isaiah 43:1-7.

After reading the text, please complete the following: "When I read verse 1, I feel ..."

Today's Treasure
"*When you pass through the waters, I will be with you; and when you pass through the rivers, they will not sweep over you. When you walk through the fire, you will not be burned; the flames will not set you ablaze. For I am the* LORD, *your God, the Holy One of Israel, your Savior.*" **ISAIAH 43:2-3**

Benefit 1
To know God and believe Him

Benefit 2
To glorify God

Benefit 3
To find satisfaction in God

Benefit 4
To experience God's peace

God's Word often tells us not to fear, yet not all our fears are unfounded. Think about it. Our present society poses many real threats. Reread verse 5. God is not suggesting that difficult things don't happen to His children.

What reason exists for not giving way to fear? Choose one.
☐ God will deliver us.
☐ God is with us.
☐ Our lives are just a breath in comparison to eternity.

Sometimes frightening things can happen to believers as well as unbelievers. If God's presence doesn't ensure that nothing frightening will ever happen to us, how could the assurance of God's constant presence still be the quieter of our fears?

Fill in the following blanks with the promises God made based on the following conditions.

When you pass through the waters,

When you pass through the rivers,

When you walk through the fire,

What can we assume from the repetition of the word *when* rather than *if* in verse 2?

Can you think of a time when you sensed God's presence the clearest? What were the circumstances?

Can you think of a time in your Christian life when you could not sense God's presence at all? What were the circumstances?

Read Psalm 139:7-12 and the promise in Hebrews 13:5. We obviously and fortunately cannot escape God's presence, but why do you think we experience times when we sense God's presence more clearly than others?

I WALK DAILY WITH MY JESUS.

God's presence is absolutely unchanging, but the evidence of His presence is not. On some occasions God may purposely alter the evidences of His presence to bring the most benefit from our experience. Sometimes we receive the most benefit from seeing many visible "prints" of His invisible hands during a difficult season. Other times, we profit most from seeing fewer evidences.

What did Christ say to one who insisted on seeing literal "prints" in John 20:24-29?

God does not love us less when He gives us fewer evidences. He simply desires to grow us up and teach us to walk by faith and not by sight. These steps are most challenging when we're delivered *through* frightening experiences rather than *from* them.

Read Matthew 14:25-32. Did the wind die down before or after Christ told His disciples not to be afraid? ☐ Before ☐ After What would be the basis of their courage since the storm continued to rage?

The point is not that we have nothing to fear and cowardice is simply an unreasonable state of mind. Christ's presence is the basis for courage in our storms. He did not say, "Take courage! I am calming the storm. Don't be afraid." Instead, with the winds still raging, He said, "Take courage! It is I. Don't be afraid."

   Christ does not always immediately calm the storm, but He is always willing to calm His child on the basis of His presence. "Don't worry! I'm right here! I know the winds are raging and the waves are high, but I am God over both. If I let them continue to swell, it's because I want you to see Me walk on the water. This set of prints can be seen only in a storm. I'm in this with you, and I love you more than you'll ever know." We'll probably never learn to enjoy our storms, but we can learn to enjoy God's presence in the storm!

 In Psalm 16:11, what did David confidently expect from God?

> We can learn to enjoy God's presence in the storm!

The New King James Version renders one phrase, "In Your presence is fullness of joy!" The Hebrew word for *joy* is *simchah*, which means "glee, gladness, joy, pleasure, rejoice(-ing)." *Simchah* comes from a word that means "(making) merry" (*Strong's*). We can learn to enjoy God's presence even when life is not presently enjoyable. I can't explain it, but I've experienced it personally over and over.

   Before we can begin to enjoy God's presence, we must accept His continual presence as an absolute fact. Are you one who always needs a set of "prints" for reassurance? The most wonderful set of fingerprints God left with His invisible hand is probably within your reach this very moment: You have His Word.

Scripture declares God never abandons His children. He is always there. When it all comes down, we either choose to believe or disbelieve God. He promised us He is always with us. Once we choose to accept His presence as a fact, we can be free to go on to enjoyment. Are you ready to accept His ever-abiding presence in your life as an absolute fact? Are you ready to begin enjoying God in your life more than ever?

If so, in the margin write a simple prayer asking Him to strengthen your faith and teach you how to enjoy Him to the fullest.

The fifth benefit of our covenant relationship, enjoying God's presence, and the other four, obviously relate to each other. I'd like to share a comparison with you that may help you draw a simple differentiation.

Benefit 1
To know God and believe Him

Benefit 2
To glorify God

Benefit 3
To find satisfaction in God

Benefit 4
To experience God's peace

Benefit 5
To enjoy God's presence

Keith and I have been married for 30-plus years. I know my husband very well, and I believe him when he tells me something (Benefit 1). In an earthly sense, I glorify him because I've lived with him so long that some of his traits now show up in me (Benefit 2). He satisfies virtually every need a husband should (Benefit 3). I often get to experience peace while he assumes the responsibility of finances and future security (Benefit 4). I could not experience the last primary benefit of our marriage without the other four, yet it is completely distinctive: I purely enjoy my husband's presence (Benefit 5). We are currently experiencing one of the most wonderful seasons of our marriage so far. We enjoy each other's company more than ever. He makes me laugh. He's intellectually stimulating. He's tender. My husband and I spend lots of time together, but so do many other couples. What makes our time together special is that we actually enjoy it.

As much as I enjoy my husband, daughters, grandchildren, family, and friends, no relationship in my life brings me more pure joy than my relationship with God. I certainly haven't "arrived" in some mystical place, nor have I made even these few steps quickly or casually. I've grown to enjoy God with time. Not every minute I spend with Him is gleeful or great fun. Intimacy with God grows through sharing every realm of experience. I've wept bitterly with Him. I've screamed in frustration. Sometimes I thought He was going to break my heart in two. But I've also laughed out loud. Wept with unspeakable joy. Gone to my knees in awe. Squealed with excitement.

I have been to every extremity and back with God. But if I had to define my relationship with Him by one general statement, I would tell you that He is the absolute joy of my life. I don't just love Him. I love loving Him. Surrendering my heart to Him has not been a sacrifice. I don't know any other way to say it: He works for me.

I am hesitant to say all of this because I would be sickened to think I might sound proud of my relationship with God. Please hear my heart when I tell you that the greatest joy in my life is the very thing I have deserved the least. I consider the ability to love Him and enjoy Him an absolute gift of grace … one He will gladly extend to anyone who offers Him her whole heart. I know a little of what the apostle Paul meant when he said in 2 Corinthians 11:2, "I am jealous for you with a godly jealousy." My friend, I am "jealous" for you to enjoy God. I want it so badly for you that I can hardly stand it. I want God to be the greatest reality in your life. I want you to be more assured of His presence than any other you can see or touch. Yes, this can be your reality. This is your right as a child of God. We were destined for this kind of relationship with God, but the enemy has tried to convince us that the Christian life is sacrificial at best and artificial at worst.

In the margin, write our definition of captivity. Review day 1 if necessary.

This week we've worked very hard to establish a five-part checklist of priority benefits based on the Book of Isaiah that should be a reality in our relationships with God.

Please write the five benefits in order in the margin. Then match the benefits to the following statements by writing number 1, 2, 3, 4, or 5 in each blank.

_____ "I can hardly believe how God has gotten me through the last year since my husband died. Slowly but surely He is filling up those horrible empty places."

_____ "I feel such a strange calm over my life right now. I remember a time not long ago when I would have panicked over this situation."

_____ "I'm learning so much about God in my study of the Gospel of John. I'm learning to trust Him so much more."

_____ "I know you've been through so much this year, Anne, but I've never seen Christ more clearly in anyone than I see Him in you."

_____ "Sorry I'm late! God is revealing some wonderful things in my quiet time right now and I lost track of time. I remember when 15 minutes seemed like an eternity in prayer! God is so good."

Benefit 1:

Benefit 2:

Benefit 3:

Benefit 4:

Benefit 5:

The enemy has no right to hold you back from any of these benefits. They are yours. In this study we are going to reclaim some surrendered ground. Are you in this one with me? As you reflect over the list of benefits and the time we've shared, do any of these benefits suggest that you may have something holding you back? Is God pointing to the possibility of an area of captivity in your life?

How does God want you to respond to what He showed you today?

Conclude with an assignment to take very seriously. Commit yourself entirely to God that He may set you free to be everything He planned. Ask Him in Jesus' name not to let the enemy steal one bit of the victory God has for you. We must not allow intimidation or fear to imprison us in any area. Remember, Satan can presume no authority in your life. He will do his best to bluff you. Don't let him. "The one who is in you is greater than the one who is in the world" (1 John 4:4).

Listen closely. The liberty bell's ringing.

BREAKING Free

session three viewer guide

Isaiah 44:20-22. With two weeks of Bible study behind us, we're prepared, if we're willing, to take one of our first leaps on the path to freedom: _freedom from self-delusion_.

A succinct definition of idolatry: *An idol is* _any trade-off for_ *God.*

A New Testament Contrast of Truth and Lies

TRUTH: John 8:31-36—Christ _sets the captive free_ through truth.

LIES: John 8:44—Satan _sets the free captive_ through lies.

Equations That Add Up to Liberty

My _environment_ + My _experiences_ = My "_Truth_"

Read 2 Chronicles 18:28-34.

Romans 6
Ephes. 4

Truth Liberty
Lies Captivity

John 8:44

"The LORD is near to all who call on him,
to all who call on him in truth" (Ps. 145:18).

My "_truth_" + 0 = _incomplete_

My "_truth_" + _satan_ _lies_ = _captivity_

God's Truth > _My "Truth"_

Compare Hebrews 4:12.

More powerful to free you than our own truth that keeps us in bondage.

James 1:22-25. Contrast "looking at himself" (v. 24) with "looks intently" (v. 25).

Verse 24. The Greek word translated *looking at himself* "indicates percep
tion. Tragically, this kind of person _ignores_ what he has perceived,
resulting in a _detachment_ from what is observed, in this case the
truth _about_ _himself_." (*New American Commentary*)

I am God and nothing is too difficult for me.

_My_ "_Truth_" + _God's Truth_ = _Freedom_

James 1:22-25
*Do not merely listen to the word
Do what it says!*

Pslm 40:11
May your love + your truth always protect me.

— *Self Delusion* —

Removing the Obstacles

my side, holding my hand.

I was filling out some paperwork in my office and it hit me: I had been sober for six years. God met me right where I needed Him to. That's not to say I do not struggle. I am still a recovering alcoholic and need God's love every day. Praise Him, that He is a God who breaks strongholds.

Day 1
The Obstacle of Unbelief

Today's Treasure
"Remove the obstacles out of the way of my people." ISAIAH 57:14

Have you read *The Pilgrim's Progress* by John Bunyan? He compared the Christian life to the journey from the City of Destruction to the Celestial City. While I'd never compare this study with Bunyan's classic, in *Breaking Free* we are pursuing the same journey. However, we travel from the City of Slavery to the Land of Liberty. Welcome to week 3 of our journey toward breaking free. Last week, we identified five primary benefits of our covenant relationship with God. The absence of any of these benefits is a possible indicator of some form of captivity.

I believe God wants to radically change us as we experience liberty in Christ. One of my worst nightmares would be for you to invest many hours in study, increasing head knowledge, but turning the last page with wrists heavy from the same bonds you had when you began. This tragedy could be a reality if we do not provide God with complete access to the innermost places in our hearts.

According to Isaiah 57:14, what must be removed?

In Isaiah's day villages prepared for a visit from their king. Workmen cleared a path and built a road to provide the access. In the Middle East valleys suddenly rise up into rugged mountains. Cracks in the mountain rocks often spill dangerous boulders into the valleys. Without modern paved roads, paths became treacherous.

If the king found the path unprepared, he'd bypass the village and withhold his blessing. God inspired Isaiah 57:14 with a different entourage in mind, however. Notice in the passage God has the commoner as the traveler rather than the king. Instead of removing obstacles for His own journey, God commanded the removal of obstacles to His people's journey. He wanted no obstructions hindering the journey of His people into His presence. To accomplish the task and reach freedom we must remove some very large obstacles. God desires to use these weeks to draw us closer to His heart. The road may get a little rough at times, but I believe we'll be glad we took it. Our destination will be worth the trip.

Yes, we face a few obstacles to remove, but we have the approval and blessing of the matchless King in our favor. We don't have to wonder if He's willing and able to deliver us from the bonds withholding abundant life. Remember, it is for freedom Christ has set us free. He's more than willing. He's ready. The question is whether we are ready to cooperate and prepare the way for our Liberator.

What are some obstacles you've battled in previous efforts to live the liberated, abundant life in Christ? Make your list in the margin.

We will seek to remove many obstacles to freedom, but this week we specify five primary obstacles that correspond with our five primary benefits. If we do not address and remove these five obstacles in advance, the personal visit of our King will be greatly hindered. Today let's focus on the first benefit. Read Isaiah 43:10.

In the margin write Benefit 1. Look back to page 52 if necessary.

Celebrate the fact that you committed to knowing God when you joined us in this Bible study. Accept a well-deserved pat on the back from the Holy Spirit! Let's focus, then, on the second portion of Benefit 1: To believe Him.

Which would be the most obvious obstacle to believing God?
☐ disobedience ☐ wrong priorities ☐ unbelief
☐ arrogance ☐ false worship

As simple as this seems, the largest obstacle to believing God is choosing not to believe Him. We're not talking about believing *in* God. We're talking about believing *God*, believing what He says. Believing He is who He says He is.

We can believe in Christ for salvation yet spend the rest of our days believing Him for little more. Eternity can be secured while life on earth remains shaky at best. Let's pinpoint what "believing God" means, and we'll have a better understanding of its greatly hindering antonym. Read Genesis 15:6 and Romans 4:3.

What do these verses tell you about Abraham? Choose one.
☐ He believed in God. ☐ He believed in the pre-incarnate Christ.
☐ He believed God. ☐ He was blessed for believing in God.

God freed me from lies of rejection.

In Genesis 15:6, the Hebrew word for *believed* is *'Aman* meaning "to make firm, … to stand firm, to be enduring; to trust, to believe." This Hebrew word is often translated *faithful* in the Old Testament. In Romans 4:3, the Greek word for *believed* is *pisteuo* meaning "to be firmly persuaded as to something, to believe … with the idea of hope and certain expectation." It comes from the Greek word *pistis,* translated *faith* throughout the New Testament. As you can see, in both the Old and New Testament, belief and faith are the same concept.

We might assume the definition of unbelief, but let's look at an interesting Scripture to offer us encouragement. Read Mark 9:21-24.

After the suffering father claimed belief in verse 24, what urgent request did he make of Christ in the next breath? Respond in the margin.

What refreshing honesty this admission must have been to Christ. First the father gave the right answer, "I do believe." But right answers don't help much with a wavering heart. As the father stood in the presence of Christ, he could no longer hold back his honest heart: "Help me overcome my unbelief!" The Greek word for *unbelief* is *apistos* meaning "not worthy of confidence, untrustworthy … a thing not to be believed, incredible." As we view this definition along with the definitions of its antonyms (belief or faith), we can safely draw the following conclusion that we can believe in Christ, accepting the truth that He is the Son of God, and we can believe on Christ, receiving eternal salvation, yet fail to stand firm, endure in belief, and choose to find Him trustworthy day to day.

Not worthy of confidence makes me shudder. God is so deserving of our trust.

In the margin write your own paraphrase of Numbers 23:19.

Has God ever proved unworthy of your confidence? If we think we've discovered unfaithfulness in God, I believe one of three conditions has resulted: (1) we misinterpreted a promise, (2) we missed the answer, and (3) we gave up before God timed His response.

I see good and bad news in the issue of unbelief. The bad news? Unbelief is crippling. Second Corinthians 5:7 says, "We walk by faith, not by sight." We take steps forward with God through faith or belief. Unbelief literally cripples our spiritual "walk," casting huge obstacles in the way of a victorious journey here on earth.

We sometimes approach Christ with the attitude of the father in Mark 9:21. Christ asked how long the demon-possessed boy had been in his present condition. Search Mark 9:22 carefully.

> The steps we take forward with God we take through faith.

How did the father reveal a lack of confidence in Christ's ability and how did Christ respond in verse 23? Respond in the margin.

You may have been battling captivity for a very long time, or you may have no clue what's holding you back from the full benefit of your salvation. You may have almost given up ever experiencing the reality of abundant life. Somewhere along the way you may have ceased believing God is able. Perhaps you secretly approach Him with the attitude "if you can do anything, take pity on me."

Now the good news! If we're willing to admit our lack of confidence in Him, Christ is more than willing to help us overcome our unbelief. Belief (faith in the abilities and promises of God) is a vital prerequisite for fleshing out the liberty we've won through Jesus Christ. Let's take a little self-test to measure our state of belief. Please answer candidly. You will not be asked to share your answers.

Beside each question write a number from 1 to 10 to indicate how strongly you believe or disbelieve the statement. After indicating your belief, look up the Scripture reference to see what the Bible says.
___ 1. Christians can have areas of captivity (Gal. 5:1).
___ 2. Christ can set anyone free from captivity (Luke 4:18).
___ 3. God is fully acquainted with you personally and wants what is best for you (Ps. 139:1-3; Isa. 48:17).
___ 4. We have an invisible but very real enemy called Satan who is a personality of evil rather than a "principle" of evil (Eph. 6:10-12).
___ 5. Our hearts can want what's desperately wrong for us (Jer. 17:9).
___ 6. The Bible is the inspired Word of God and true (2 Tim. 3:16; Ps. 18:30).

No matter how you answered, I can relate. At some time in my life I probably would have answered as you did. At one time, I couldn't answer any of them with a confident 10; but now God has made a full believer out of me. If we believe the Bible, we can believe the concepts represented by each question.

Your struggle may be that you are not utterly convinced that the Bible is God's inspired Word. If so, scriptural "proofs" may mean little to you. Believe it or not, I was not always convinced either—although I never would have admitted it. Not coincidentally, my uncertainty accompanied a sizable lack of knowledge. I knew what I had been taught and wholeheartedly believed the basics; but I did not become convinced about the glorious inspiration of God's complete Word until I really began to study.

Instead of discovering loopholes and worrisome inconsistencies, I have been awed to my knees over the beauty of God's Word and the perfect blending of the Old and New Testaments. The study of Scripture has increased my faith at least one-hundredfold. I've continued to grow increasingly amazed at His Word. See how important belief can be in the matter of freedom. Read Matthew 9:27-29.

 In the margin describe the theme of this encounter.

Please understand. Christ is fully God. He can heal anyone or perform any wonder, whether the person's belief is great or small. Christ isn't asking us to believe in our ability to exercise unwavering faith. He is asking us to believe that He is able.

When it comes to bringing us to a life of freedom, I believe God is also willing. If we were focusing on physical healing, I would not have such certainty. Sometimes God heals physical sicknesses and sometimes He chooses greater glory through illness. He always can heal physical diseases, but He does not always choose to bring healing on this earth. Scripture is absolutely clear, however, that God always wills the spiritual captive to be free. God's will is for us to know Him and believe Him, glorify Him, be satisfied by Him, experience peace in Him, and enjoy Him. For God to have utmost cooperation from us on this freedom trail, we must believe that He is willing and completely able.

> God always wills the spiritual captive to be free.

Today where would you place your belief on the following diagram?

unbelief	still struggling	growing in confidence	certainty

If you are not struggling with belief, be careful not to judge another's weaker faith (Rom. 14:1). Many reasons can exist for unbelief in the area of freedom from captivity. Because some believers have been in chains for so long and have tried so hard to break free in the past, they almost have given up hope for the future.

If you are having difficulty believing you really could live out the liberty of Christ, would you make the same plea the father made in Mark 9:24? Spend some time in prayer asking the Father to overcome your unbelief.

If you are not struggling with belief, in your prayer finish the sentence, "Lord, help me overcome my …"

Glance at Isaiah 43:10 one more time. God wants us to know and believe Him. The most effective key to believing God is right before our eyes: The more we know Him, the more we will believe Him. The apostle Paul said it best: "I know whom I have believed, and am convinced that he is able to guard what I have entrusted to him for that day" (2 Tim. 1:12). We tend to run to God for temporary relief. God is looking for people who will walk with Him in steadfast belief. Beloved, choose to believe. Those who trust in Him will not be put to shame.

Day 2
The Obstacle of Pride

We are preparing for a mighty work of God by seeking to remove five major obstacles. We will benefit most from the weeks that follow if we remove each in advance of the material to come. Each of these obstacles corresponds as a direct hindrance to one of the five benefits of our covenant relationship with Christ.

On day 1 we focused on the hindrance to Benefit 1: To know God and believe Him. Based on the example of the father of the demon-possessed boy, if we have difficulty believing God our fervent prayer needs to be "I do believe; help me overcome my unbelief!" (Mark 9:24).

Today we consider the primary obstacle hindering Benefit 2: To glorify God. First remember what it means to glorify God. God is glorified when He is allowed to show Himself … and show Himself great or mighty. How can we be assured of living a God-glorifying life? By adopting a God-glorifying attitude. God tucked a wonderful Scripture in the Book of Isaiah that beautifully illustrates an attitude through which God will undoubtedly be glorified.

Today's Treasure
"I live in a high and holy place, but also with him who is contrite and lowly in spirit, to revive the spirit of the lowly and to revive the heart of the contrite." **ISAIAH 57:15**

In Isaiah 26:8, what do the people desire or value?
☐ God's name and renown   ☐ God's honor and blessing
☐ God's healing and power

God will show Himself "great and mighty" in those whose heart's desire is His name and renown. The original word for *name* is *shem*, which means "definite and conspicuous position … honor, authority, character … fame" (*Strong's*). Those who possess a God-glorifying attitude have allowed Him to assume a *definite position* in their personal lives that can't help becoming conspicuous.

Place an X on the scale below to indicate how you would estimate the visibility of God in you at this point in your life.

practically invisible   *conspicuous*

Please don't think you're alone if He's rather inconspicuous in you. Few things are more contrary to our human natures than desiring anyone's "fame" or "renown" above our own. Nothing could be more natural than self-seeking. Believers sometimes stop short of a God-glorifying life because we want to share in God's glory.

How does Isaiah 42:8 say God responds to this mentality? (margin)

According to Isaiah 43:7, we are called to allow the King of all creation to reveal Himself through us. He will not share His glory with another, not even with His own children. Not because He's egotistical but because He's interested in our eternal treasures. By demanding that we seek His glory alone, He calls us to overcome the overwhelming and very natural temptation to seek our own.

What do you think would be the biggest obstacle to glorifying God?
☐ pride   ☐ indifference   ☐ ignorance
☐ rebellion   ☐ disobedience

Alexander Pope called it "the never-failing vice of fools."[1] Pride—a destroyer of ministries, marriages, friendships, jobs, and character. God will be most readily seen through those who desire His fame above all else. Sounds simple, but it's not. In fact, few things are more contrary to our human natures than desiring anyone's fame above our own. Even when we desire the fame of our spouses or children, deep inside we are often yearning for the fame they might lend to us.

To fulfill our God-given destinies—to allow the King of all creation to show Himself through us—we must overcome the temptation to seek our own glory by desiring His instead. If we are to recognize and allow God to free us from any areas of captivity, we must recognize pride as more than self-promotion. It is a dangerous lure to captivity. Read Jeremiah 13:15-17 very carefully. I want you to feel the weight or seriousness of this reference.

> We must overcome the temptation to seek our own glory by desiring His instead.

According to verse 16, why would the arrogant be wise to quickly seek the remedy of giving glory to God?

What did God say would ultimately happen if His people, due to pride, did not listen to Him (v. 17)?

Can you think of several reasons why we would have to cast down pride to break free from any areas of captivity? In the margin list as many reasons as you can.

Beware of the fact that pride often disguises itself. For example, I have known people who thought they were too far gone to save, too wicked, too sinful. Such people would be shocked to hear that their attitude is a form of pride as well. They think their sin or problem is bigger than God.

I want nothing to hinder God's work in your personal life through these weeks. My convictions concerning this Bible study are bone-marrow deep. I know the reality of captivity, and I know the reality of liberty. I will stop at nothing biblical to beg you to let freedom ring loudly in your life. Pride will be a huge inhibitor to the journey ahead. God wants to…

- get to our hearts. Pride covers the heart.
- free us from hindrances in our past. Pride refuses to look back.
- treat us with His Word. Pride doesn't like to be told what to do.
- set us completely free. Pride thinks he's free enough.
- bring us out of dark closets. Pride says secrets are nobody's business.
- help us with constraining problems. Pride denies there is a problem.
- make us strong in Him. Pride won't admit to weakness.

Only God could have changed my heart.

We are on a journey to freedom. As we embark on our road trip, let's imagine that we have everything we need packed and ready to go: Bible, book, pen, anticipation, time set aside. But before we can take our first few steps, we run into a boulder in the road. The size of this boulder differs with each of us according to the degree to which we struggle with pride. I can hardly imagine that any of us see only a small pebble in our way. To go forward from here, God must empower each of us to roll the boulder of pride off our road to liberty. I believe this stone will roll if we give it three mighty shoves.

1. The first shove is to view pride as a vicious enemy.

What motivation does each of the following Scriptures provide for viewing pride as an enemy?

Proverbs 8:13

Proverbs 11:2

Proverbs 13:10

Proverbs 16:18

Obadiah 1:3

2. The second shove is to view humility as a friend. Often our society reviles biblical humility as a sign of weakness. Nothing could be further from the truth. Being filled with pride is easy. It comes naturally. Humility takes a supply of supernatural strength that comes only to those who are strong enough to admit weakness.

What motivation does each of the following Scriptures provide for viewing humility as a friend?

James 4:6,10

Isaiah 57:14,15

Isaiah 66:2

Esteem basically means to "have respect." Can you imagine being one whom God "respects"? What a wonderful thought!

Humbling ourselves before God means bowing before His majesty.

3. The third and final shove is humbling ourselves before God. James 4:10 and 1 Peter 5:6 plainly tell us to humble *ourselves*. You see, humility is not something we have until humbling ourselves is something we do. This step necessitates action before possession. Humbling ourselves certainly does not mean hating ourselves. Humility can be rather easily attained by simply opening our eyes to *reality*. I have plenty of reasons to be humble, far more reasons than I have to be proud.

A simple reality check should make humbling ourselves achievable. Just read a few chapters of Scripture boasting in the greatness of God; Job 38 is one of my favorites. We certainly don't have to hate ourselves to see how small we are in comparison to God and to respond appropriately by bowing down before Him. In a nutshell, that's what humbling ourselves before God means: bowing down before His majesty. We don't have to hang our heads in self-abasement to humble ourselves. We simply must choose to lower our heads from lofty, inappropriate places. We choose to humble ourselves by submitting ourselves to His greatness every single day.

How does God want you to respond to what He showed you today?

The last sentence of Daniel 4:37 provides one of the most effective motivations for humility in my personal life. What does it say?

I look at it this way: I'd rather humble myself than force God to humble me. Let's allow the circumstances and weaknesses, and any thorns in the flesh God has chosen to leave, to do the job they were sent to do—provoke humility. This is not so we can be flattened under God's doormat but so He can joyfully lift us up. Find a private place to get down on your knees and humble yourself before your mighty and glorious God. The hosts of heaven are sure to hear a thunderous rumble as boulders of pride roll off our road to freedom.

Day 3
The Obstacle of Idolatry

Today we place the spotlight on a third obstacle blocking our path to freedom. This obstacle hinders the third benefit of our covenant relationship with God. In week 2, day 3 we saw God wants us to find our satisfaction in Him rather than things that cannot satisfy. Let's begin our reading today with Isaiah 55:1-9.

In the margin, list everything these verses teach us about our God.

In Isaiah 55:2 God posed a concern to His own children: people who knew Him but were not coming to Him to receive all He desired to give. Sound familiar? God asked, "Why spend money on what is not bread, and your labor on what does not satisfy?" Then, like a frustrated parent determined to get through to his child, He said, "Listen, listen to me, and eat what is good, and your soul will delight in the richest of fare." Isaiah 55:6 implies God's prescription for those with an inner thirst (Isa. 55:1) and hunger they cannot fill.

What should those who are spiritually thirsty and hungry do (Isa. 55:6)?

Isaiah 55:3 issues the perfect invitation for all those who cannot find lasting satisfaction: "Come to me." I believe God creates and activates a nagging dissatisfaction in every person for an excellent reason. According to 2 Peter 3:9, God doesn't want anyone to perish. Rather, He wants everyone to come to repentance. He gave us a will so we could choose whether or not to accept His invitation: "Come to me." God purposely created us with a need only He can meet. One of the most common and overt human experiences is the inability to be completely satisfied.

Many come to Christ out of their search for something missing; yet after receiving His salvation, they go elsewhere for further satisfaction. Christians can be miserably dissatisfied if they accept Christ's salvation yet reject the fullness of daily relationship that satisfies. Just as He offered the children of Israel, God offers us so much more than we usually choose to enjoy.

Our wise and merciful Lord creates every one of us with a God-shaped void in our lives so we will seek Him. Dissatisfaction is not a terrible thing. It's a God-thing. The terrible thing is when we don't let it lead us to Christ. He wants us to find the only thing that will truly satiate our thirsty and hungry hearts.

Has dissatisfaction ever led you to discover Christ in a new and satisfying way? ☐ Yes ☐ No **If so, when?**

Today's Treasure
"Who shapes a god and casts an idol, which can profit him nothing?"
ISAIAH 44:10

In retrospect, can you think of a time when God was trying to lead you to find fullness in Him but you settled for something less? ☐ Yes ☐ No If so, in the margin describe what happened.

Realizing God desires for us to find genuine satisfaction in Him helps us discover the third primary obstacle on our road to freedom: settling for satisfaction with anything else. God gave this practice a name I was unprepared to hear: idolatry. After serious meditation, I realized the label made perfect sense no matter how harsh it seemed.

Anything we try to put in a place where God belongs is an idol. God created us so that He alone fits our deepest needs. Each of us have succumbed to idolatry at times. Before you hang your head in shame, remember the Holy Spirit does not convict us of sin to condemn us. Rather, He convicts us of sin so we'll become aware, seek forgiveness, and be set free!

We must remove the obstacle of idolatry. We begin by recognizing the obstacle as idol worship, but we may find removing it difficult. The first two obstacles to freedom—unbelief and pride—can be removed effectively by a choice: we can choose to believe God and we can choose to humble ourselves before God. I am not minimizing the difficulty, but I am suggesting the obstacles are removed by volition. Some of the idols in our lives—things or people we have put in God's place—can take much longer to remove. Some of them have been in those places for years and only the power of God can make them budge. We hope to work on removing them over the weeks to come.

We must begin by choosing to recognize their existence and admitting they cannot keep us satisfied. I'm hoping that the more we study, the more convinced we'll become that God is perfectly suited to displace every idol we possess.

The nation of Israel struggled horribly with the sin of idolatry. We saw some of the results in the lives of Uzziah, Jotham, Ahaz, and Hezekiah. Idolatry permeated the lives of God's people. Read Isaiah 2:1,6-9.

In verse 6 Isaiah said God had abandoned His people. The prophet saw no sign of God's presence. God had promised not to abandon them, and He didn't. But where sin is rampant God can certainly shrink the presence of the Holy Spirit and leave virtually no signs of His presence. I've experienced God withdrawing His obvious presence in my own life in seasons of sin.

> Anything we try to put in a place where God belongs is an idol.

✳ What signs of idolatry did Isaiah see in the people (Isa. 2:8)?

In the margin describe how you think we can figuratively bow down to the work of our hands.

Isaiah was so upset by the idolatry that he blurted out, "Do not forgive them." When God shows us the wickedness in and around us, we appreciate His mercy and grace. We may occasionally see as He sees, but we can hardly comprehend how He continues to forgive. The Israelites had been given everything, yet they refused to be satisfied. They traded in what their hearts could know for what their eyes could see. Isaiah 44:10 reminds us that "a man's idols can profit him nothing." The next verse says that idols ultimately reap shame. Read Isaiah 44:6-23, then complete the following.

How do our idols, substitutes for God, ultimately bring shame? (margin)

People can become so engrossed in their idols that they no longer pay attention to their physical needs (v. 12). What idols could displace common sense regarding physical health?

Idols can take the form of humans (v. 13). We can apply this point literally. At some point we've all exalted someone to a place where only God belonged.

Can you think of someone you once idolized? In the margin describe why you think you idolized that person.

Read verse 21 carefully. Why do you think God wants Israel to remember these things?

The mercy of God is indescribable, isn't it? Even when His people turned to idols, He swept away their offenses like a cloud, their sins like the morning mist. As we must face some of the idols we have worshiped in our quest for satisfaction, we need never doubt God's mercy. He asks one thing: "Return to me, for I have redeemed you" (v. 22).

See the strong tie between our quest for satisfaction and idol worship? The void in our lives God created for Himself will demand attention. Whether or not we realize it, we look desperately for something to satisfy us and fill the empty places. Our craving to be filled is so strong that the moment something or someone seems to meet our need, we feel an overwhelming temptation to worship it.

One of the most thought-provoking verses in Isaiah 44 is verse 20. Reread it carefully. Fresh conviction washes over me like a squall. How many times have I fed on ashes instead of feasting on the life-giving Word of God? How many times has my deluded heart misled me? How many times have I tried to save myself?

What about you? Does this verse cause any kind of strong response in you? ☐ Yes ☐ No If so, in the margin describe your feelings.

I could fall on my face and praise God through all eternity for finally awakening me to say, "This thing in my right hand is a lie." I remember one thing in particular I held onto with a virtual death grip. I also remember the harrowing moment God opened my eyes to see what a lie I had believed. I cried for days.

I originally thought this lie was a good thing. My heart, handicapped in childhood, had deluded me. Although I didn't realize it at the time, I eventually bowed down and worshiped it. My only consolation in my idolatry is that I finally allowed God to peel away my fingers and to my knowledge have only grasped His hand since.

Had I not discovered what a lie I held, I would never have run to Him to fill the void. I've discovered the glorious satisfaction only the Lord Jesus Christ can bring. I can truly say to you at this moment that I love Him more than anything or anyone in this world. Jesus is the uncontested love of my life. Yes, I plunged to the depths to discover satisfaction. Sadly, I often learn things the hard way, and I'm very aware that Satan will constantly cast idols before me. I hope never to forget that I could fall again to the same one I bowed down and worshiped before.

Beloved, whatever we grip to bring us satisfaction is a lie—unless it is Christ. He is the Truth that sets us free. If you are holding anything in your craving for satisfaction, would you be willing to acknowledge it as a lie? Even if you feel you can't let go of it at this moment, would you lift it before Him—perhaps literally lifting your fisted hand as a symbol—and confess it as an idol? Beloved, if what you're grasping isn't Christ, it's the worst kind of cheater. The kind that appears as a friend but secretly steals your treasures with no remorse. God does not condemn you. He calls you. Will you open your hand to Him? He is opening His to you.

> How does God want you to respond to what He showed you today?

Day 4
The Obstacle of Prayerlessness

Today's Treasure
"Foreigners who bind themselves to the Lord to serve him, to love the name of the Lord, and to worship him, all who keep the Sabbath without desecrating it and who hold fast to my covenant—these I will bring to my holy mountain and give them joy in my house of prayer." **Isaiah 56:6-7**

We're working to roll away some huge stones from our road to freedom. I deeply desire for you to approach this study of God's Word with attention to detail, retaining truths for the rest of your life. Remember, we not only want liberty in Christ to become a present reality, we want it to be permanent. Some stones in the path are so huge, they must be removed in advance. The obstacle we study today is no exception. First recall the benefit it obstructs. God wants us to enjoy His peace.

The key to peace is authority. Peace is the fruit of an obedient life. Disobedience and rebellion against God's authority complicates the life of a captive. I can tell you from personal experience that at times of greatest captivity, I most wanted to be obedient to God. I was miserable in my rebellion, and I could not understand why I kept making wrong choices. Yes, they were my choices and I've taken full responsibility for them as my sins. However, Satan had me in such a vice-like grip I felt powerless to obey. Of course, I wasn't powerless; but as long as I believed the lie, I behaved accordingly.

Read Philippians 4:6-7. Let's have a little fun for a moment and paraphrase the verses from a negative standpoint. In other words, turn this prescription for peace into a no-fail prescription for anxiety.

Begin with the following words, and in the margin complete the two verses accordingly. "Do not be calm about anything, but in everything ...

"Do not be calm about anything, but in everything ..."

I know I'd get a kick out of your prescription for anxiety. If you're like me, you know it by heart because you've filled it so often! No matter how you worded your remedy, you probably cautioned those seeking anxiety to avoid prayer.

I might have written something like this: "Do not be calm about anything, but in everything, by dwelling on it constantly and feeling picked on by God, with thoughts like 'and this is the thanks I get,' present your aggravations to everyone you know but Him. And the acid in your stomach, which transcends all milk products, will cause you an ulcer, and the doctor bills will cause you a heart attack and you will lose your mind."

Without a doubt, avoiding prayer is a sure prescription for anxiety, a way to avoid peace. To experience the kind of peace that covers all circumstances, the Bible challenges us to develop active, authentic (what I like to call "meaty") prayer lives. Prayer with real substance to it—original thoughts flowing from an individual heart, personal and intimate. We often do everything but pray. We tend to want something more "substantial." Even studying the Bible, going to church, talking to the pastor, or receiving counsel seems more tangible than prayer.

What victory the enemy has in winning us over to prayerlessness! He'd rather we do anything than pray. He'd rather see us serve ourselves into the ground, because he knows we'll eventually grow resentful without prayer. He'd rather see us study the Bible into the wee hours of the morning, because he knows we'll never have deep understanding and power to live what we've learned without prayer. Satan knows prayerless lives are powerless lives, while prayerful lives are powerful lives!

The apostle Paul was zealous for others to know Christ in the satisfying way he knew Him. Paul was thoroughly convinced that certain blessings of God came through prayer alone, and he prayed diligently for these to be realities in the lives of other believers. Read Ephesians 1:17-20.

In the margin record the specific blessings that come through prayer.

Can you see ways in which any of these blessings or manifestations of the Holy Spirit could replace anxiety with peace? Please be specific.

Without infringing on any points you've made, I'd like to make one very general observation based on these verses. The better we know God (v. 17), the more we will trust Him. The more we trust Him, the more we will sense His peace when the wintry winds blow against us.

You paraphrased Philippians 4:6-7. Read these two verses again, out loud if possible. Sounds like a promise to me. Has the world ever promised you anything that really delivered an authentic and lasting peace when turmoil continued around you? ☐ Yes ☐ No

At the grocery store recently I was amused by the label on a lotion that claimed it was an effective stress reliever. I could hear a baby screaming on the next aisle. I had a brief notion to offer the lotion to the poor mom pushing the cranky cargo, but I feared I might get a little stress reliever thrown on my face. This world can't seem to come up with a real, lasting solution to the stresses and strains of life.

Just a few days ago I again saw the best advice the world seems to have— Just remember two things: (1) Don't sweat the small stuff. (2) It's all small stuff.

I'd like to stuff a sweaty sock in the mouth of the person who first said that. It's not all small stuff. I have a friend whose son was paralyzed in an accident his senior year in high school. I pray almost daily for a list of people, from age 4 to 74, who are battling cancer. Two recently came off my list and into heaven. My precious friend's husband, an honest, hardworking believer with a son in college, just lost his job—again. Not long ago, three tornadoes whipped through my hometown—stealing, killing, and destroying. No, it's not all small stuff.

Worldly philosophy is forced to minimize difficulty because it has no real answers. You and I know better than the small-stuff philosophy. We face a lot of big stuff out there. Only through prayer are we washed in peace.

It's time to roll away the stone of prayerlessness. It is the most prohibitive obstacle in the road to victory and forms a crippling obstacle in our present pursuit toward making liberty in Christ a reality in life.

> Worldly philosophy is forced to minimize difficulty because it has no real answers.

Why do you think prayerlessness is such an obstacle? (margin)

In addition to the reasons you noted, let me share one of mine. When Satan takes perfect aim at our "Achilles heel," picks the perfect time, and wears the perfect disguise, none of the following will work effectively to keep us out of a snare:
- Discipline. At times of great temptation and weakness, discipline can fly like a bird out the nearest window.
- Lessons we have learned from the past. We don't think that straight when we get a surprise, full-fledged attack.
- What is best for us. Our human nature is much too self-destructive to automatically choose what is best at our weakest moments.

Our strongest motivation will be the person with whom we walk. Staying close to Him through constant communication, we receive a continual supply of strength to walk victoriously—in peace even as we walk through a war zone.

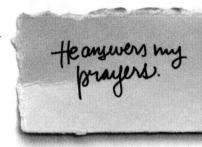

Beloved, let me give you another reason we need prayer as we seek to break free. Satan will try to stir up what our faithful Refiner wants to skim off. Remember, Christ came to set the captive free. Satan comes to make the free captive. Christ wants to cut binding ropes from our lives. Satan wants to use them to tie us in knots. We must walk with Christ step-by-step for the sake of protection, power, and a resulting unparalleled passion in our lives. None of these will be realities in our lives any other way. The enemy will be defeated. Believe it. Act on it.

Read Ephesians 6:10-18, giving special attention to verse 18. Notice the words, "With this in mind." Paul was referring to his words about warfare.

In the margin describe why you think prayer was especially important in matters of warfare.

 Now take a look at Ephesians 6:15. We are to keep our "feet fitted with the readiness that comes from" what?

Our feet keep us balanced as we stand. This passage is about standing against the devil's schemes. God wants us to be alert and powerful in His Spirit, not filled with fear. Do we need to fear the enemy? Paul answered confidently in Romans 8:37: "No, in all these things we are more than conquerors through him who loved us." We are more than conquerors. Our balance out on the battlefield comes from knowing that—although we are at war with Satan, who is admittedly powerful—we are at peace with God, who is gloriously omnipotent and fights our battles for us. Our feet are fitted for battle by resting snugly in the gospel of peace. We won't experience that peace without prayer. For this reason, Paul said, "With this in mind, be alert and always keep on praying" (Eph. 6:18).

Can you imagine how different Paul's life and the infant church would have been if he allowed fear to rule him? Through faith, the opposite of fear, Paul was spiritually loosed even when he was physically chained. Had he given way to fear, he may have been physically loosed; but he would have been spiritually chained.

Read Ephesians 6:19-20. In these verses what was Paul depending on to help him be fearless? ☐ wisdom ☐ strength ☐ prayer ☐ friends

Prayer matters. The Spirit of God released through our prayers and the prayers of others turn cowards into conquerors, chaos into calm, cries into comfort. The enemy knows the power of prayer. He's been watching it furiously for thousands of years. In preparation for this lesson, I searched for all the uses of the word *pray* in its various forms from Genesis to Revelation. I nearly wept as I saw hundreds of references.

> Abraham prayed … Isaac prayed … Jacob prayed … Moses left Pharaoh and prayed … So Moses prayed for the people … Manoah prayed to the Lord … Samson prayed … Hannah wept much and prayed … So David prayed … Elijah stepped forward and prayed …

The last thing God wants for His children is a spirit of fear regarding the enemy.

71

How does God want you to respond to what He showed you today?

Elisha prayed, "O, Lord" … After Job had prayed for his friends … Hezekiah prayed to the Lord … Daniel got down on his knees and prayed … From inside the fish Jonah prayed … Very early in the morning, while it was still dark, Jesus got up, left the house and went off to a solitary place, where He prayed … Going a little farther, He fell with His face to the ground and prayed.

If Christ sought to have the divine life strengthened in Him through solitary times of intimacy with the Father, how much more should I? I am hopeless to live the victorious life without prayer.

Look back at the names of the Bible characters who prayed. The list could have gone on and on. Without exception, prayerful lives were powerful lives. The Bible is a book of prayer. As Today's Treasure reminds us, God's presence is a house of prayer. O, Beloved, when our lives are over and the record of our days stands complete, may the words written of us be, she prayed …

Day 5
The Obstacle of Legalism

Today's Treasure

"*The Lord says: 'These people come near to me with their mouth and honor me with their lips, but their hearts are far from me. Their worship of me is made up only of rules taught by men.'*"
ISAIAH 29:13

Today we conclude our emphasis on removing the obstacles in the way of God's benefits. This week we have exerted spiritual muscle rolling away the stones of …

> **Unbelief** … *so we may know God and believe Him.*
> **Pride** … *so we may glorify God.*
> **Idolatry** … *so we may find satisfaction in God.*
> **Prayerlessness** … *so we can experience God's peace.*

This week's memory verse reminds us why we want to exert the spiritual, emotional, mental, and physical energy this journey demands.

Below write Isaiah 64:4 from memory (compare 1 Cor. 2:9).

Every time you are tempted to let worldly priorities overshadow God and His Word, say this verse out loud! He is worthy of our utmost attentions and the study of His Word will liberate and revitalize us as nothing else can do. He is faithful!

We have one last boulder to roll off the road before we are free to move ahead unhindered on our journey to liberation. As you recall, each obstacle we study this week directly hinders one of the five primary benefits of our salvation.

What is Benefit 5?

Many elements or conditions can keep us from truly enjoying God's presence. For instance, not spending adequate time with Him greatly affects our pure enjoyment of His presence. Having an underdeveloped prayer life robs our joy as does harboring bitterness or anger at another person, but the person who studies God's Word in depth and experiences a consistent lack of enjoyment of God often suffers from a condition with an ugly name—legalism.

To the best of your understanding, what does legalism mean when used in a negative, religious context? Respond in the margin.

The term *legalism* does not appear in Scripture, but perfect illustrations of it are scattered throughout the Word. Each of the following references teaches us something about legalism either directly or by example.

Record what you learn about legalism from each one.

Matthew 12:9-14

Acts 15:1-2,6-11

Galatians 2:15-16

With what you've learned about legalism from the references above, interpret Ecclesiastes 7:15-20 to the best of your understanding.

In my opinion, legalism results when three conditions occur:

1. Regulations replace relationship. The Pharisees in Matthew 12 revealed that they had a superficial understanding of God and no enjoyment of His presence. The Sabbath belonged entirely to God. He established it for man's benefit, not to imprison him. The greatest benefit Christ could bring to the man with the shriveled hand was a relationship with the Savior. He initiated this relationship through healing. We don't have to wonder who enjoyed Christ more that day—the Pharisees or the man with the shriveled hand!

How could a student of God's Word squeeze the enjoyment out of her Christian walk by replacing relationship with regulations? (margin)

2. Microscopes replace mirrors.

Based on Matthew 7:1-5, what do you think I mean by this expression?

He fills the hole in my heart.

Note the words from Matthew 12:10, "looking for a reason to accuse." Modern-day Pharisees sometimes practice religious voyeurism, looking for a reason to accuse others. They tend to love a church "soap opera" because their own relationship with God is so unexciting. They look to the faults of others to keep things interesting.

I am thankful to say I've seen far more genuine examples of true Christianity in the church than unfeeling legalists. Unfortunately, I have also seen many caring Christians intimidated by the occasional legalist. Concentrating on the shortcomings of others can cheat a Christian of truly enjoying the presence of God.

3. Performance replaces passion. If our motivation for obedience is anything other than love and devotion for God, we're probably up to our eyeballs in legalism and in for disaster. Obedience without love is nothing but the law. The Israelites often demonstrated how short-lived righteousness for righteousness' sake tends to be.

Read God's description of legalism in Isaiah 29:13. In the margin write what you believe to be an example of this kind of legalism.

Let's search our hearts for a moment. God does not take our spiritual temperature under the tongue by the words we say, or in our ear by the impressive teachings we hear, or under our arms by the service we perform. God takes our spiritual temperature straight from the heart.

In the margin you'll find a drawing of a thermometer. Let's see if we can take our own temperatures for a moment. I won't tell if you won't. I don't want you to label any mark I ask you to make. Only you will know what each mark represents. Let's take four "temperatures."

First, if you could take your temperature based on the spiritual or "religious" words you say, where would you estimate it on the thermometer? Draw a line at that point. Again, do not label anything on this drawing. This exercise is for personal use only.

Second, if you could take your temperature based on the good biblical teaching to which you expose yourself, where would you estimate it on the thermometer? Draw a line at that point.

Third, if you could take your temperature based on your service or works for God, where would you estimate it on the thermometer? Draw a line.

Last, if you could take your temperature for God straight from your heart, where would you estimate it on the thermometer? Again, draw a line. No one knows which temperature each line represents but you.

I don't know about you, but this little experiment has caused me to do some thinking. Three strong reasons exist for rolling the large obstacle of legalism out of our way before we go any further in our study.

1. This journey is about a relationship—not regulations. I want you to thoroughly enjoy God's presence through the next seven weeks. I'm praying for you to sense His presence more than ever. If you ask Him to make Himself so real to you through His Word and lavish you with His love, you will enjoy God even when you don't enjoy the confrontation! God is going to get very personal with us over these next weeks. Sometimes you're going to have your eyes opened to things you'd rather not see. How do I know? Because I've been on this journey! Truth sets us free, but sometimes Truth is pretty confrontational! When this study is complete and someone asks you if you enjoyed it, I want you to be able to say with all sincerity, "I enjoyed God!"

2. This journey is about you. My rendition of the journey is about me. In the past, I've written studies on biblical figures like Moses, David, and Paul. This time each of us is the human protagonist. (Sometimes you may think I'm your human antagonist!) If you are taking this journey with a small group, please fight the temptation to place their lives under a microscope. Simply let God's Word become a mirror of what you want reflected in your life. You may hear group members share things that are completely foreign to you. Let's resist judgment and gossip at all costs. Many people have been badly injured by life. Let's have mercy for one another and avoid analyzing others' problems.

3. This journey is about the heart. The last thing I want this study to represent is another means of increasing biblical knowledge. I pray you will grow in knowledge, but that is not our purpose. Anyone who is taking this study for the pure satisfaction of completing another Bible study won't stay interested long. In fact, if you're still with me, you're probably not one of them!

This Bible study is for the heart—to loosen any chains keeping the heart from enjoying abundant liberty in Christ's salvation. If we let our mouths grow close to Him through churchy conversation and even theological discussion in small groups but we keep our hearts far from Him, this journey will not mean a thing. I'm not fussing. I'm just pleading with you to withhold nothing from God for the next seven weeks.

Precious student of God's Word, you've worked hard shoving those obstacles off the road this week. Are you still having trouble budging one or two? Then remember, God's specialty is rolling away a stone. Show Him which one is causing you trouble, put your hands on top of His, and on the count of three …

How does God want you to respond to what He showed you today?

1. *Bartlett's Familiar Quotations* (Boston: Little, Brown & Co., 1980), 332.

BREAKING Free

session four viewer guide

New Testament parallels from the confrontation between Sennacherib, the king of Assyria, and Hezekiah, the king of Judah: We'll view Sennacherib symbolically as the enemy captor and Hezekiah symbolically as the covenant child of God.

Isaiah 36:13-16. Our captor tries to coax us into _____ _____ with our _____.

Isaiah 37:10-11. Our captor likes to _____ _____ of all who _____ _____ and poses the question, "And you think you _____ ____ _____?"

Isaiah 37:14-22,23,28,35-37. Over and over Scripture portrays _____ as the _____ _____ ____ _____ when under attack.

God has reserved momentous victories and great rewards for us. But we'll never make it _____ _____ _____ if we can't make it _____ _____ _____.

See 1 Corinthians 10:13. "Way of escape." The Greek word *ekbasis* (escape) comes from the same origin as the English word _____. In the Greek language the term also implies an _____.

Making It Through the Moment: The Role of Prayer

1. Prayer changes _____.

   Two reasons we often don't take the exit:

   • We don't _____ _____ (Ps. 40:8).

   • We don't feel like we _____ (Rom. 8:1).

2. Prayer activates _____. Compare Jude 24-25.

Week 4

Rebuilding the Ancient Ruins

He is standing by my side, holding my hand.

The Lord wants bind up my

I am so thankful that God loves us. He knows our every hurt, and He cares! He has set me free. For the first time ever in my life, I have hope that my life can be different.

Day 1
Touring the Ruins

"Rebuild the ancient ruins and restore the places long devastated" (Isa. 61:4). Something about those words touches a deep longing in my heart. Do they stir something in you? Do they make you want to climb up on the Master's workbench? This week we look into old ruins in our lives. Don't let that scare you. We're looking back to see how God wants to transform the mangled into monuments to His glory. Your memory verse this week points the way. Memorize Isaiah 61:4 and celebrate your reconstruction.

The Master Craftsman awaits. The captivity Isaiah foretold occurred when the Babylonians captured the people of Judah. We want to apply to our internal captivities the principles related to their physical captivity. Isaiah speaks of rebuilding and restoring ancient ruins that have been devastated for generations. The last segment of time offers the most specific invitation for personal application. Allow the Holy Spirit to meddle for a moment. Can you think of any ruins in your life that have been in your family line for generations?

I can think of a few ancient ruins in mine. We'll be discussing some. You might think of ruins like alcoholism, gambling, pornography, racism, or passive aggression. Until then, let's explore this concept to clarify how we can personally apply the idea of rebuilding ancient ruins to our lives and families.

I'm thankful for God's uncanny timing; I've just returned from Greece and Rome. God allowed us to trace many of the apostle Paul's travels where we gazed on the ruins of ancient cities like Ephesus, Corinth, and Rome. I was intrigued by the ruins for the lives they represented. Without historical context the remains are just old columns that no longer gird roofs, stone streets that no longer feed the market, and cities that have long since been defeated by human or natural foe.

Why do people flock to see ancient ruins? Because unlocking any society's heritage is important to understanding the development of its present inhabitants. Looking back for the right reasons with the right attitude helps us become better equipped to look forward. That's exactly what this portion of our series is all about—looking back. Don't get antsy on me now. We need to muster the courage to stop by the ancient ruins and see what we can learn about ourselves.

We need to examine areas of devastation or defeat in our family lines. Then we can explore resulting bonds that need breaking. Yokes can often be caused by severed relationships, lives left in ruins because of a loss or a tragedy, ancient family arguments and inheritances of hate, or generational debris scattered by a bomb that dropped and a life that refused repair.

Virtually all of us have some family ruins that only Christ can rebuild, but we could be unaware of them. A crucial reason exists for facing generational strongholds: Unless we purposely seek them, they can remain almost unrecognizable.

Think about generational strongholds for a moment. In the margin describe why they could be hard to recognize.

Perhaps you thought of several reasons, but we are going to highlight this: we tend to think of hand-me-down baggage as part of who we are rather than how we're bound. In many cases, we grew up with these chains so they feel completely natural. We consider them part of our personalities rather than a yoke squeezing abundant life out of us. Consider the following example.

God has changed my life in many ways.

> Claire's parents died in an epidemic. She was forced to live with her older brother. Money was scarce, so in Claire's behalf and without her consent, the brother accepted an offer of marriage from a prosperous older man. This husband turned out to be cruel and abusive; and after fathering two daughters, he left the family penniless because he wasn't given a son. Claire found refuge in Christ as her Savior, but she never let Him rebuild her life. Claire died before her granddaughter and great-granddaughters ever knew her. They were never orphaned nor beaten by a spouse, yet all but one of them battled a distrust and fear of men they hardly recognized, let alone understood.

You may think, *That seems more like a learned behavior than a stronghold.*

Anything passed down to us that inhibits the full expression of freedom in Christ qualifies as bondage. Our aim is not to argue genetics versus environment; our aim is to be loosed from anything limiting our lives in Christ. All things qualify as God's specialty, that's part of His beauty.

In the margin briefly describe another possible scenario of generational bondage—perhaps one you've witnessed personally.

You and I would both quickly agree; these are sad scenarios. Do you know what makes them even sadder? They were unnecessary to those in Christ. The cross of Calvary is enough to set us free from every yoke; and His Word is enough to make liberty a practical and perpetual reality, no matter what those before us left as an "inheritance." But His Word must be applied to specific life needs. Too often Christians have sought Jesus as Savior but ignored Him as deliverer.

I promised that we were going to approach our look at the ancient ruins for the right reason and with the right attitude.

What might be a right reason or attitude for looking back at family history, and what would be a wrong reason? Respond in the margin.

Let's allow the Word of God to help us formulate the right approach through two considerations. We can see the first in Matthew 1:1-16. Jesus' family tree includes such imperfection as Rahab the prostitute (Josh. 2:1-7) and Manasseh, an indescribably vile king (2 Chron. 33:1-17).

Point 1: Even Christ had a blend of the negative and positive in His lineage.
Beloved, we each have a concoction of good, bad, and ugly in our family lines. No one, no matter how whole he or she may seem to be, can boast a spotless, blameless, perfectly healthy lineage. Our purpose is not to drag old skeletons out of the closet or engage in family bashing of any kind. We need to make sure we didn't inherit any hand-me-down chains that interfere with the priceless benefits of our covenant relationship with Christ. He broke the chains of all kinds of bondage when He gave His life for us on the cross; however, many of us still carry them in our hands or have them dangling from our necks out of pure habit, lack of awareness, or lack of biblical knowledge. We purpose to recognize any generational bonds and ask God to remove them.

I use the word *inherit* from time to time. I want you to understand what I mean. When I refer to something we may have *inherited,* I mean anything we may have learned environmentally, anything to which we may be genetically predisposed, or any binding influence passed down through other means. Again, I don't come to you on the basis of science or psychology but on behalf of a statement declared in Galatians 5:1: "It is for freedom that Christ has set us free."

You may have *inherited* so much bondage that you can hardly stand looking back. My special prayer for you is that God will help you see some positives as well. I remember when I first dealt with the memories of my childhood victimization. My first inclination was to believe Satan's lie and think my entire childhood was ruins. Eventually, I realized I was wrong. Yes, I experienced some very ugly things, but I also can see the merciful hand of God as many positives have also surfaced. Glance back over Christ's lineage in Matthew 1, giving special attention to verses 1 and 2. Then read Galatians 3:26-29 very carefully.

What is your relationship to the lineage recorded in Matthew 1?

In response to the realization of your lineage in Christ's own family line, how do you feel about the words of Psalm 16:6?

Point 2: We don't have to disinherit or dishonor our physical lineage to fully accept and abide in our spiritual lineage.
God fully recognizes and desires to use both "lines" to His glory. Our spiritual lineage can overpower and disable any continuing negative effects of our physical lineage. We all have a "goodly heritage" in Christ (Ps. 16:6, KJV). For those who inherited many negatives, joyfully accepting this truth takes the edge off the pain of looking back.

Today I want you to take a first look back at both the positive and the negative in your heritage. Do not let the enemy get to you with a spirit of heaviness. Teachers and preachers have too long overlooked this bondage because the enemy has convinced us we will open the proverbial can of worms.

The Five Benefits

1.

2.

3.

4.

5.

I stand against all fear and intimidation of the enemy. He knows that issues left in shrouds of secrecy never get exposed to the healing light of God. We are going to stand on a positive approach even to our negatives, because bringing them before God is the first step to healing exposure and gaining freedom. If you have to list anything painful, thank God immediately that He is ready and willing to diffuse all things in your heritage that are binding you.

Recall the five benefits of our covenant relationship with Christ. Please write them in the margin.

Our purpose is to recognize what we've inherited or how we've been influenced—not to cast blame. When I ask you to review positives and negatives, I want you to think in terms of the influence each of these people had on enhancing or inhibiting the five benefits in your life. Please pause and ask God to reveal to you or remind you of any information pertinent to our study. Also ask God to disallow the enemy any ground in this or any step we take together, then believe God and receive the victory. The following exercise will help you identify any ancient ruins. Leave anything blank that doesn't apply.

Fill in the diagrams below describing both the positive and negative influences from your grandparents and parents. If you never knew your parents or grandparents, substitute the caregivers you have experienced.

Maternal Grandparents

Grandfather
Positive influence

Grandmother
Positive influence

Negative influence

Negative influence

Paternal Grandparents

Grandfather
Positive influence

Grandmother
Positive influence

Negative influence   Negative influence

Mother   Father
Positive influence   Positive influence

Negative influence   Negative influence

Can you think of any reasons why the negatives may have been present in either your grandparents' or parents' lives? ☐ Yes ☐ No
If so, describe in the margin.

Today have you recognized any ancient ruins in the last few generations? If so, what are they?

How does God want you to respond to what He showed you today?

Thank God that although you cannot change the past, He can help you change what you're doing with it! And the changes He makes in you in the present can certainly change the future! Hallelujah! Our God reigns!

Day 2
The Ancient Boundary Stone

As we journey toward the land of the free, we may have to become the brave! Our tour will take us by the ancient ruins this week for a few history lessons. Again, our purpose is not to condemn or dishonor people of our heritage but to recognize barriers in our present caused by bondage from our families' past. In our previous lesson, we highlighted two considerations that we want to remember throughout our fourth week.

Today's Treasure
"Do not move an ancient boundary stone set up by your forefathers."
PROVERBS 22:28

Point 1: Even Christ had a blend of the

_____ and

_____ in

His lineage.

Point 2: We don't have

to _____

our physical lineage

to fully _____

our spiritual lineage.

In the margin complete the two points we highlighted yesterday.

Today's lesson takes us back to the basics. Please read Exodus 20:1-21 with a fresh heart and teachable mind at this time. Perhaps a while has passed since we looked at these familiar Scriptures in their proper context. Remember, God is the Master of perfect order. Before He delivered the Ten Commandments to the children of Israel, He identified Himself in verse 2.

How did God identify Himself? Complete the verse.
"I am the LORD your God, who brought you out of Egypt, out of the ..."

The Commandments represent an ancient boundary stone we are not free to move to fit our lifestyles.

You see, one vital way we can look at the Ten Commandments is as a plan for staying out of slavery. Read the words of wisdom in Today's Treasure. An ancient boundary stone was similar to a fence. It served as a visual reminder of what belonged to the landowner and what was beyond the legal limits. It reminded people when they were crossing the line.

God's commands are the ultimate ancient boundary stones—not the ten good thoughts for the day. He is the Lord our God and His Word is eternal, which means it applies to every generation. The Ten Commandments represent an ancient boundary stone we are not free to move around to fit our lifestyles.

You may wonder what boundary stones have to do with a study on ancient ruins—practically everything. Notice the troubling warning about generational sin. Those who live beyond the boundaries will not only return to bondage, they will leave a well-trodden path for generations to follow in their footsteps.

To understand generational bondage, let's risk the discomfort of taking a look at generational sin. They intertwine for at least two reasons:

- *All bondage begins with sin.* In Exodus, the nation of Israel was in bondage because of its cruel taskmasters' sins. In Isaiah, the nation of Judah was heading into bondage because of their own sin.
- *All bondage promotes sin.* Not necessitates but promotes. Let me use an illustration to explain. All television commercials promote products. I don't have to buy, but I'd have to be pretty strong to resist at least some of the products. Likewise, all bondage highly intensifies the pull toward sin. I believe that a person raised in generational bondage rarely does not struggle in some way with the sin it promotes.

Moved Boundary
Own rules
Move Bondage
Bondage
Sin

The tie between generational bondage and generational sin is what creates such a difficult cycle. Someone moves the ancient boundary stone and decides to abide by his or her own set of rules. Life beyond the stone leads to bondage. Bondage leads to sin. Sin leads to more bondage. The cycle does not stop until someone has enough courage to move back to the ancient boundary stone God ordained.

Describe in your own words how Exodus 20:5 reflects the cycle I have just identified.

I want to be part of breaking negative cycles in my family line. I believe you want the same for your family. One reason our study is called *Breaking Free* is because many of us are dealing with ancient cycles that need breaking. Perhaps on our own determination and strength we've bent them a little, but they'll never break without God. And He ordinarily will not rebuild what is not broken.

God's commands—His ancient boundary stones—were given not to enslave us but to keep us free. He is a good and wise God who knows what's best for us. Even His jealousy is for us and not against us. Exodus 20:5 sounds very harsh and unlike God until we look deeper into His Word. Our first stumbling block here is the word *jealous*. We tend to think of this word only in negative, even sinful, terms; so we might be disturbed when it is used to describe God. Read what 2 Corinthians 11:2-3 says about godly jealousy.

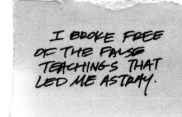

 In the margin explain the difference between ungodly and godly jealousy.

The word *godly* means Godlike; therefore, God is only capable of godly jealousy. Having a godly jealously means being jealous for someone, not of someone. When God referred to Himself as the jealous God as a warning against idol worship in Exodus 20:4-5, He wasn't jealous *of* idols. He is jealous *for* His children. He knows all other "gods" of this world possess no glory and can offer no salvation.

Idols detract attention from the one true God, the only One worthy of our praise, the only real Deliverer. God is also a Giver by His eternal super nature. He desires to bless. When we turn away to other "gods," we often force Him to hold back His blessing and stay His giving hand. Ungodly jealousy is to be jealous of someone. Godly jealousy is to be jealous for someone for her highest good.

I knew a mother who displayed the best of godly jealousy. Her daughter became entangled in a destructive cult. She worked and prayed tirelessly until her daughter was restored to freedom. She was jealous for her daughter, not of her.

The second stumbling block in Exodus 20:5 is the word *punishing*. *Visiting* (KJV) is a little more reflective of the Hebrew. The original word is *paqadh* and some of its meanings are "inspect, review, number, to be deposited … to visit in the sense of making a call." It was a word also used for taking a census.

God does not punish children for their parents' sins. We will see this truth clearly in Ezekiel 18 on day 4. I believe in Exodus 20:5 God says He can review or take a census of all the times the effects of the parents' sins can be seen in the next several generations. He can count those who have been adversely affected by the sins of their parents or grandparents. For instance, if a pollster took a census of the number of alcoholics in three generations of an alcoholic father's family, the head count would very likely be high. Why? Because alcoholism had been deposited in the family line. It came calling and an unfortunate number of children and grandchildren answered the door. Sins of the parents and grandparents add up in the next generations.

Before we parents die of fright, let's remember God is the only perfect parent. He's not cursing three or four generations over a little parental irritability. In fact, I don't believe He's cursing anyone. God is referring to a natural phenomenon placed in poignant words in Hosea 8:7, "They sow the wind and reap the whirl-wind." Parents and grandparents must be very careful what they sow because it may bear wind in their lives and a whirlwind in the lives that follow.

Notice the context of the warning in Exodus 20:5. His edict concerning generational sin follows on the heels of which commandment?

Why do you think parents and grandparents must be seriously warned against seeking other "gods" and bowing down to idols? (margin)

Keep in mind that idolatry involves anything or anyone we worship, use as a replacement for God, or in any way treat as our god. Only Christ can set us free, all other gods or idols can only enslave; therefore, enslaved parents teach their children how to live in bondage even with the best of intentions to do otherwise. For many years I have kept an excerpt from *It's Always Something* by the late Gilda Radner. The last few paragraphs share a lesson on life every parent should heed.

> When I was little, my nurse Dibby's cousin had a dog, just a mutt, and the dog was pregnant. I don't know how long dogs are pregnant, but she was due to have her puppies in about a week. She was out in the yard one day and got in the way of the lawn mower and her two hind legs got cut off. They rushed her to the vet and he said, "I can sew her up, or you can put her to sleep if you want, but the puppies are okay. She'll be able to deliver the puppies."
> Dibby's cousin said, "Keep her alive."
> So the vet sewed up her backside, and over the next week the dog learned to walk. She didn't spend any time worrying, she just learned to walk by taking two steps in the front and flipping up her back-side, and then taking two steps and flipping up her backside again. She gave birth to six little puppies, all in perfect health. She nursed them and then weaned them. And when they learned to walk, they all walked like her.[1]

Go ahead and laugh a few seconds, then take it very seriously.

How could the moral to this story parallel what we've talked about concerning generational bondage and generational sin? (margin)

I read that excerpt on July 13, 1989. Do you know why I remember it so well? Because after crying myself into a heap, I resolved to do anything and everything God willed—no matter how difficult—to make sure my two precious pups would not grow up to walk like their mother, the victim. Or like her mother, the victim. I say this with deep love and all due respect. I was trying to do my best before that pivotal period in my life, but I still had remaining areas of bondage I had convinced myself would not affect my children. I finally faced the fact that I had to break all chains. Even a thin chain can strangle the life out of you.

To the praise and glory of our redeeming God, as I write this study, Amanda and Melissa are both young adults. So far, I see no signs of their living like victims; but don't worry, I intend to keep watching. With deep earnest, I pray that if they walk like me now, they will walk wholeheartedly in liberty with God. I have found freedom right next to His side. Breaking the cycle has been such hard work, but the glorious freedom God has given is indescribable! It is worth it, my friend, because He is worth it. And He happens to think you are worth it.

Today's lesson has been heavy, but we're not taking this series just to learn the Bible. God wants whole hearts, not big heads. We're taking a journey so we can pack up and move to a place where we can freely enjoy our covenant relationship with Christ, the place secured by the ancient boundary stones.

Take courage if these subjects are hard for you. The enemy is hoping we'd rather remain in denial than face the truth and let God's Word penetrate our lives and set us free. If the subject of generational bondage and sin doesn't seem to apply to you, ask God how He desires to use these lessons in your life. To grow compassion? deeper understanding? In my opinion, few of our family "lines" couldn't use a little "realignment." Let's invite God into our private business. He's the perfect family Counselor.

> How does God want you to respond to what He showed you today?

Day 3
That Ancient Serpent

I have several reasons for approaching Satan's role in bondage the way we will. I don't want him to be glorified in any way. This study is about who we are in Christ, the benefits of our covenant relationship with God, and learning to live in the freedom we've been given. I have chosen to focus on some of the enemy's schemes today because I believe he is deeply involved in matters of generational sin and bondage.

> **Today's Treasure**
> *"In order that Satan might not outwit us. For we are not unaware of his schemes."*
> **2 Corinthians 2:11**

How does Revelation 12:9 portray Satan? Check all that apply.
☐ a fish   ☐ a dragon   ☐ a whirlwind   ☐ a serpent   ☐ a liar

Satan is both ancient and misleading. Revelation 12:9 refers to Satan as "that ancient serpent." He has been around a very long time. We can safely assume he and his cohorts know more about our family heritage than the most extensive genealogical research could uncover. If knowledge is power, our enemy is pretty powerful. If he can use our earthly heritage against us, I have very little doubt he will. Revelation 12:9 tells us of another of Satan's behaviors. Isaiah 53:6 tells us "we all, like sheep, have gone astray, each of us has turned to his own way."

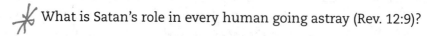 What is Satan's role in every human going astray (Rev. 12:9)?

We can be sure Satan will do everything he can to lead us astray. After thousands of years of existence, I don't think the ancient serpent has a wealth of new ideas. He probably tries the same general lure on us that he used on those who came before us in our family lines. He starts with the obvious and sees if what worked with the parents will work with the children. Not very creative, but highly effective.

What more do you see about Satan in Luke 4:13? Choose one.
☐ He constantly tempts people to sin.
☐ He waits for opportunities when we are vulnerable.
☐ He tempts us through the actions of others.

My husband was never close to one of his grandfathers. According to Keith, this grandfather allowed his unrestrained temper to totally destroy the family home. I can remember my husband saying, "The scariest times of my life were when I saw glimpses of that same kind of anger displayed in one of my parents."

When Keith became a father, every time he reacted with the least degree of anger, the enemy would attack with accusing thoughts like, *You're just like them!* Keith often felt depressed afterward. I admire my husband for the way he has taken this potential problem to the Lord and let Him treat it with truth so the chain could be broken.

You see, every time Keith got angry, Satan saw an opportunity. If he could tempt Keith to lose his temper and raise his voice, the enemy would win in a doubleheader: He'd tempted Keith to sin in his anger and to feel hopeless about ever changing his behavior. Based on Luke 4:13, Satan is an opportunist.

Personalize this experience for just a moment. "Imagine" that you sometimes see in yourself something you have not liked in a parent or grandparent.

What behavior might you see in your life that you disliked in your parents or grandparents? Respond in the margin.

We don't need to be afraid of Satan's opportunism, just aware of it. Always remember that any opportunity for Satan to work is an even greater opportunity for God to work. May we offer our opportunities to the only Opportunist we can trust.

How does 2 Corinthians 11:3 portray Satan?

Satan is a deceiver, leading our minds astray. He is *cunning* (NIV) or *subtle* (KJV). The more undetected Satan's work remains, the less we'll resist him. One of the dangers of a generational yoke is that it blends in so well with the rest of our lives and families. God gave me a frightening visual aid just a few days before writing this entry. Keith and I were walking in the country. He suddenly grabbed me and said, "Don't move!" The biggest copperhead Keith had ever seen was curled up on the path just a few feet in front of us. Why didn't I see it? Because it was exactly the color of the path. Why did Keith? He is a hunter. He has an eye for camouflaged creatures!

We can think of Satan's subtleties as times his work is well camouflaged. Generational yokes often go undetected because they blend in so well with our personalities. We excuse some of these yokes as simply being the way we are. We might even say, "My mother was like this and so was hers! We're just outspoken women who know our own minds!" Or a man may say, "My grandfather raised my father not to take a handout from anyone. We're proud people and I'm not going to take a handout either. Thanks, but my boy doesn't need an instrument to play in some band. He has honest work to do."

Perhaps you're beginning to see a well-camouflaged chain inherited through the family line. You don't have to decide *well, I'm stuck with it, so I may as well be proud of it.* In Christ, you are not stuck with anything but Him, praise His name!

Are you aware of some ways Satan has worked subtly to perpetuate a chain in your family line? ☐ Yes ☐ No If so, explain in the margin. You may be general on paper as long as you agree to be specific with God!

What do you think God could do to keep that ancient serpent from continuing to strike your family in this way?

What do you see about Satan in 2 Corinthians 2:10-11?

Verse 11 says if we refuse to forgive, Satan finds an open door to outwit us or take advantage of us. Satan is scheming, particularly in matters of unforgiveness. Now we see a concept arise that will help us understand the possible relationship between generational sin, bondage, and Satan. Exodus 20:5 proves that God has allowed the sins of the fathers to visit the children to the third and fourth generations. The following statement is a safe assumption we can make based on many biblical evidences concerning God's allowances and Satan's schemes:

Satan is out to take advantage of virtually anything God allows.

This explains the relationship between Satan and generational sin. Because God has allowed the possibility, Satan tries to increase the probability. The enemy specializes in taking advantage of someone's refusal to forgive. Here's an all too common example. A family has a feud over the family business. The grown siblings cease speaking to one another and do not allow their children to associate. They harbor

My liberty in Christ has become my reality.

bad feelings so long that those who refused to forgive become unforgiving people. The cancer spreads to other relationships as well. The grandchildren and the great grandchildren know very little about the original feud. In fact, they know very little about each other. They have little in common, except most of them are mad at someone all the time.

Please allow me to pen a penetrating question and trust that it comes from the Holy Spirit and not from me. Your answer will be for no one besides you and God.

Has your extended family ever experienced a feud resulting in short- or long-term division? ☐ Yes ☐ No If so, is your extended family close now? Whether your answer is yes or no, explain your answer briefly.

If we come from an extended family full of disassociations, we may feel unaffected by it, but we're probably not. A feeling of detachment is a negative effect all by itself. Perhaps alienation has been your family's way of life for so many generations, it doesn't even seem strange! Let's be courageous and ask God if we are perpetuating division and unforgiveness in the family line.

Part of finding wholeness is coming to terms with our heritage Christ's way. In Him, we can take the best and leave the worst behind. We need to love and accept family members even though we may not always approve of their lifestyles or spend lots of time together. Even if unity is not possible, we need the peace Christ can bring. For liberty to be a reality, we need to be free of wrongdoing, even if no one else in the family follows suit. If this is an issue in your family, let's begin praying about it and ask God to use the remainder of our journey to help.

First Peter 5:8 tells us Satan is like what?

Our final point today broadens the scope of our previous point. We've been talking about Satan taking advantage of unforgiveness. Based on 1 Peter 5:8, Satan is hunting for prey. I don't know much about lions; but from my limited knowledge, I can tell you this: They are looking for anything juicy and vulnerable! The implication of 1 Peter 5:8 is that Satan is looking to devour anything that is, if you'll allow me to make up a word, devourable! Or vulnerable.

The sins of the fathers increase the vulnerability of the children to the third and fourth generations (Ex. 20:5). As a child, my maternal grandmother lost both her parents. Years later, she lost her husband and finished raising my mother all by herself during the Great Depression. My dear mother battled insecurities all her life. When I was about nine, she began having health problems that caused her to be somewhat detached for several years. When I began to seek wholeness in Christ, I finally mustered the courage to ask Him where I was vulnerable. He revealed that I feared having no one to take care of me and if I didn't let Him heal this part of me, I would be vulnerable to unhealthy relationships. This only makes sense in terms of a chain of insecurity passed down through several generations.

God and I worked very hard on this issue and I'm so glad we did. Although my parents have been wonderful and my husband is an excellent provider, the reality is this: God is my only guarantee. The Knower of all my needs is the sole Meeter of all my needs. Only He can fully and wholly provide, but we cannot drop chains we do not even know we're carrying! Remember John 8:32, just facing the truth of our past or present will not heal us. It's facing our truth in the light of God's Truth (His Word and His Son) that sets us free! Whenever the enemy tries to use your physical lineage against you, use your spiritual lineage against him! As a child of God and a joint heir with Christ, refuse the enemy a single inch of the ground we are taking back.

How does God want you to respond to what He showed you today?

Day 4
Surveying Ancient Ruins

Today we begin looking at blueprints for rebuilding our ancient ruins. Earlier I promised we would see biblical proof that Exodus 20:5 does not mean children bear the guilt of their fathers' and forefathers' sins. Feeling the effects of their sins and shouldering the guilt are two very different repercussions. God brings healing to the former and relieves the unnecessary burden from the latter. Today we study Ezekiel 18. This chapter addresses the sins of the fathers and sons (not to the exclusion of the mothers and daughters). The most obvious place to discover signs of ancient ruins is in the generation before ours because it is more recent.

Before we address these biblical issues, let's acknowledge the fact that some of you have descended from an unusually healthy family line and will be able to relate very little from personal experience. Perhaps you could view today's lesson educationally. On the other hand, you may have descended from the opposite extreme and see absolutely nothing positive in your family lineage. I pray that you will seek healing from God and let Him shed a little light on the shades of grace and goodness in your physical heritage.

I assume, however, that most readers will be somewhat like me. I am a blend of the best and worst of my earthly lineage. I am asking God to help me discern the difference and allow Him to break all negative bonds in my generation. Like you, I want to pass down the very best to my children, both physical and spiritual. In straining ahead for an ideal, we are sure to reach positive change.

Please read Ezekiel 18 in its entirety. In the margin write a one-sentence synopsis of this Old Testament chapter.

Today's Treasure
"Yet you ask, 'Why does the son not share the guilt of his father?' Since the son has done what is just and right and has been careful to keep all my decrees, he will surely live." **EZEKIEL 18:19**

Let's organize our thoughts. Write in the margin your own basic outline of this chapter any way you wish using words, phrases, or sentences.

Do your children ever accuse you of being unfair about something? Every once in a while mine do—and it hurts! Then just in case I don't get the point, they'll go on and on with the subject until I'm weary of hearing it. At those times, I could be caught fussing at my children using words like these: "I've heard that out of your mouth more times than I ever wanted to! What you're accusing me of isn't even true! Now let that be the end of it!"

What verse in Ezekiel 18 quotes God responding in a similar way?

What evidence of God's mercy do you see in the chapter?

Do you detect a pleading coming from the heart of God at any point in this chapter? If so, what was He pleading for people to do?

When I'm attempting to apply Old Testament concepts to the New Testament believer's life, I sometimes find that a figurative application seems to fit more than a literal application. For instance, Moses stood in the presence of God and came down from the mountain with a face literally beaming (Ex. 34). Although our faces don't literally shine from the presence of God when we've spent lots of time with Him, I do believe we are somehow more radiant. Likewise, when God speaks of a father or son "dying" for his own sins and not for the other's in Ezekiel 18, we are challenged to apply the principle figuratively as New Testament believers.

We who have trusted Christ don't "die" for our own sins. Thankfully, Christ has already done that for us. Figuratively speaking, we can experience the death of self-respect over our sins or the death of an earthly relationship, but our physical deaths are only means of passing from this life to our citizenship in heaven.

Most of us have probably discovered a few ancient ruins this week. In today's lesson and on day 5, we are going to study how to begin rebuilding our ancient ruins. We begin rebuilding when we do four things:

1. Agree to take an honest look back. Many well-meaning Christians take out of context the exhortation in Philippians 3:13, "forgetting what is behind," and apply it as a command to never look at the past. Paul was talking about all the trophies of life he had to leave behind in order to follow Christ. God's Word clearly expresses what a good and effective teacher the past can be. The past will be a good teacher if we will simply approach it as a good student, from the perspective of what we can gain and how God can use it for His glory.

Take another look at Ezekiel 18:14,31. In very simplified terms, in the margin describe how the chain of destructive behavior is broken.

> I am free from anger at my parents for causing me childhood pains.

I see four important steps the son took toward breaking the cycle his father may have created or perpetuated:
- He saw the sins his father committed.
- He made the firm decision not to practice the same habits.
- He got rid of his own offenses.
- He pursued a new heart and new spirit.

You may be thinking, *Easier said than done!* You're right. I've never seen a construction worker who wasn't covered in sweat; but if he worked diligently, the result was something beautiful. Rebuilding happens no other way. Each of these subjects will be studied over the course of our journey to breaking free, but let's look at the first one now. The Hebrew word for *sees* in Ezekiel 18:14 is *ra'ah,* which means to "view, inspect … to learn … gain understanding."

Remember point 2 on day 1 of this week's study? How do these synonyms differ from the concept of dishonoring a parent?

Fill in the blanks according to Proverbs 30:11: "There are those who

_____ their fathers and do not _____ their mothers."

God told us to honor our parents in Exodus 20:12, just seven verses after He described generational sin, so we cannot pretend that our subject matter is the exception to the rule. As we consider any "sins" of our parents that we don't want to imitate or pass down, we should be careful not to curse them. The concept of cursing in this context reflects demeaning them and belittling them. We can be honest with ourselves and with God and still avoid belittling a parent.

   Would you be willing to ask God to help you view any sins of your parents for the sake of the high risk they run of repeating themselves in your life or your children's? Would you be willing to take a deeper inspection than we've taken so far to learn and gain understanding?

Without dishonoring anyone, what further enlightenment on chains you need to break has the Holy Spirit given you?

2. Believe the truth over the enemy's lies. If breaking the chain of generational sin or bondage was impossible, God would never hold us responsible for repeating the sins of our parents. But we can be freed from the effects and practices of the sins in our lineage. Allow me to say this gently and with much compassion: You are not the exception and neither is your situation. In all things we can be overcomers but, indeed, only through Him who loves us (Rom. 8:37).

Look at the potter's house in Jeremiah 18. Compare verses 1-5 with verse 12. God was so willing to remold and remake, but what was their reply?

In weeks 2 and 3, we talked about belief versus nonbelief. We will continue to echo the same truth from different mountains throughout our journey. Down in the deepest part of our hearts, do we look at old habits and behaviors that have been snares to us and our parents and think, *It's no use*? Please, Beloved, turn from any unbelief or it will keep liberty from being a reality.

If this does not apply to you, would you stop and pray for someone who has virtually given up all hope of breaking a negative chain and seems to be responding, "It's no use"? Write his or her first name or initial in the margin and circle it after you have interceded for the person.

3. Discern the difference between rebuilding and preserving the ancient ruins. You may be thinking, "Beth, believe me, I've taken plenty of looks back and I continue to get angrier or more depressed." I understand. I've done exactly the same. Then I learned the difference between rebuilding and preserving. I was reminded of the difference as I stood at the Acropolis in Athens. Our guide estimated how much money they spend every year "preserving the ruins." God never called us to preserve our ancient ruins. Rather than inspect the ancient ruin and then work with God to rebuild, we just keep revisiting and preserving and we never get over it. Without God, our only sure Restorer, that's about the best we can do.

Do you think you have been preserving or working on rebuilding the ancient ruins? ☐ Yes ☐ No Explain your answer briefly.

4. Accept God's appointment as a reconstruction worker.

Write this week's memory verse, Isaiah 61:4, in the margin.

Now check your context by rereading Isaiah 61:1-4. To whom does the pronoun "they" refer in Isaiah 61:4?
☐ those who imprisoned God's children
☐ the Father, Son, and Holy Spirit
☐ the captives who have been set free

Once again, we can apply something figuratively that applied literally to Israel: Just as God appointed the Israelites to rebuild the wall around Jerusalem, He appoints you to rebuild your ancient ruins.

In the margin, list reasons why you think He requires our cooperation.

I believe one reason God requires our cooperation is that He deeply desires our involvement with Him. He created us for this purpose. Rebuilding ancient ruins is impossible for us without God. We are unqualified for the task, but as we draw near to Him, He rebuilds our lives and characters. Remember, God's primary purpose in healing us from our hurts is to introduce us to new depths of relationship with Himself.

Although we are focusing on rebuilding the ancient ruins this week, I am praying that every week will place tools in your hands for this important and sometimes ongoing task. Perhaps you're still wondering how our ancient ruins can ever be rebuilt. After all, we can't change the past. Right? Beloved, as we begin cooperating with God in the process of rebuilding, we might not be able to change the past, but we can change a few things more impressive:

- We can change how we look at it.
- We can decide how we're going to build on it.

Let's covenant to stop preserving and start rebuilding. The hammer is passed down into our hands.

> How does God want you to respond to what He showed you today?

Day 5
The Ancient of Days

Studying freedom from strongholds can be overwhelming. Our enemy does his best to make it so overwhelming that we'll feel defeated from the start. Satan can do nothing about our salvation once we have received Christ, so he hopes to handicap us so we won't be a threat. Just as God's primary agenda is redemption, Satan's primary agenda is to blind people to the Redeemer. Once we are redeemed, God's primary agenda becomes our completion.

 Based on God's priority in our lives, what might be Satan's priority in the lives of people who are already Christians?

Today's Treasure
"I have revealed and saved and proclaimed—I, and not some foreign god among you. You are my witnesses," declares the LORD, *"that I am God. Yes, and from ancient days I am he."* **ISAIAH 43:12-13**

As God began stirring the tremendously heavy burden in my heart to write this study, He gave me two statements on which to build:

- Christ came to set the captives free.
- Satan came to take the free captive.

We are the free. Our liberty is a fact, but according to Galatians 5:1, we can return to a yoke of bondage. Satan can't take authority over us. He is a defeated foe, but he unfortunately gets lots of cooperation. One of the priority goals of this study is to help us learn to cease cooperating with the enemy and start living in the reality of our liberty.

If you are feeling overwhelmed, you need a spiritual shot in the arm! Now hear this: That ancient serpent is powerless against the magnificent "Ancient of Days!" All week we've been talking about rebuilding the ancient ruins that we've compared to generational bondage or sin. On day 3 we studied that ancient serpent who takes advantage of anything God allows.

Today we get to conclude our week's emphasis with the One who, according to Today's Treasure, has been God from ancient days. Let's begin our lesson today from the tip of Mount Perspective!

Read Daniel 7:9-10 and list the descriptions the prophet gave in his vision of God and His surroundings.

I've always thought "Ancient of Days" was a peculiar name for God. Reflect on the name for a moment. What do you think it reflects?

The enemy, that ancient serpent, has been around a very long time and knows man's tendencies and vulnerabilities. Far more impressive, however, is the "Ancient of Days!" When she was in the second grade, my daughter Amanda illustrated a truth about the centrality of God. She was telling me something she had prayed over at school that day while standing in the lunch line. I said to her, "Oh, Amanda, do you know how much it means to Mommy for you to make God a part of your day?" I'll never forget her answer. "You're so silly, Mommy. You know God made the day. I'm just glad He made me part of His."

I was stunned. She expressed the meaning of God's wonderful name, the "Ancient of Days." Every day the sun rises by God's permission. He's never had a wink of sleep, and nothing has been hidden from His sight. God has been God through every single day of your heritage. If you're dealing with some ancient ruins, He was there when they first crumbled. He knows every detail. He knows exactly how you've been affected, and His expertise is reconstruction. After all, Christ was a carpenter by trade. Nothing has ever been allowed to crumble in a Christian's life or heritage that God is unable to reconstruct and use. Let's consider several primary catalysts that take us from cursings to blessings in our physical family's lineage.

Read Psalm 78:1-8, a springboard for the catalysts we'll name today.

Two immensely important facts float to the surface in these eight verses:

- Every generation has a new opportunity to exert positive influence. No matter what atrocity has taken place in your family line, God can raise up a new generation and turn the cycle in the direction of godly seed. Your great-grandfather could serve a life sentence for murder and your grandchild could serve a life sentence of faithful evangelism through which thousands come to know Christ! A certain link lies between the unfaithful and the faithful. Consider the second fact.

- Between every unfaithful generation and faithful generation is one person determined to change. My friend, you could be that link. So could I. Perhaps no one in your family was overtly sinful, but they were simply uninvolved in Christ's kingdom agenda. Maybe you would like to be a link that takes your family line from an unfulfilling life of religion to a passionate life of relationship with Christ. Perhaps your prayer for your grandchildren and great-grandchildren might be a love for missions. Whatever it may be, you can be that link!

What is your dream or desire for your grandchildren and great-grandchildren?

If this dream is in keeping with what you know of God's will, then you have the endorsement and approval of Christ to begin acting on it. Cooperate with God and pray toward the fulfillment of the dream.

You can be absolutely certain that God's will is for your generation to give way to godly seed. I aggressively pray for godly seed to come from my offspring. I love my parents and grandparents so much, and I want to pass down many wonderful things they've given me. We faithfully attended church and were exposed to many positive things, but my parents were never taught how to walk with God daily through prayer and His Word. They did not possess intimate relationships with God that released power to overcome some big obstacles. I hope to give my children and their children many of the positive things handed down to me, but Keith and I also hope to give them a few new gifts.

One of Keith's greatest priorities is handing them down an example of greater wholeness and a secure identity in Christ. I pray constantly for my children and theirs to love God passionately and serve Him fervently. I hope they will inherit a burden for world missions and a commitment to love and accept all races.

On the other hand, I'm not naïve enough to think we won't hand down a few unwanted "gifts." I pray they also will be able to discern and reverse any negative cycles they see in Keith and me. God certainly blesses our prayers and our hopes, but to break cycles and provoke lasting change we must also be willing to deliberately cooperate with Him. Among the most treasured gifts we could pass down to the next generation is authenticity. We accomplish little good when we praise the deeds of the Lord, but we live lives inconsistent with His Truth.

I know it was my Lord and Savior rescuing me again.

In what ways are you allowing the next generation to see authenticity in your life?

We're about to see why the work is so very worth it! Look back at Exodus 20:5-6. Many readers are so disturbed by verse 5 that verse 6 never sinks beyond the skull! Write Exodus 20:6 in the space below.

How many generations suffer from the sins of the fathers?

How many generations benefit from one who loves God and is obedient to His commands?

I think we all get the point! We tend to characterize God as harsh because of His allowances to the third and fourth generations of those who are unfaithful, but look at His blessings on future generations of the faithful! Not much comparison between three or four and a thousand! God is clearly more gracious in His blessings than He is stern in His chastisements. Do you realize that your walk with God could affect great numbers of future generations?

How many of your descendants could be blessed because you agreed to be a link to a new cycle of faithfulness to God? _____

Amazing. Take another good look at verse 6. Compare John 3:16. Whom does God love?
☐ the faithful ☐ the repentant ☐ the world ☐ the obedient

To whom does God show love? Choose any that apply.
☐ those who love Him   ☐ those who search for Him
☐ those in the world   ☐ those who obey Him

He loves the world, but He shows love to those who love and obey Him. God lavishly loves every person, but He reserves the right to demonstrate His loving mercy to those who love and obey Him.

How is the teaching in John 14:21 consistent with Exodus 20:6?

In future weeks we will address in far more depth the subjects of loving God and obeying Him. For now, let's dig out a beautiful jewel embedded in Exodus 20:6. The Hebrew word for *showing* in this verse is *asah*. Guess what it means? It means "to construct, build." Right there in the context of generational influence, God promises to build blessing on the lives of those who love Him and obey Him.

Oh, believer, do you see that the "Ancient of Days" is anxiously waiting to build a solid foundation your descendants can live on for years to come if they choose? He's not asking us to rebuild ancient ruins by ourselves. He's simply asking us to be one of the tools He uses. God knows exactly what went wrong, exactly where the cracks are in the foundation. He was there, remember? He was completely God then, and He is completely God now.

So many people yearn to be part of something significant. Something important. We want to make useful contributions to society. We look at people who do and we're envious, yet do we realize what kind of contribution we could make to our own family lines? I can't think of anyone to whom I'd want my life to be a blessing more than my children's children and their children's children. Ten generations later our names might be forgotten, but one day in heaven I believe they'll get to meet the link that changed the direction of the chain.

Sometimes we're willing to criticize what happened before us, but are we willing to take the challenge of positively affecting those after us? The little slice of time God offers each generation is a trust. Those before us who were not faithful with their trust will be held accountable, but we're still here. We still have a chance to positively affect the generations that follow us. Reread the ending of the story of Hezekiah we encountered in week 1, Isaiah 39:5-8.

What kind of "link" was Hezekiah?

I think you'll agree, Hezekiah blew it. God gave him an extra slice of time, but he was only faithful with the trust for a little while. His actions caused his own children to be carried away captive. Many parents have done the same because they viewed their few years of occupation of this planet as the only years that mattered. The virus of self-centeredness is very contagious, but each generation has the option not to catch it.

How does God want you to respond to what He showed you this week?

I am praying so hard that you and I will not be like Hezekiah. I pray we don't recommit just for a while, then lapse back into carelessness and ultimately captivity. Please believe God for lasting change. If you do your part for one generation, He'll do His for a thousand. Sounds like a pretty good deal to me.

I don't know how much longer Christ will tarry; but according to the biblical signs of the times, I don't think any expert would expect Christ to linger a thousand more generations. Do you know what that means? If you are willing to be the link through whom God works to bring a greater depth of faithfulness and effectiveness, your life could affect every generation in your family line until He comes. Pretty impressive. The blood's already been shed. Isn't it worth a little sweat and tears?

---

1. Gilda Radner, *It's Always Something* (New York: Avon Books, 1989) 268-269.

99

BREAKING *Free*

session five viewer guide

In the journey to freedom, nothing has greater potential to weigh us down than the _____ _____.

If we dare to break free while some of our family members remain in bondage, we are going to have to exercise some _____!

"The spirit which they then received, the new nature and life that God gave them, was not 'a _____-_____,' the two words being a practical compound." Instead, "we received 'a spirit of _____,' the opposite of 'a spirit of _____.' "[1]

1. Courage to believe we can be _____
   • We often feel the family chains will never fall _____ _____ _____ because they're _____ _____.
   • In the context of the Potter reshaping the clay, God said to His people, " 'turn ... each one of you, and reform your ways and actions.' But they will reply, '_____ _____ _____' " (Jer. 18:11).

2. Courage to be _____
   We may be mistaken as ...

   a. _____

   b. _____ (See Isa. 3:5-7.)

   c. _____

3. Courage to "extract the _____ from the _____"
   (Jer. 15:19, NASB).

Let's camp on a common generational stronghold that is poisonous: _____.

   a. _____ is grievous sin fueled by _____ and _____.

   b. _____ propagates from the false notion that, if people are
   _____, someone _____ _____ _____ _____.

4. Courage to deal a _____ _____ with _____ _____

"Memory ... is vigorously _____ _____, selecting out of the
_____ _____ _____ _____, retrieving and arranging images
and insights, and then hammering them together for use in the _____
_____."[2]

In Isaiah 33:6, God offers a second storehouse. Every time you draw something
painful from your storehouse, draw something priceless from God's:

   • _____, also translated _____—*yeshu 'a'*

   • _____

   • _____

1. R.C.H. Lenski, "St. Paul's Epistle to the Romans" in *Commentary on the New Testament* (Peabody, Massachusetts: Hendrickson Publishers, 1998), 521-522.
2. Eugene H. Peterson, *Answering God* (New York: Harper Collins, 1989), 117.

Binding up the Brokenhearted

God has sewn a thread of love in my heart. Sometimes the only strength I possessed was to hang on to that thread. I didn't know then what a master weaver God could be with a torn and bleeding heart, but His hand remained steadfast. He has sewn me a new heart.

Day 1
Straight to the Heart

Can you remember when you lost your first tooth? rode your first two-wheeler? lived through your first day of junior high? Monumental experiences, yet you may or may not recall them. But if I asked about the first experience that shattered your heart, you'd likely remember everything—down to the last detail. Somehow having your heart broken is an injury in a class all by itself.

How about you? What was your first real heartbreak in life? (margin)

As I think back on a few of my own heartbreaks, I can almost feel the ache all over again. Not only is a broken heart inevitable from time to time, but it is one of the primary emotional rites of passage into maturity. Sadly, many individuals are introduced to mature emotions long before they should be.

Our first reactions in times of tragedy tend to be, "Don't You care, God?" Though our minds may never comprehend, our tear-swollen eyes and willing hearts can accept the words: "He has sent me to bind up the brokenhearted."

The term *brokenhearted* in the original language means nothing intellectual. Nor does it mean anything deeply spiritual. It means exactly what it says: One of the primary reasons God sent His Son to this earth was to bring tender salve and relief to those whose hearts have been broken.

On days 2 through 5 we will study New Testament examples of Christ's ministry to the brokenhearted. Today, however, we will view several places in the Old Testament where God displayed His ministry to the brokenhearted.

In the following passages, record the circumstances involved, and how God bound up the brokenhearted.

Reference	Circumstances	Bind Up
Genesis 16:1-13		
Genesis 39:11-23		
Ruth 1:3-18		
2 Samuel 12:15-25		

Today's Treasure
"He has sent me to bind up the brokenhearted."
ISAIAH 61:1

People often contrast the God of the Old Testament with the God of the New Testament. Actually, He's the same God. Christ's death on the cross and resurrection from the dead fulfilled the demands of the Law and unleashed the gates of boundless grace, but God has always loved and been compassionate. Only God can truly and completely heal shattered hearts. He uses different methods, but according to Isaiah 61:1, one of His greatest priorities is binding up the brokenhearted.

Now that we've had a chance to see the consistency of God's loving and tender heart toward the emotionally injured or devastated, let's take an in-depth look at this wonderful part of the ministry He assigned to His Son: "The Spirit of the Sovereign Lord is on me … He has sent me to bind up the brokenhearted." I pray you will be as blessed as I am over the original meanings God led me to discover. Don't proceed quickly. Take in the following truths slowly. Meditate on them and feel vastly ministered to and loved.

Read Isaiah 61:1 again. Take notice of the second active verb in verse 1: "He has sent me." The Hebrew word for *sent* is *shalack,* meaning "to shoot (forth)."

Read Psalm 127:3-4. How do these verses describe "sons"?

In John 3:16, Jesus is called God's _____.

John 3:17 tells us God gave His Son for the salvation of people by sending Him into the world. You see, God only had one arrow in His quiver. The most perfect arrow ever to exist. This arrow was a masterpiece, priceless to Him. Cherished far above all the hosts of heaven. Nothing could compare. His only heritage. His only Son. But as God looked on a lost world—desperate, needy, and in the clutches of the enemy— His heart was overwhelmed. Though we sinned miserably against Him and few sought Him, God could not love us less.

Love reached sacrificially into the quiver and pulled out the solitary arrow. The quiver would now be empty, His cherished arrow in the hands of hateful men. Yes, God so loved the world, but God also loved His only begotten Son with inexpressible, divine affection. The divine dilemma: two loves. And one would demand the sacrifice of the other. Only one weapon could defeat the enemy of the soul—God's arrow. He positioned the weapon, pulled back the bow, steadied His grip, aimed straight for the heart, "And she brought forth her firstborn son, and wrapped him in swaddling clothes, and laid him in a manger" (Luke 2:7, KJV).

Oh, what unfathomable love! What sacrifice! All who will lower their veiling shields of unbelief and let the healing arrow penetrate shall be saved. I don't know if you're feeling what I am right now, but I've had to stop, picture, meditate, and respond to God.

Use the margin if you'd like to thank Him for looking down from heaven, seeing your need among the millions, aiming His priceless arrow straight at your heart, and sending Christ forth just for you.

The next Hebrew word I'd like you to see is the adjective we're using continually today for the heart. Isaiah 61:1: "He sent me to bind up the *broken*hearted." Today we've seen examples of broken hearts in Scripture, but now let's see what God characterizes as a broken heart. The Hebrew word for *broken* in Isaiah 61:1 is *shavar,* meaning "to burst, break into pieces, wreck, crush, smash; to rend, tear in pieces (like a wild beast) ..."

Have those words ever described your heart? ☐ Yes ☐ No

They certainly describe mine and it hurts to even think about it! The definition also says "This verb occurs with a broad range of violent meanings." Please don't misunderstand. This latter part of the definition does not mean that a broken heart occurs only when something violent happens to you. As you and I both know, broken hearts can result more frequently from words than actions. The idea is that a heart is almost always broken in a specific moment over a single action. Let me explain by example:

> David and Teresa struggled in their marriage almost from the start. David feared that Teresa married him for security rather than affection, but he loved her too much to face the problem. He hoped she would learn to love him but, sadly, she didn't. She grew colder and colder. For six years he fought for the marriage and carried most of the weight of the relationship. One day he walked in from work to find her clothes gone and a note on the table. "I'm sorry, David. I can't help the way I feel. I don't love you and I never have. I tried for as long as I could. We'll both be better off."

Based on the definition of the word "broken" in Isaiah 61:1, at what point do you imagine David's heart was "smashed" or "torn into pieces"?

If your answer is "When he realized Teresa left him," according to our context today, you're probably right. This doesn't mean that he didn't hurt before nor does it mean he hadn't suffered long-term misery. *Shavar* simply means that in the most technical sense, we can usually trace a time of heartbreak to a single moment. The heart may remain broken for years, tragically, even for the rest of our lives; but the heartbreak can usually be traced back to a particular breaking point.

Can you relate to this definition? Think of a time when you suffered through a season with a broken heart.

Can you remember one particular moment when you felt your heart break? ☐ Yes ☐ No Did you have any idea at the time that God cared so much that He aimed His Son straight toward your heart? ☐ Yes ☐ No

I don't think anything hurts like a broken heart. I've experienced times of brokenness still too painful for me to share. One I can share happened when my longtime

God knows my heart so well.

friend and coworker said good-bye. God purposed for us to divide and multiply our ministries. We both discerned God's direction several months earlier. As God made His will clearer and clearer, the ache in our hearts increased. Then one day she called me and said as tenderly as she could, "After much prayer, I believe God is leading me on from Living Proof at this time." I tried so hard to keep a strong upper lip just as she did. After we could finally compose ourselves enough from all the complicated emotions we felt, we sat down and tried to do business.

Finally, in the middle of sorting out the details of her departure, we both burst into tears. Memories of so much laughter, so many good and meaningful times together, so much prayer, and such a deep partnership flooded our minds and came crashing like a tidal wave against our hearts. Even though I knew God was right, at that moment my heart broke into pieces. I don't doubt hers did too. I do not have many opportunities to form close relationships, so the loss of one is monumental to me. Over the months that followed, God put our hearts back together separately but faithfully. Every now and then, I can still cry about it. I imagine you can cry over the memory of a broken heart or two yourself.

During those difficult months that followed, God ministered so tenderly to me. As a matter of fact, He worked in the very ways so beautifully depicted in the last Hebrew definition I'd like you to see today.

Isaiah 61:1: "He has sent me to _____ the brokenhearted."

The original word for *bind up* is *chavash,* meaning "to bind on, wrap around; bind up as a wound, bandage, cover, envelope, enclose." *Strong's Dictionary* adds a very visual definition to the same word: "to compress … to stop." How can we biblically characterize the difference between an aching heart and a broken heart? God defines a broken heart in our context today as one that is hemorrhaging.

God ministers to His children willingly and lavishly whether our hurt is minimal or unbearable, but all of us would likely characterize a broken heart as one of life's most painful experiences. I simply want you to see that God characterizes it as such too. The idea of compressing the hemorrhaging heart is very much like the practice of applying pressure to a badly bleeding wound. What a wonderful picture of Christ! A crushing hurt comes to our heart and the sympathizing, scarred hand of Christ presses the wound; and for just a moment, the pain seems to intensify … but finally the bleeding stops. Oh, my friend, are you beginning to see the intimate activity of Christ when we're devastated? And to think, this is the same One we accuse of not caring when the crushing moment occurs.

Let's conclude our lesson with a last thought on Christ binding up the brokenhearted. Notice the first definition includes the concepts of covering, enveloping, and enclosing. Have you ever noticed that when your heart is broken, you tend to feel exposed and less in control of your emotions? I certainly have and, frankly, I hate losing control of my emotions in front of people! Few things feel more vulnerable than a broken heart. Life's way of reacting to a crushed heart is to wrap tough sinews of flesh around it and tempt us to promise we'll never let ourselves get hurt again. That's not God's way. Remember, self-made fortresses built to protect our hearts not only keep love from going out but they keep love from coming in. We risk becoming captives in our own protective fortresses. Only God can put the pieces of our hearts back together again, close up all the wounds, and bind them with a porous bandage that protects from infection … but keeps the heart free to inhale and exhale love.

Are you in bondage to a broken heart you have never let Christ bind and heal? Right now, you could conclude today's lesson with a bandage instead of bondage. Go ahead. Expose your heart one more time … just to Him. After all, this is what His Father sent Him to do. The bow's stretched back and the arrow's ready. But it's up to you to drop your shield.

> How does God want you to respond to what He showed you today?

Day 2
Hearts Broken in Childhood

The remainder of this week will focus on broken hearts resulting from three different catalysts: childhood abuse, betrayal, and loss. We will deal with a fourth catalyst in video session 5. I think we can learn volumes about Christ's ministry to the brokenhearted through these four examples. We will spend today and day 3 on hearts broken by childhood victimization or abuse.

God does not minimize the things that break our hearts. He is not looking down on us thinking how petty we are because some things hurt us so. If we're so "heavenly minded" that we grow out of touch with earthly hardships, somewhere we've missed an important priority of Christ. God left our bare feet on the hot pavement of earth so we could grow through our hurts, not ignore them and refuse to feel our way through them. Begin your reading today with Matthew 18:1-11.

In the margin list every piece of evidence you can find to support the statement: "Christ loves children."

Based on Christ's statement in verse 6, how do you think one person could cause another person to sin?

In Matthew 18:5-9 I believe Christ's words specifically apply to child victimization or abuse because, in my opinion, anything that directly causes a child to have an increased tendency toward sin can be characterized as victimization or abuse.

Today's Treasure
"At that time the disciples came to Jesus and asked, 'Who is the greatest in the kingdom of heaven?' He called a little child and had him stand among them." **MATTHEW 18:1-2**

107

i was always picked last at recess.

In the margin describe why it would be better for one who causes a child to sin to have a millstone hung around his neck and be drowned.

Which of the following statements best reflects verses 8 and 9?
☐ Our prison systems should have harsher penalties for crimes.
☐ We must take sin seriously, especially sins that so easily affect others.
☐ Maiming the body will help us cease from sin.

I never share the details of my childhood victimization for two reasons: First, I want the Healer glorified, not the hurt; and second, a greater number of people can relate to more general terms. However, I did not choose this subject for our study because of my own experience. The staggering statistics of those who encounter childhood victimization drove me to the topic. Unfortunately, many of you have suffered abuses much like mine. If you haven't, you know someone who has.

God used Matthew 18 mightily to answer some questions for me. Let me tell you how I deal with "why's?" to which I can't find answers: I find as many answers as I can in God's Word, fill in those blanks, and trust Him with the rest. Sounds simple but it's not. It's something I practice by faith every single day of my life, and my heart finds such solace and rest in this method. Go with me through Matthew 18:1-9, and let's see if we can fill in enough blanks concerning childhood victimization to trust God with the rest.

1. Children are the apple of Christ's eye.

Based on Luke's account of the same scene in 9:46, what was the disciples' motive for asking who would be greatest?

The disciples often tried to get Jesus to choose one of them as the greatest. Instead Jesus "called a little child and had him stand among them" (Matt. 18:2). He essentially said, "You want to see my idea of greatness? Look at this child."

Why might the disciples have been a little insulted by Christ's example, based on the insight you can gain from Mark 10:13-16?

Savor Christ's tenderness toward children. He could have simply spoken a blessing over the children, but He chose to demonstrate His love for them instead by taking them in His arms, touching them, and blessing them. I believe Christ not only loved children, but they loved Him. How many children would be willing to leave their playtime and step up in front of 13 men to be used as an example? Not many, unless they completely loved and trusted the One who summoned them.

I think Christ was one of those people who attracted all the kids in the neighborhood. I like to imagine He went few places without swinging around several kids in a quick game of "Flying Dutchman." In fact, the attraction children had to Christ may have been the very reason why the disciples rebuked them in Mark 10:13. The disciples may have been sick of constantly maneuvering around a bunch of kids. Maybe I'm wrong, but based on the blanks we can fill in, I have a feeling the missing blanks are in favor of children. I find humor in the fact that Christ pulled a real child forward to express His idea of greatness, while His chosen twelve were acting like a bunch of children. Next notice:

2. Children are uniquely accompanied by Christ.

What do you think Christ meant in Matthew 18:5?

Christ basically said, "What you do for them, you do for Me." What is another way God tenderly cares for children in Matthew 18:10?

3. Abuses to children may as well have been personally applied to Christ.
Based on the contexts of Matthew 18:6 and 10, I believe we can assume that He was saying not only, "What you do *for* a child, you do *for* Me," but "What you do *to* a child, you do *to* Me." He obviously takes harm to children very personally.

If you were victimized as a child, did you ever think about how Christ felt about what happened to you? ☐ Yes ☐ No

How could the enemy benefit from tempting you to believe wrongly about Christ's attitude toward child victimization? (margin)

Based on what you've read today, what is the truth about Christ's attitude toward children and all that happens to them?

How does Zechariah 2:8 state God's defensiveness toward His own?

4. Christ is never the author of abuse. The Bible teaches us that some hardships are specifically ordained by God for the purpose of our growth and refining. Child abuse is not one of them. When you are trying to discern whether God or Satan is the author of a hardship, one of your best clues is whether or not sin is involved. God never entices us to sin nor does He employ sin or perversion as a means of molding us into the image of Christ. Impossible!

Allow me to use my own experience as an example. Two of the factors that most affected my childhood were abuse and a fall that mangled my teeth. My teeth became a source of insecurity and embarrassment for years. I know without a doubt that Satan was the author of my childhood abuse because such heinous sin was involved and because shame resulted. Remember, shame is Satan's "stamp of approval." On the other hand, my fall placed many difficult challenges in front of me, but sin played no part in the cause. As a result of the fall, God allowed me to experience what I call the "underdog syndrome" and placed in me a deep compassion for people who are teased harshly and treated unmercifully. God somehow made the truth register in my young heart that He thought I was beautiful. Without a doubt, I gained abundantly from that childhood disaster.

Think about your own childhood. Identify an experience that would be characteristic of:

God

Satan

In week 7 we're going to study the sovereignty of God, but now I want to make a point that may be difficult yet necessary for our liberation. I'll personalize it to my own experience for clarity: God permitted both of those childhood experiences whether or not He authored them. No, God could not have authored my childhood victimization, but obviously He allowed it. Why? He may have other reasons I do not yet know, but until those blanks are filled in, I know the following:

1. He knew that I would have to seek Him diligently for healing and in that healing I would come to know my Healer.
2. He knew glory would come to His name through the miracle of restoration and subsequent ministry.
3. He knew I would be compassionate to people hurt in childhood.
4. He knew that the crime of childhood victimization would "come out of the closet" in this generation, and He desired to call forth Christian spokespeople to address it from His Word.
5. He wanted me to teach how to make freedom in Christ a reality in life from the passion of personal experience.

Beloved, I know no better way to say it. Until the rest of the blanks are filled in, those are enough for me. God's good from life's bad is one of the most liberating concepts in the entire Word of God. We'll never be free until we truly believe that God can do something with anything. God has promised to bring good out of anything we encounter as long as we love Him and if we allow Him to use it for His purpose (Rom. 8:28).

I so much encourage you to completely surrender your hurt to Him, withholding nothing, and invite Him to work miracles from your misery. Then you must be patient and get to know Him through the process of healing. You will see fruit. I promise! But more than that, Christ promises. You may or may not have experienced childhood victimization, but virtually everyone has suffered some kind of hurt in childhood.

Shame is Satan's "stamp of approval."

Have you ever surrendered every part of that hurt to Him? ☐ Yes ☐ No
If not, would you surrender that hurt now? Use the space below to write
a brief prayer, offering something that hurt you as a child to the One
who loves children so much. You are His child, no matter your age.

How does God want you to respond to what He showed you today?

Today's study is incomplete without day 3. Please don't fail to complete your next
lesson. Matthew 18 has far more to teach us about Christ and child victimization.
Until then, thank you for being courageous enough to study a difficult subject
with me. It is for freedom that Christ has set us free. You and I will never be free
until we accept how much Christ cares about us and despises the yokes that have
held us captive.

Day 3
Hearts Mended by Truth

Today we continue our study of God's ministry to those whose hearts were broken
by childhood victimization. Please read Matthew 18:1-11 again.

Christ healed in many ways during His incarnation. Sometimes through
touch. Sometimes through speech. Matthew 18 is a perfect example of Christ
offering healing through truth. I found significant healing in the study of this
Scripture. I learned how important I was to Christ when I was a child and accepted
how much He despised what happened to me. Scripture is the strongest bandage
God uses to bind hearts broken in childhood. I believe that those who have fallen
victim to abuse are less likely to find instantaneous healing. They are more likely
to find progressive healing through the study and application of truth. Renewed
minds and positive habits are a necessity to lives pressing onward in victory.

Since today is a continuation of day 2, please refresh your memory of
our first four truths by completing the statements in the margin here
and on page 112.

Let's continue with the remainder of our healing truths.

5. *Christ avenges the abuse or victimization of children.* (Reread Matt. 18:6.)

Today's Treasure
"Woe to the world because of the things that cause people to sin! Such things must come, but woe to the man through whom they come!" **MATTHEW 18:7**

Children are

Children are uniquely

Abuses to children
may as well have been

Christ is never

I don't think
confessing sin
that resulted from
victimization is
primarily about
fault. It's about
freedom!

God has never made empty threats. He hates victimization. I believe Christ is referring to childhood victimization in Matthew 18:6-10 for at least two reasons:

- He specifically infers something one person can do to another. In this reference, the "other" is a child.
- He speaks of an action that "causes one of these little ones … to sin."

I believe each of us who have been victimized in childhood can testify that the tendencies toward certain sins dramatically increase as a result. As part of my healing, I had to take responsibility for my own sin, whether or not another person's actions escorted me to those sins. Perhaps you are like I was at one time. You don't want to take responsibility for your sins because you don't think they were your fault. You may wonder, *How else would I have responded after my reference point had been so distorted?* But, you see, I don't think confessing sin that resulted from victimization is primarily about fault. It's about freedom!

Yes, my sins were my own fault. But more important to God, I believe, was my willingness to confess how badly I hated those sins and how I wanted to be free from the power the abuse held over my decisions. Confession allowed me to bring sinful behaviors to the table for open discussion with God. He instantly forgave me and completely cleansed me, then He began to teach me day-to-day how to change my responses.

You may be thinking, *But the complications and repercussions of victimization are so overwhelming. It's just so hard to deal with!* I agree. And that, my friend, is a primary reason why it would be better for any victimizer to have a "millstone hung around his neck and to be drowned in the depths of the sea."

Undoubtedly, childhood victimization is a giant to battle. I believe we can safely say it is one of the biggest of all giants, especially if the giant was someone who was supposed to protect you. However, just as surely as God empowered young David to slay Goliath, He'll empower you if you let Him. Just remember David's words in 1 Samuel 17:47, "For the battle is the LORD's" also speaks to the victim who knows the Lord. Read Lamentations 3:58-59.

In the margin paraphrase the passage in your own words:

Forgiving my perpetrator didn't mean suddenly shrugging my shoulders, muttering, "OK, I forgive," and going on as if those things didn't happen. They did happen. And they took a terrible toll on my life. Forgiveness involved my handing over to God the responsibility for justice. The longer I held on to it, the more the bondage strangled the life out of me. God saw every bit of it, and He can far better represent me and uphold my cause. Forgiveness meant my deferring the cause to Christ and deciding to be free of the ongoing burden of bitterness and blame.

Many people who were victimized in childhood have asked me: "Are you really OK when no one's around or are you putting on a good act?"

No, I'm not putting on an act. The memories are still painful to me at times, but they no longer have power over me. I am free from their control and, yes, I have forgiven. You know one of the primary reasons I finally forgave my perpetrator? This may be hard for some of you to stomach, but it is the absolute truth: I finally came to a place where I felt sorrier for him than I did for myself. I can tell you that if I had to be in the scenario of Matthew 18:6, I'd rather be the loved and cherished victim than the victimizer. As my nephew used to say when he was little, "Dat dude's in bid trouble."

6. We can sadly assume victimization will continue in this world system.
Several very important clues to understanding the fact of child abuse in our world are hidden in Matthew 18:7.

First fill in the following blank: "Such things, _____ but woe to the man through whom they come!"

The Greek word for *must* is *anagke* meaning "compelling force, as opposed to willingness … that as a result of the depravity and wickedness of men, there is a moral inevitability that offenses should come."

In your own words, why will some level of child victimization probably continue to occur in our world as we know it?

Another reason for child victimization is impossible to overestimate. What other forces are at work according to Ephesians 6:12?

If you don't believe in the existence and ardent activity of the vile prince of this world system (John 12:31) and his evil underlings, you will never comprehend the origin and ongoing problem of childhood victimization. Until Christ's kingdom comes, we can and must reach out to victims and support laws that restrain evil and "expose deeds of darkness," but we will never be able to completely stop it. While he is the prince of this world, Satan has far too much to gain from it.

The next word may help you understand why the enemy benefits so viciously from the kinds of hurts we're addressing. Matthew 18:7 says: "Woe to the world because of the things that cause people to sin! *Such things* must come, but woe to the man through whom they come!" The KJV renders the word *offenses*.

Either way, get a load of this word and meaning. *Skandalon:* "The trigger of a trap on which the bait is placed, and which, when touched by the animal, springs and causes it to close causing entrapment … *skandalon* involves a reference also to the conduct of the person who is thus trapped. *Skandalon* always denotes an enticement to conduct which could ruin the person in question." You don't have to have your doctorate in biblical studies to recognize the work of the enemy in victimization. Ironically, the host of the shame game is shameless.

God wants to bind up my broken heart.

✳ Compare 2 Timothy 2:26. According to this Scripture, why does the devil try to trap people? Choose one. To …

☐ tempt them to turn from God   ☐ make them hate their own lives
☐ take them away from Christ   ☐ do his will

Satan has enticed all of us to sin, but have you ever experienced a time when, in retrospect, you believe Satan was trying to "ruin you"?
☐ Yes ☐ No If so, in the margin explain in general and discreet terms.

The fact that you are in an in-depth Bible study tells me that he did not succeed in the long run. Why didn't he?

In your opinion, how could childhood victimization eventually trap someone by enticing conduct that could ruin the person in question?

We know from research that large numbers of both men and women who turn to scandalous behaviors such as prostitution, promiscuity, and homosexuality were victims of sexual abuse in childhood. I'm not making excuses, but sometimes explanations for such a lack of self-respect help us understand and know how to respond to such destructive behaviors. Please understand that Satan is always looking for a scandal. He delights in scandals, particularly when they involve believers in Christ, because he wants to ruin our testimonies.

Satan wants to keep people from receiving Christ as Savior. Certainly, childhood victimization is an effective deterrent since many victims feel they "cannot believe in a God who could let such a thing happen." If they only knew how anxious the Father is to heal and vindicate! The enemy can try to keep them blinded, but if they respond to the Holy Spirit's call, the veil is removed and Christ becomes theirs (2 Cor. 4). Since the enemy cannot keep salvation from anyone who wants to believe, he tries to ensure that they will be either too emotionally handicapped to turn into an effective witness, or perhaps better yet, too driven by destruction to avoid a scandal. The enemy's hope for Christians is that we will either be so ineffective we have no testimony, or we'll ruin the one we have.

Isn't the enemy's gain one more reason we must refuse to let him have another inch of ground over something in our past? It's time to direct our indignation toward the author of abuse: Satan himself. I want to make a statement I believe with my whole heart concerning childhood victimization: Ultimately the accuser is the chief abuser.

> Ultimately the accuser is the chief abuser.

Who is the "accuser" according to Revelation 12:10? _____

Why might the accuser be the chief abuser?

I was abused more times than I would like to count, but I was accused every day of my life from that time on until I finally said, "Enough!" and agreed to let God bring healing and forgiveness. My friend, read these words carefully and accept them with your whole heart: You are not defined by anything that happened to you or anything you have done. You are defined by who you are in Christ. You are God's beloved child. He has seen any wrong done to you, and He will uphold your cause. And as for that perpetrator? "Dat dude's in bid trouble."

We've talked about a difficult subject, but until the truths of our pasts converge with the truth of God's Word, we will never be whole. When Christ said, "You will know the truth and the truth will set you free," He was referring to His truth, the Word of God. If I am a believer in Christ, I cannot know the truth about myself until I know the truth of God's Word. Please make me a promise. Do not allow Satan to get an inch of ground from this lesson. The last thing your enemy wants is for you to be free.

Remember, Christ came to set the captives free and Satan came to make the free captive. He could try to counterfeit what we've learned by trying to sow fear in you regarding your children or heaviness in you because of difficult reminders. Refuse to let him pluck away any of the seeds God has planted today. Let these truths take root in your heart, then water and cultivate them with belief.

As we conclude today's lesson, you may be thinking, *But I still don't have all the answers.* Neither do I, but God has filled in enough of the blanks to invite us to trust Him with the rest.

In closing, fill in each of the following blanks with your first name.

My child, _____, I loved you before you were born. I knit you in your mother's womb and knew what your first and last words would be. I knew every difficulty you, _____, would face. I suffered each one with you. Even the ones you didn't suffer with me. I had a plan for your life before you were born. The plan has not changed, _____, no matter what has happened or what you have done. You see, I already knew all things concerning you before I formed you. I would never allow any hurt to come into your life that I could not use for eternity, _____. Will you let Me? Your truth is incomplete unless you view it against the backdrop of my truth. Your story, _____, will forever remain incomplete ... until you let Me do what only I can do with your hurt. Let Me perfect that which concerns you.

I remain,

Your Faithful Father

You are not defined by anything that happened to you or anything you have done.

How does God want you to respond to what He showed you today?

115

Day 4
Hearts Broken by Betrayal

Today's Treasure

"If an enemy were insulting me, I could endure it; if a foe were raising himself against me, I could hide from him." **PSALM 55:12**

Christ binds up the brokenhearted. Choosing any means other than the work of the Great Physician to treat brokenheartedness is an invitation to bondage. We could boil this unit down to one motto: Bandage or Bondage? We have addressed hearts broken in childhood. Psalm 107:20 gives a perfect synopsis of God's primary prescription for overcoming childhood victimization: "He sent forth His word and healed them." After my season of healing from childhood abuse, my scriptural testimony became Psalm 119:92.

In the margin write your own paraphrase of Psalm 119:92.

I pray that you and I will always be able to boast about Christ through our afflictions. I don't like tribulation one bit more than you do, but, not coincidentally, the road signs marking a positive change in my personal journey all appear in places of difficulty. Today we focus on another painful catalyst for a broken heart. I want the psalmist to introduce our subject matter before we center on the corresponding ministry of Christ.

Read Psalm 55:1-11. How would you describe David's frame of mind at this point in his life?

Without looking any farther in Psalm 55, list three or four circumstances that could cause this frame of mind.

David faced two primary emotions: fear and anguish. Fear is a very distressing emotion and one we are wise to confess to God with great urgency, just as David did. Fear in this example, however, was not David's problem. Anguish was.

David's heart had obviously been wrenched by an experience exceeding the fear of his enemies. Read the remainder of the psalm now. According to verse 12, David found his present situation almost unendurable. The reason for his anguish of heart and his inability to "endure" may have surprised you.

What was causing David such pain?
☐ the threat on his life
☐ the loss of his son's respect
☐ the betrayal of a close friend
☐ other _____

Describe the kind of relationship David once had with this friend.

How did David then describe his close friend in verse 20?

Only a person who has had intimate access to your heart can betray you to the point David described. The deeply damaging, heart-anguishing kind of betrayal is the kind that can shatter your heart. If you've ever encountered this kind of betrayal, most likely the mere recollection of it stabbed your heart again, no matter how long ago you encountered it. Just as we saw in David, the betrayal of someone close to us can be so shocking and upsetting that we can feel momentarily paralyzed by it.

Both the examples today single out betrayal in a friendship, but the point on which we'll relate and apply is not the kind as much as the depth of relationship. If you've ever been betrayed by a sibling, parent, spouse, child, or good friend, you've probably experienced the kind of anguish we're talking about.

Have you ever been betrayed by someone very close to you? ☐ Yes ☐ No

Please do not retreat emotionally over this question. I am not going to ask you to identify the person or exact situation. I do, however, ask you to work with the Holy Spirit as He penetrates our hearts regarding the subject of betrayal to ensure we've healed properly. If we haven't, perhaps today's lesson will help.

Recall the definition of a broken heart from day 1. Remember that the original intent suggested a moment when a violent break came to the heart.

In your situation, can you recall the moment your heart broke over the betrayal? If you remember, fill in the blanks below with adjectives describing exactly how you felt when the break of your heart came.

_____ _____ _____

Whether or not you fell to the temptation, chances are good you were tempted to react destructively over the days, weeks, or even months to come. What are a few things you felt like doing whether or not you did?

According to Hebrews 4:14-16, on what basis and with what assurance can you go to the throne of grace when you are painfully betrayed?

I see at least four reasons why Christ is the perfect choice to turn to when I am betrayed and want to react destructively:

1. He is sympathetic. We can't always count on sympathy from others when we're suddenly shattered. Our heartbreaks really aren't anyone else's full responsibility. They are Christ's. Remember, He came to bind up the brokenhearted. All anyone can really do is sit with us and watch our hearts bleed! Others can only take that kind of intimacy for a short time!

2. He knows I am weak. Unlike people, Christ is never intimidated by the depth of our need and the demonstration of our weakness. I am so glad that I don't have to have a "stiff upper lip" and set a good example for others to follow when I'm all alone with God and hurting.

3. He has been tempted in every way I have. Take another look at your answer to the earlier question, What are a few things you felt like doing whether or not you did them? If I'm reading Hebrews 4:15 correctly, Christ has also been tempted to react just like you were. I find great comfort in knowing Christ doesn't throw His hand over His mouth in shock when I wish I could act a certain way.

4. He met my same temptation without sin. No matter how I have reacted to betrayal or any other kind of heartbreak in the past, I am so glad to know that a way exists to be victorious. Christ has already done it. If I follow Him through my situation, I too can do it. If I blow it or react wrongly in the immediacy of the hurt, I can choose to follow Him the rest of the way, and in His mercy He will still bless and honor my choice.

Beloved, it's never too late to start following His lead in your crisis. We've established that Jesus has walked in the sandals of those sinking in the sand of betrayal. Let's look at the specifics. You probably know the story, but don't let familiarity cause you to miss a fresh application. Read Matthew 26:14-56 carefully.

Compare verses 21 and 31. Fill in the following blanks: Christ said that

one would _____ and all would _____ on account of Him.

Here is a question to provoke some thought. Why do you think Christ only considered Judas a betrayer even though all the disciples deserted Him and fled (v. 56)?

A true betrayer is motivated most by selfishness.

I don't know the correct answer to the question either, but one clue was left at the scene. Clearly Judas's actions were planned and deliberate while the remaining disciples reacted in fear. Judas showed premeditation.

I usually think of betrayal as something the alleged betrayer knew would devastate but did not care enough to act differently. Isn't that a large part of the reason we feel so betrayed at times? Because the person knew his or her actions were going to devastate, yet did it anyway?

God's love healed me in ways I can't express.

If you've ever felt betrayed, was part of your injury knowing that the other person would have been aware how hurt you would be?
☐ Yes ☐ No

You see, Judas was a betrayer in every sense of the word. A true betrayer is motivated most by selfishness. Simply put, his or her gain is worth more than the other's loss. Judas knew what his betrayal would cost Jesus, but his premeditation revealed he decided it was worth it. A second reason Christ may have considered Judas's actions as betrayal and the other disciples' actions as a falling away appears in Matthew 9:4.

What was Christ capable of doing?

Which of the following do you think motivated the disciples' falling away? ☐ fear ☐ evil ☐ indifference ☐ carelessness

Christ could see evil in Judas's heart. I don't believe He saw evil in the disciples. Rather, I think He saw fear. Big difference. I believe all betrayal is motivated by selfishness but not always motivated by evil.

I don't believe every spouse who has an extramarital affair means to devastate the betrayed husband or wife. Indeed, a betrayer may be sincerely regretful of the pain selfishness caused. Furthermore, not every alleged "betrayer" sees himself as one. Sometimes betrayal is a matter of perception. In Christ's case, however, the betrayal by Judas took the worst of all forms.

Even though Christ knew Judas would betray Him, I believe He was still devastated by it. He came to this earth in the form of human flesh not only to die in our behalf but also to live in our shoes. Heart-shattering betrayal is one of the hardest experiences we ever encounter. To best know how to bind up the heart broken by betrayal, He chose to experience it. That's what Hebrews 4:14-16 is all about. Christ ministers to the betrayed through His example.

We will conclude our lesson by attempting to enact the exhortation given to us in Philippians 2:5. What is it?

Let's see if we can determine Christ's attitude as He faced betrayal "yet without sin." Read Matthew 26:53-56 again. Obviously, Christ had the power to open the earth and swallow His opposition, but He didn't.

Why didn't He?

Jesus trusted the sovereignty of His Father. To get through difficult times that seem to defy explanation, we are helped greatly when we choose to trust God's sovereignty. Trusting God's sovereignty means trusting that if He has allowed something difficult and shocking to happen to one of His children, He plans to use it mightily *if the child will let Him.*

God did not cause Judas to be a thief and a betrayer, but He used the fraudulent disciple to complete a very important work in the life of Christ.

Scripture clearly tells us Satan used Judas, but God ultimately took it over for His good work. If your spouse has betrayed you with infidelity, my heart aches for you. I know my words may be difficult to read, but I believe God can use the betrayal to complete a very important work in *your* life too. How? Only you can find out. I've seen good ultimately evolve from the ravages of unfaithfulness several times. I never cease to be amazed at the *bad* God can use for *good*.

Read Philippians 3:10 and Colossians 1:24.

I pray continually to be Christlike; then when He allows me to "fellowship" in a few of His specific "sufferings," I tend to whine and carry on. Christ experienced betrayal. If we're going to fellowship in His sufferings, we are also going to experience betrayal. Here's the question that draws the bottom line. Few of us will escape betrayal in one way or another, but will we choose to fellowship with Christ in the midst of it? Will we choose to trust the sovereignty of our Heavenly Father who allowed it? Betrayal can either hurt and hurt. Or hurt and help. The choice is up to us.

> How does God want you to respond to what He showed you today?

Day 5
Hearts Broken by Loss

Today's Treasure
"Jesus said to her, 'I am the resurrection and the life. He who believes in me will live, even though he dies.'" **JOHN 11:25**

God introduced a season of loss in my life that spanned the most difficult two-year period of my adulthood to date. This painful season began with the excruciating loss of our son Michael to his birth mother—a loss so difficult that I still wrestle with it. On the heels of Michael's departure came the news that my mother's cancer had entered the bones and was incurable. For the ensuing months we watched helplessly as our tiny "Queen of Everything," as we called her, suffered terribly.

God moved one of my two best friends, leaving a tremendous void of laughter and foolishness in my life. My mother's illness continued to steal more and more of her until God, in His tender mercy, received her home. One week later, my other best friend moved to Mississippi. The second week I moved my oldest daughter to college and kissed a treasured season of my life good-bye. I've never recorded the experiences in sequence before. My lower lip is practically quivering, but I speak to people whose suffering far exceeds anything I've imagined.

My good friend Shirley says we can't compare losses. Anything that breaks the heart is a legitimate reason for seeking the healing only Christ can bring.

Have you ever experienced a season when you seemed to face one loss after another? If so, in the margin describe when and what it involved.

I'm learning so many things from God through this season of letting go. I know God's timing purposely corresponded with the writing of this study. Many emotions have swept over me during the last two years, but if you asked which emotion served as the common denominator, I would not hesitate to say *grief.* In fact, I was somewhat taken aback over the feelings of grief accompanying the moving of my two best friends. The grieving seemed out of place to me in relation to my other losses yet oddly unavoidable.

What about you? Have you ever experienced feelings of grief that surprised you or almost seemed inappropriate through a change in jobs, homes, health, or relationships? ☐ Yes ☐ No If so, explain.

God finally opened my eyes to see that grief was not inappropriate. Each of my experiences represented a kind of death. With the loss of Michael I experienced the death of being the mother of three, the mother of a son, a dream, and, overall, the death of a relationship that had practically consumed me for seven years.

With the departure of my two best friends I experienced the death of instant camaraderie, of expected company at many women's events, of relationships I had known for many years, and of pure togetherness. Best friendships with long histories are not easy to replace. The death of my mother has been the death of my head cheerleader, of my children's maternal grandmother and best friend, of a daily relationship, of someone who undoubtedly loved me with all her heart. In essence, hers was the death of a relationship impossible to replace. Two weeks later when I drove away from Texas A&M University leaving behind my firstborn, I knew I was facing death to family life as we had known it. I knew many wonderful times lay ahead and trusted that Amanda and I would always be close, but I knew the nature of my role must change. She was only an hour and a half away, but that's farther than right up the stairs where she'd been for all those years!

Life involves change. Change involves loss. Loss involves death of one kind or another. Before we conclude, I believe we will discover a new way to personally apply the words of the apostle Paul in 2 Corinthians 4:11, "For we who are alive are always being given over to death for Jesus' sake, so that his life may be revealed in our mortal body." Every time we are delivered over to a death of any

The most debilitating loss for a Christian is the loss of faith.

kind, we encounter a challenge to allow the loss to bring gain for Jesus' sake. We accomplish this task by allowing His life to be revealed in our mortal bodies. I hope to prove this hypothesis through a fresh look at one of the old, old stories.

Read John 11:1-44. List every evidence you can find to suggest closeness of relationship between Christ, Lazarus, Martha, and Mary.

What reasons did Christ cite or imply for waiting until Lazarus was dead before He returned to Bethany?

Verse 4:

Verse 11:

Verse 15:

Verse 40:

What other reason can you safely assume based on verses 19 and 45?

Imagine that Christ came the moment Mary and Martha sent word to Him, immediately healing Lazarus of his threatening illness. How do you think the results would have compared to Jesus' raising Lazarus from the dead?

I'd like to offer three fresh breaths of life for those times when we experience the death of something or someone we cherish.

1. Christ never allows the hearts of His own to be shattered without excellent reasons and eternal purposes. Surely one reason God detailed the story of Lazarus is so we could look for a precedent to help us in our losses. Christ dearly loved Mary and Martha, yet He purposely allowed them to suffer a loss. Our Father would never allow our hearts to break for trivial reasons. We may never see the reasons like Mary and Martha did, but could we walk by faith and believe the best of Christ? You see, the most debilitating loss for a Christian is not the loss of a loved one but the loss of faith.

✳ **How do you think the loss of faith could turn into a form of bondage?**

Has the enemy turned any of your losses into bondage? If so, in the margin describe how.

2. Christ never allows any illness to end in death for a Christian. Death seems so final. Even if we believe that death is not the end, our hearts often lag far behind. All believers in Christ will rise from the dead. What made Lazarus unique was his return to mortal life. Please don't think me morbid, but I'm not sure Lazarus got the better end of the deal! When I die, I would rather not wake up and do it all over again! Either way, however, death is never the end of anyone's life in Christ. Neither does it have to be the end of the life of the loved one left behind—but too often, it is. My primary purpose in this lesson is to convince anyone who feels she can hardly go on living that Christ desires to raise you from the living dead.

By what new name did Christ reveal Himself to Martha in John 11:25?

3. Any kind of "death" is an invitation to resurrection life to the believer. Thank goodness, the loss of something or someone dear never has to mean the end of abundant, effective, or even joyful life for any Christian.

Joy and effectiveness may seem to pause for a while as grief takes its course, but those who allow their broken hearts to be bound by Christ will experience them again. Our Savior is the God of resurrection life, no matter what kind of death has occurred in the life of any believer!

Nothing is more natural than grief after a devastating loss, but those of us in Christ can experience satisfying life again. When our hearts have been shattered by loss, we have an opportunity to welcome a supernatural power to our lives. It doesn't come any other way. That is the power to live again when we'd really rather die. It is a power that displays the life of Christ in us like no other because it defies all odds. God becomes the only explanation for our emotional survival and revival. Perhaps the most profound miracle of all is living through something we thought would kill us. And not just living, but living abundantly and effectively—raised from living death to a new life. A life indeed absent of something or someone dear but filled with the presence of the resurrection and the life.

No, my life will never be the same. I no longer have a son. My mom is in heaven. My two best friends have moved. My firstborn went off to college and now has a family of her own. But, you see, the life of a Christian is never about sameness. It's always about change. That's why we must learn to survive and once again thrive when change involves heartbreaking loss. We're being conformed to the image of Christ.

When our hearts are hemorrhaging with grief and loss, never forget that Christ binds and compresses it with a nail-scarred hand. Life will not ever be the same, but I have the invitation from Christ to rise to a new life—a more compassionate life, a wiser life, a more productive life. And, yes, even a better life. Sound impossible? It is without Christ.

As we close our lesson today, I can almost hear Christ calling out a name. Is it yours? By any chance have you been among the living dead? The stone's been rolled away. Resurrection life awaits you. Will you continue to sit in a dark tomb or will you walk into the light of resurrection life? Lazarus, come forth!

How does God want you to respond to what He showed you today?

I FINALLY GAVE IT ALL TO JESUS.

BREAKING *Free*

Today we will talk about the brokenness of heart that can result from the frantic

search for something _____ ____ _____ _____ _____.

John 4:1-18.

1. All _____ is rooted in _____.

2. _____ does not _____ _____.

Compare John 4:10,14 to John 7:37-39.

" 'Welling up' is inadequate. The verb … does not appear to be used elsewhere

of the action of _____. The word indicates springing up or _____."

(New International Commentary on the New Testament)

"The life that Jesus gives is no _____ and _____ thing. It is

much more than merely the _____ into a new state, that of being

saved instead of lost. It is the _____ life, and the living Spirit within

people is evidence of this." *(New International Commentary on the New Testament)*

3. _____ _____ is at the heart of all bondage.

In his book *Addictions: A Banquet in the Grave,* author Edward T. Welch refers

to all addiction as "____ _____ _____."

4. The continued search for something _____ to fill our empty places

is _____.

Romans 6:19-21

John 4:25-30

5. Christ knows _____.

Jeremiah 2:13

6. A new response is one _____ _____ away.

Conclude with a glance at John 4:31-33.

Week 6

Beauty from Ashes

I tried to think of ways to get her to counseling, ways to help her. Then I realized I couldn't make that decision for her. She had to make it herself. It is no longer my responsibility. In fact, it never was. I will mourn and pray for her, but I will not lose hope. I rejoice that He makes beauty from ashes and I am excited about how He is taking me to a deeper level of faith and trust in Him.

Day 1
Ashes Instead of Honor

Today's Treasure
"Tamar put ashes on her head and tore the ornamented robe she was wearing. She put her hand on her head and went away, weeping aloud as she went."
2 Samuel 13:19

I'm shocked and humbled by the men who have done the women's Bible studies I've written. Many commented that our Bible studies were as applicable for men as for women. Isn't God glorious? However, I'm afraid this week will not be nearly as gender friendly for men, so I apologize in advance to any dear brother who has joined us so far. I'm not, however, offering you a week off. I believe a man can profit from what we are about to study. Men need to know the unique struggles of women just like women need to know the unique struggles of men.

We will study God's desire to restore the virtue and dignity of women. At no time will my intention be to blame men for the demeaning of women. I want to shed light on Satan's scheme to demoralize women and steal their God-given dignity. Many women are in terrible bondage to a growing societal ploy by the evil one. I hope to identify it today and emphasize God's liberating intentions for us in days 2 through 5.

This week's memory verse is Isaiah 61:3. Write the verse in the margin.

Note the phrase: "to bestow on them a crown of beauty instead of ashes." Our emphasis is God's desire to crown us with beauty. Before we can understand His desire, however, we will consider what this "crown of beauty" will replace.

Identify why each of the following covered themselves in ashes:

Esther 3:8-9; 4:1

Job 42:1-6

Daniel 9:1-3

Ashes symbolized mourning, but the cause could differ dramatically. In Esther, Mordecai mourned the plot to destroy the Jews. Job mourned his own small view of God. In Daniel, God's prophet mourned over the vision of Jerusalem's 70-year desolation. We also mourn for different reasons. Sometimes over our own sins. Sometimes over the suffering of others. Sometimes over the future.

Ancient Hebrews commonly wore sackcloth and ashes as a symbol of grief. The uncomfortable sackcloth reminded the individual of the call to grief. Ashes showed the mortality of man, especially in view of his omnipotent, eternal God. To cast ashes on one's head was the humble symbol of man's desperate need for God's mercy and his ever-pending covenant with destruction. Those covering themselves in ashes demonstrated that without God they would be nothing.

We have few western practices that compare, and I'm not sure we're the better for it either. Even wearing black during a time of mourning has become somewhat outdated. Tangible evidence sometimes grants an added freedom of expression. The old ways may have been healthier in this respect.

In ancient days people also repented of sin with obvious demonstrations of sorrow. I can't think of any such practice in the modern church. In fact, we all tend to be more comfortable when we each keep our repentance to ourselves! Perhaps the reason I have a favorable view of some of the ancient practices is because I am so demonstrative, but I can't help believing we can all find a little freedom in expression at times.

How about you? In the margin describe tangible ways you practice your mourning over sin, loss, or concern for others.

I am purposely making an issue of this point because our society is tending toward a frightening reduction of emotions. Squelching emotions only stores them in explosive containers. God's Word constantly recognizes our emotional side.

Today we look at a heart-wrenching expression of grief in Scripture. We can assume women in ancient times, just as men, practiced putting on sackcloth and ashes as they mourned. The Bible describes in detail only one time, however, when a woman covered herself in ashes. Read 2 Samuel 13:1-22.

In the margin describe the emotions this tragedy stirs in you.

✳ **In what ways did Tamar symbolize and express her grief?**

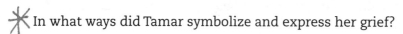

What is your personal opinion regarding the advice Absalom gave Tamar? Respond in the margin.

What was the significance of the richly ornamented robe in verse 18?

Even though Tamar's brother Absalom loved her, he could not restore her dignity. How does Scripture characterize Tamar's life at Absalom's?

Tamar remained the daughter of a king, yet she lived like a desolate woman. Amnon's actions could not change Tamar's bloodline, but she apparently lived the rest of her life believing she could never be restored.

The quality of our lives usually grows from *what* and *who* we believe we are. Tamar's father, the king, was highly responsible for her unchanging sense of desolation. He was furious, but he did nothing tangible and positive with his appropriate emotions. You can rest assured that our God is also furious when women are abused and mistreated. The difference is that we can trust Him to do something about it—His way, His time. Imagine Tamar's life in the long run. If we assume her dignity was never restored, what do you think she might have been like by the time she was 40 years old?

Consider how much like Tamar we are in this generation. Those of us who have received Christ are literally daughters of royalty. In fact, every woman who has been renewed in Christ through faith and repentance is spiritually a virgin daughter of the King. The biblical image and intent of womanhood is honor and purity. Whether or not you have ever been personally and individually victimized, dear sister, you are living in a time of victimization of women.

Can you list any evidences suggesting the demoralization of women in our society? Respond in the margin.

Satan is actively and progressively pedaling the demoralization of women. Consider a few examples:

- From my office window I see several billboards suggesting women were made for sensual pleasures and little more. A growing number of advertisements blatantly push their products through sex appeal. My husband has been floored over the growing use of suggestive advertisements in his fishing magazines! (He's a fishing purist, so he sees this method of sales as virtually sacrilegious!)
- Girls are starving themselves to death to be model-thin to fit the world's definition of attractive. I'll never forget the time I took two happy, well-adjusted, size-6 daughters to the mall to find prom dresses. Three hours later I took home two devastated girls crying about how "fat" they were. I couldn't believe it. I marched into one of the stores and checked the dress size on the mannequin in the window. Guess what size? Size 2!
- Alarming numbers of young teens are seeking breast implants and liposuction *with the approval of their parents.*
- Many influential women teach the hatred of men almost as a religion. The mentality that all men are bad is neither accurate nor healthy. Individuals commit crimes—not entire genders. A hatred or fear of men is symptomatic of poor emotional health. A blatant sign of unhealthy emotions among many women is the *need* of some to conjure up a female *god*. A Bible has been rewritten with female references to God rather than male!
- Adult women are becoming more and more convinced that they must forsake femininity for professionalism. Acting less like women is not an effective way to combat the demeaning of women.
- Women who are homemakers sometimes feel they are looked down on as unsuccessful and unmotivated.
- Lesbianism has growing acceptance as a way to strike out against the demoralization of women. What a deception! What could be more demoralizing than turning to homosexuality? The answer is not in turning from men. The answer is in turning to God.

After intense Bible study, I am no longer in Satan's bondage.

129

Read Ephesians 6:12. Who is our struggle against? Respond in the margin.

My dear sister, you may think you're unaffected by the enemy's demoralization of women, but I ask you to consider this question on behalf of your gender: If we're not buying into the mentality society is selling about women, then why are we working so hard and spending so much money to be desirable? or feeling so guilty and ugly if we don't? I believe we are internally affected whether or not we externalize the struggle.

Those of us who have been individually and physically victimized know the desolation Tamar experienced. Many of us were convinced by the enemy that we were no longer fit to have honor and dignity. In my situation, by the time I learned what a virgin was, I shuddered with the shock that I wasn't one. I never had the chance. What I'm asking you to recognize, though, is that you have also been hurt and affected by the frightful experiences of other women.

Several years ago an article appeared in our local paper exposing a secret network for the victimization of little girls in areas of the Orient. Many Americans were patrons of this horrific crime. I was devastated for my gender. What's more, so was every other woman who read it, even those who had never been personally violated. Why? Because we've all been innocent little girls at one time or another, and the terror they face is unimaginable. We are all violated by crimes like these. Certainly, many men who read the article were outraged too.

Satan desires to have women in a stronghold of exploitation, sexploitation, distortion, and desolation. He knows how effective and influential women can be, so he works through society to convince us we are so much less than we are.

Take a look at Isaiah 6:1-4. By what other descriptions could you call "the Lord seated on a throne" based on your knowledge of Scripture?

☐ King of kings ☐ Creator of the universe
☐ Lord of hosts ☐ Sovereign Ruler of all the earth
☐ the Holy One ☐ your personal Heavenly Father

How does God want you to respond to what He showed you today?

Oh, sister, I hope you feel as free to describe Him as your personal Heavenly Father as the other names. Christian, if you are not royalty, He is not King. Let's learn how to start fulfilling our destinies. This week's study is very important.

If Satan has convinced you to see yourself as anything less than the hand-picked daughter of the King, you have something in common with Tamar. If you think anything could happen to you that could steal your royal heritage, you have something in common with Tamar. If you think you deserve mistreatment or disrespect, you have something in common with Tamar. What you may have in common is a stronghold. My prayer is that the Holy Spirit will be free to mend the torn coats of the daughters of royalty. And that He will also restore lost dignity, teach us our true identity, and liberate us to live in purity.

Conclude your lesson today by reading aloud Psalm 45:13-15. That, my dear sister in Christ, is your destiny.

Day 2
To be a Bride

We are studying the tender—and if I may say, romantic—ministry of Christ given to Him in Isaiah 61:3: "to bestow on them a crown of beauty instead of ashes." The mourner poured the ashes on his or her head as Tamar did after the crime Amnon committed against her. Come with me for an imaginary look back.

Imagine Tamar: grief-stricken, sobbing, ashes on her head. Her body in a heap on the cold floor. Soot covers her beautiful face and smears the rich colors of her torn robe. Her outward appearance echoes the cavernous darkness in her soul. Hopelessness and death well up in her. She is nothing but a tomb.

The door of her room slowly creaks open. A stream of cloudy sunlight pours through the door. A figure of a man takes form within it. Not Absalom. No, she would recognize Absalom anywhere. Her heart jumps with sickening terror; then the figure steps through the door and His visage becomes clear. Tamar has never seen Him before, yet He looks so familiar. Not frightening. And she should be frightened. No man should be entering her chamber. She should run, but she cannot seem to move.

She glances down at the hands that seem paralyzed on her lap, her palms covered with ash. She suddenly becomes shamefully aware of her appearance. Wretchedness sears her heart. She is certain her violated estate is obvious. She despises herself.

"Tamar," the man speaks gently and with warm familiarity.

Her heart sobs, "She is dead!" A slave of shame has taken her place.

He approaches and takes her face in His hands. No one has ever done that before. The overwhelming intimacy turns her face crimson, not with shame but with vulnerability. His thumbs sweep over her cheeks and wipe the tears from her face. As He takes His hands from her face and places them on her head, her throat aches with fresh cries as she sees the filth on His hands. Her filth. He draws back His hands and she senses something on her head. Perhaps in His mercy He has hooded her disgrace.

The man offers her His hands, still covered with soot, and she takes them. Suddenly she is standing. Trembling. He leads her to the brass mirror hung on the wall. She turns her face away. He lifts her chin. She gives the mirror only a glance. Her heart is startled. She begins to stare. Her face is no longer streaked with dirt. Her cheeks are blushed with beauty; her eyes are clear and bright. A crown sits on her head, and a veil flows from its jewels to her shoulders. Her torn coat is gone. A garment of fine white linen graces her neck and adorns her frame. The King's daughter, pure and undefiled. Beauty from ashes.

"I delight greatly in the LORD; my soul rejoices in my God. For he has clothed me with garments of salvation and arrayed me in a robe of righteousness, as a bridegroom adorns his head like a priest, and as a bride adorns herself with her jewels." **ISAIAH 61:10**

God wants to surpass our dreams.

No, I do not believe in fairy tales. But I do believe in God. He sent His Son for just such a purpose. Whatever the cause of our mourning, Christ can be the lifter of our heads. He can give us beauty instead of ashes. This was not Tamar's story, but it might have been. Beloved, it can be yours. Does it seem too silly for you? Oh, Sister, have you bought into the hardness and cynicism of this world? In your attempt to give up on girlish dreams, you may have given up on a few that were meant to come true.

God wants to restore dignity, virtue, and honor to women in a world that demoralizes them. You don't have to be personally violated to buy into the world's negative propaganda. If the humble dignity of Christ is not a reality in your daily life, you are living short of your rights and your destiny. This week we're seeking the restoration of feminine honor and virtue. Each day we will recapture a girlish dream God gave us so He could show us His glory by surpassing it.

I believe practically every little girl has at least four dreams: (1) to be a bride, (2) to be beautiful, (3) to be fruitful (which we usually define as having children), and (4) to live happily ever after. Satan wants to destroy our dreams. God wants to surpass our dreams. I believe God gives us dreams so we'll long for God's reality.

We'll examine all four of our common girlish dreams. We start with the first: to someday be a bride. I can almost sense some contented singles bristling up on me. Could you admit that you had dreams of being a bride when you were a little girl? God instituted marriage so we could comprehend a greater relationship (Eph. 5:25-33). Only two individuals can make up a marriage. Our heavenly union with Christ is common to all believers, but the intimacy of this relationship is expressed between Christ and individual believers. Whether we are male or female, we are the bride of Christ.

I love the term *bride*. Interestingly, God's Word does not refer to us as *wives of Christ*, but as the *bride*. Let's look back in the context of Isaiah 61.

Practice Scripture memory by writing Isaiah 61:3 in the margin.

The *crown of beauty* in its original meaning is an ornamental headdress like a crown or a wedding veil. The original term comes from the Hebrew word *pa'ar*, meaning "to gleam ... to explain oneself ... to beautify" (*Strong's*). The kind of headdress a woman wore explained who she was. In Isaiah 61, the crown of beauty is symbolic of an elaborate ornament identifying a woman as both bride and queen. In ancient days the only way a woman could be queen was to be married to the king. Isaiah 61 portrays God blowing away the ashes of mourning and replacing them with a crown. A crown identifying the woman as the bride of the King. In this case we are the bride of the Book of Isaiah's Prince of Peace!

Read Isaiah 61:10, relishing every single word. If you have received Christ as your Savior, describe your symbolic appearance.

This is how Christ sees you. I also believe this is how the enemy sees you. He just doesn't want you to know it. His job is to deceive us into believing we are so much less than we are because he knows we'll act like who we think we are. No matter what has happened to us, what we have done, or where we have been, you and I are brides! It's high time we see ourselves as we really are. I don't know about you, but the simple reminder of who I am in Christ causes me to delight greatly in the Lord! If you've not yet discovered it, part of the freedom I hope you'll find in this Bible study is the liberty to let your soul rejoice in your God.

In the margin write a prayer expressing what you're feeling about our lesson so far. If you're not feeling anything, tell Him! A lack of reaction to freeing truth can indicate a stronghold! The sooner you identify any strongholds, the sooner you'll be free.

Think once again of the implications of the term *bride*. What are a few things the word *bride* implies that the word *wife* may not?

Of course, this question has no one correct answer. To me, *bride* indicates lots of things *wife* doesn't. *Bride* implies newness and freshness. A crisp, beautiful dress. The fragrance of perfume. Richly colored lips. Sparkling eyes. I usually picture youthfulness. Perhaps innocence. I believe all these things will characterize our relationship with Christ and the ultimate consummation of marriage.

Scripture implies that our relationship to Christ, though enduring eternally, will remain fresh and new. We will somehow always be brides, somewhat like my mother-in-law. Keith's parents have been married 56 years, but my father-in-law always refers to his wife as his bride. To me, his tender expression implies a lasting romance. He loves to bring her gifts. They still embrace, kiss, and date!

Let's look at two insightful references. First read Jeremiah 2:2.

What is a young bride in love usually willing to do? Respond in margin.

One of the characteristics of a loving bride is her willingness to follow her groom to places that at times may seem like wilderness. Our Bridegroom sometimes leads us to difficult places, but we can trust Him always to have purpose in our stay and never to forsake us. Remember, Christ can't lead us somewhere He refuses to go.

This year I followed my Bridegroom to a place of aloneness. I'm presently living in a place or phase of my relationship with Christ where I spend lots of time alone. All the losses of the past year have introduced me to a new and unfamiliar place. I've grown closer to my Bridegroom than ever before, which miraculously makes me closer to my earthly mate. Yes, I feel that I followed Christ to a wilderness in this present season of my life; but, in seeking Him more frequently than ever, I've experienced His fulfillment of Isaiah 41:18.

Isaiah 41:18 tells us God can "turn the desert into pools of water." We can't truly appreciate a spring until we discover one in a desert. I don't think I'll always be in this place. It's looking less and less like a wilderness now. Anyway, you've probably noticed that our Bridegroom doesn't allow us to grow too comfortable in one place! But I'm learning to enjoy it while I can.

How about you? Describe a place where you followed your Bridegroom. What did He have for you there?

Usually our earthly grooms move us to new places to seek a higher quality of life. The same is true of Christ. All His moves offer you a better quality of life.

Now read Revelation 19:4-8. These verses describe the corporate gathering of all believers and Christ at the marriage supper of the Lamb. Though this wedding feast is a future event, verse 7 implies a very important responsibility of the bride—one that cannot wait until the last minute!

Notice the qualifier of the bride's actions: "She has made herself ready." Past tense. We cannot make ourselves ready the moment we see Christ any more than a woman can be prepared to meet her groom at the altar with three minutes' notice. If we belong to Christ, we'll still see Him, whether or not we've prepared ourselves to be fitting brides, but I want to be ready. Don't you? I don't want to be caught with spiritual curlers in my hair!

When I was preparing for my wedding, I often thought about being a wife. Not just any wife. Keith's wife. Mind you, we don't just get married. We get married to a man! A wedding is not about a lovely ceremony. It's about a long-term relationship. I could not think about being married without thinking about Keith.

Sometimes I thought about how different we were. He was such an outdoorsman. Frankly, my hair does better in air-conditioning. I also thought about a few similarities. We both liked to be in control. We both liked to be right. Hm-m-m. So much for things in common. But he was the cutest thing I had ever seen and when he smiled, my heart melted. And, after all, we both enjoyed a hot cup of coffee. In hopes that he thought I was cute too, I prepared myself as best I could to be darling and make a good cup of coffee. Make fun of us if you want, but 30 years later it's still working! I still send him out the door with a fresh cup of coffee in the morning and put on a little blush when he drives up in the evening.

The same is true as we prepare to be eternal brides. We won't just be part of a beautiful ceremony. We will be the bride of Christ. God's Word doesn't imply that we are to make ourselves ready for the wedding but for the Groom. Thus, we cannot make ourselves ready without thinking all about Him—meditating on our similarities (which hopefully are multiplying), thinking about our differences and how we might adjust—simply thinking about how wonderful He is.

Yesterday I asked you to conclude by reading Psalm 45:13-15. I purposely avoided asking you to read verses 1-12 so you could end with them today. Remember, making ourselves ready means studying and knowing our Groom.

✳ Read Psalm 45:1-15. Write the specific characteristics or descriptions of your Groom that compel each of the following:
your love for Him

your respect for Him

your awe of Him

your joy in Him

Behold your Groom, the One for whom you're preparing. Make yourself ready!

How does God want you to respond to what He showed you today?

Day 3
To Be Beautiful

The benefits of our covenant relationship are internal and spiritual, but those who are free to believe God, glorify God, find satisfaction in God, experience God's peace, and enjoy God's presence display a noticeable difference in their lives.

I want to share something about women who live free that I hope will be encouraging. Most of them have experienced a serious stronghold or hindrance they fought to overcome. Every person I've met who really seems liberated to love, enjoy, and obey God as a lifestyle has been on the battlefield. They usually appreciate and apply victory more readily because they've experienced the misery of defeat firsthand. I rarely meet a person who has come to trust God fully without painfully confronting the fact that she can't trust herself.

The enemy is an expert archer with lots of practice aiming fiery darts. For women often the bull's-eye is childhood dreams or expectations. We grew up believing in Cinderella, yet some of us feel as if our palace turned out to be a duplex, our prince turned out to be a frog, and the wicked stepmother turned out to be our mother-in-law. Our fairy godmother apparently lost our addresses. Anyway, what we'd like to do to her with that wand of hers might not be pretty.

I'm hoping to prove to you this week that some of your girlish dreams were meant to come true in Christ—in ways far grander than the obvious. In fact, I'd like to suggest that God sometimes allows us to be let down and disappointed in life so we will learn to set our hopes more fully in Him.

In the margin list the four girlish dreams in our lesson yesterday. Place a check beside each of the dreams you remember having as a little girl.

Today's Treasure
"How beautiful you are, my darling! Oh, how beautiful!"
SONG OF SONGS 4:1

1.

2.

3.

4.

Even my friends who preferred baseball to dolls still dreamed of being a bride, being beautiful, having fruitful lives, and living happily ever after. Often those who say they never wanted those things fell victim at an early age to a negative influence, distorting their dreams. Today let's consider the second dream. Almost every little girl dreams of being beautiful. Long into adulthood we harbor hurts if we feel that no one thinks we are.

Watching my daughters go through high school reminded me of the insecurities I felt back then. To feel I looked OK, everything had to be right. No humidity, good hair, lots of makeup, no clumps in the mascara, cute clothes—preferably new. And if someone had on the same outfit? Oh, misery! I worked so hard trying to look good. Too hard. I believed that nothing about me was naturally beautiful.

How thankful I am for the freedom God has increasingly given me in Christ. I'm in the throws of middle age—a friend says, "Time is a great healer but a lousy beautician." Yet I'm happier and more satisfied than I've ever been. I'm far more likely to go without makeup or wear shorts that reveal 50-something legs. The secret? I'm learning to see myself as beautiful to Christ.

Don't try stuff on me like, "You're thin and your hair goes into all sorts of styles—of course you feel pretty!" Listen here. I had the worst pigeon toes and buck teeth in the free world. My legs looked like knobby sticks with fur. I may look different, but I know who's inside! Without Christ every woman has intense insecurities. Unless we find our identity in Christ, we are just as prone to appearance insecurities as unbelievers. Think about a season of your life when you struggled with feelings of unattractiveness, whether or not your feelings were accurate.

When was it? What influential variables in your life at that time added to your feelings of unattractiveness?

We try to act as if we don't care and that feeling unlovely doesn't hurt, but it does. Today we're going to go barefooted in the waters of the Bible's most provocative book: The Song of Songs. Before we take the first look, allow me to remind you this book is as inspired by the Holy Spirit as Matthew, Mark, Luke, and John.

Read Song of Songs 2 and 4. List every term of endearment (not figurative descriptions) the Lover gives His Beloved Bride (i.e. "my darling").

In the margin write every phrase that uses the word *beautiful* in both chapters and identify the Scripture reference.

If I really believed no men would dare tread through the waters of this week, I'd dare to have a little good, clean fun with you over a few things in these chapters! However, I know a tad about human nature. If I were doing a Bible study with Keith and one chapter said, "For men only," that's exactly where I'd begin! Therefore, I will limit my commentary on the ancient eastern poetic descriptions. Suffice it to say, if Keith ever looked romantically into my eyes and said, "Your teeth are like a flock of sheep just shorn," I'd run for the dental floss.

We missed one of Solomon's most visual comparisons. It's in 1:9.
To what did he compare his beloved?
☐ a swan ☐ a gazelle ☐ a horse ☐ a platypus

Men were into wheels then just as they are now. I'll never forget what a blast Keith had with the 1969 classic car he got Melissa for her 16th birthday. I complained about being old and he retorted, "So is Melissa's car, but you're just as good lookin'!" I didn't know whether to hit him or hug him. The men of Solomon's day had chariots. He was telling his beloved she looked as good as Pharaoh's best horse!

The Song of Songs is a wonderful book, isn't it? It makes me laugh, blush, and long for real romance. We're almost shocked that God even knows about these things, much less writes about them. God created love between a man and a woman. The full expression of that love in sexual intimacy was His idea—His gifts offered freely with complete blessing to every couple He unites in marriage. But wait a minute. Earthly marriage represents far more. Look at Ephesians 5:32.

✳ What is far more profound than a man and woman coming together in marriage? Respond in the margin.

God often teaches the unknown through the known. The Song of Songs helps us relate to our union with Christ. The book is ultimately a story about Christ and His beloved bride—us. We will share an intimacy with Him that we can only begin to comprehend by comparing it with the greatest earthly intimacy.

Real romance awaits all of us. Single and married women alike can celebrate that some dreams will really come true. One of them is perfectly portrayed in this inspired book. Christ is completely taken with you. He sees you as His beloved, His bride. Take another look at several beautifully expressive verses that show Christ's feelings for you: *"I am a rose of Sharon, a lily of the valleys"* (2:1). Notice these are the expressions of the woman.

Compare the response of her lover in 2:2. She was not being egotistical. She simply saw herself as her lover saw her. Her mirror was the face of her mate.

What is your present basis for defining how you look? If you began to allow Christ to become your mirror, do you think you'd stop taking care of yourself? ☐ Yes ☐ No Explain your response in the margin.

"His banner over me is love" (2:4). The word *banner* comes from the Hebrew word *dagal* meaning "to flaunt, that is, raise a flag; figuratively to be conspicuous" (*Strong's*). Have you ever been pretty sure someone loved you, but you longed for them to show it more? Song of Songs foreshadows the kind of relationship in

I am healed. I am whole.

which Christ's love for each of us will be completely conspicuous. He will flaunt His love for us. The visual of the banner might be pictured as Jesus waves His hand over you, signaling to all in sight that you are the one He loves. Hallelujah!

Who is someone you are absolutely certain loves you? _____
What are a few ways you know?

Do you struggle to imagine Christ becoming your ultimate soul mate? Can you picture that He will walk by your side, hold your hand, and talk with you?

On this earth, He became like us, but what does 1 John 3:2 tell us we'll become when we see Christ?
☐ like angels ☐ like spirit creatures
☐ like glorified humans ☐ like Christ

Read Song of Songs 5:10-16. In the eyes of His beloved, which will be you, how will Christ look? In the margin give your own description based on these verses.

Isaiah 53:2 (KJV) describes Christ's appearance during His first advent with these words: "There is no beauty that we should desire him." How wonderfully fitting that Christ will be the fullness of splendor and beauty when we see Him.

Compare Exodus 33:18-23 to Song of Songs 2:14. What do these two passages have in common? What is different in the two passages?

What glorious images of Christ hiding His own in the cleft of the rock! Now think of Him coming for the bride He has protected with His hand. He longs to see her face and hear her voice. The face of the bride was always veiled in the ancient eastern world. Often the groom had never seen the face of his bride unveiled. He had only been told of her beauty.

Lifting the veil was one of the most intimate parts of the wedding night. Isn't that romantic? Song of Songs implies that Christ will long to see the lovely face of His bride, His beloved. And He will not be disappointed. You will be a beautiful bride. The intimacy we will share with Christ is beyond our comprehension. We do not know what form it will take. We simply know that we will experience oneness with Him in complete holiness and purity.

One of the grandest miracles of having a wonderful, fulfilling relationship with Christ now instead of waiting until heaven is the stress Christ relieves from other relationships. Loving Christ does not cause me to love Keith less. On the contrary, through Christ I love him more. Christ helps us see each other more like He sees us. Christ takes up the slack in imperfect relationships and reminds

Have you ever received something you desperately wanted but still felt an unsatisfied longing you couldn't identify? ☐ Yes ☐ No If so, explain in the margin.

3. *God created every life to be fruitful* and multiply, but remember—God-given dreams are the realm from which God can bring an even greater reality! Most little girls dream of having children, but this God-given dream represents more than physical offspring.

Let's meditate on this for a moment. Why do most women want to have children? List as many reasons as you can.

4. *I believe our girlish dreams to have babies represent even more than the obvious.* They represent a desire to have fruitful lives, to invest ourselves in something that matters. Something that affects. Something that grows. If not, wouldn't God be cruel to allow any woman to dream of children yet disable her to have them?

I don't believe God allows surrendered hearts to continue to long for things He will not ultimately grant in one way or another. Our disappointment with God is often the result of our small thinking. The remainder of today will be devoted to a biblical basis for this belief system.

With God, we can face our giants.

Read Isaiah 54:1-5. How in the world could a barren woman have more "children" than a married woman who actually gave birth?

Let me give you a few examples. My dear friend Johnnie Haines has two fine sons who are her pride and joy. She always longed to have a daughter in addition to her sons, but she never had that daughter. One day she said to me, "My boys are virtually grown and I love them so much, but I still wonder from time to time why God never gave me the daughter I longed for too." But, you see, He did! For 10 years she led the women's ministry at a large church in Houston. She mothered numerous young women! The women under her direction are now mature believers who are serving God effectively in their homes, workplaces, and churches.

I have another friend by the name of Dr. Rhonda Kelley, author of *Life Lessons from Women in the Bible*. God never gave the Kelleys physical offspring, but He has given them more spiritual offspring than any parents I know! Her husband is a seminary president and she teaches and mentors on the campus both professionally and personally. Only heaven will boast the number of offspring Chuck and Rhonda really have. Their loss was glory's gain. At this point, I believe both of them would testify that God ultimately did not restrict them from childbearing. Rather, He loosened the restrictions and made them enlarge their tents! The potential for spiritual offspring in the lives of those physically barren is virtually limitless. If He restricts you from physical offspring, He desires to set you free from restrictions in order to bear spiritual offspring.

God created you to bear much fruit. God often applied the physical truths of the Old Testament as spiritual truths in the New Testament. Offspring is a perfect example.

Compare and contrast the following Scriptures:

Genesis 9:1 and Matthew 28:18-19

Exodus 1:6-13 and Acts 8:1-8

In the Old Testament, God promised great numbers of physical descendants. God doesn't often speak in terms of physical offspring in the New Testament. His emphasis is clearly on spiritual offspring. "Therefore go and make disciples of all nations" (Matt. 28:19) is our equivalent to the Old Testament's "Be fruitful and increase in number; fill the earth" (Gen. 1:28).

Infertility cannot be scripturally interpreted as some kind of curse for New Testament believers. In fact, those willing to have their eyes pried open may see the opportunity being physically childless affords. As we've seen today, even the Book of Isaiah says that those who are barren can have more offspring than those who are able to conceive and give birth. In fact, barrenness at any point in life affords great opportunity for spiritual offspring. If we live long enough, each of us will be barren. Are we to assume our fruitfulness has ended? Do we exist on memories and large doses of fiber until death? Why, then, does barrenness come to all women around 50 years of age? Were we meant to sit around for the next 20 to 30 years and twiddle our arthritic thumbs? God is far too practical for that!

What can older women do, according to Titus 2:3-5,11-15?

When older women pour their lives into younger women and their children, they are birthing spiritual offspring! Older women are a necessity in the body of Christ! I don't see the slightest hint that older people should retire from serving God or witnessing to the lost. Quite to the contrary, they have opportunities that far exceed those of younger men and women. God calls us to be fruitful and multiply until He calls us home.

If you are in your 20s or 30s, in the margin list a few people God has used to "rear" you spiritually. If you are over 40, list a few people in whom you've invested your life as a spiritual parent or mentor.

When I was a little girl, I wanted to be a mommy more than anything in the world. Now my children are grown. Recently my older daughter and I were enjoying fellowship together when she paused and asked, "Mom, now that Melissa and I are both grown and moving away from you and Daddy, will you be OK?"

A lump welled in my throat but I still answered confidently, "Yes, Darling. Most people just need to feel useful. As long as I have Jesus, I will always feel useful—even if I occasionally feel lonely."

I have tried my hardest to keep my children from growing up, but all my efforts have failed. Sometimes I think, *What will I ever do? I was born to be a mommy!* Then I remember God has called me primarily to women's ministry and I will always have the opportunity to "mother" a few spiritual offspring as long as I'm willing to invest myself.

What about you? Are you discovering a few opportunities to rear spiritual children? ☐ Yes ☐ No If so, explain.

At this time in my life I do most of my mentoring through my teaching and writing. I do, however, have a spiritual daughter or two in whom God has called me to invest my life. The joy of these daughters has been indescribable! One has a particularly dry and delightful wit. She is a gifted Bible teacher at only 27 years of age and hardly ever misses an opportunity to affectionately rib me about my age. I introduced her once as a spiritual daughter and later she said, "Since you led the person to the Lord who, in turn, led me to the Lord, wouldn't that make you my spiritual grandmother?" After I called her a smart aleck, we had a great laugh and every card or gift I've sent to her since has been signed, Love, Granny.

What blessing comes from the body of Christ! If God chose for you to have physical children, prepare yourself! They will grow up! Then it's time to enlarge your tent and invest in spiritual children! If God chooses for you never to have physical children, He's calling you to a far bigger family!

God purposely placed the dream of fruitful lives in every little girl's heart. Oh, how I love the paradoxical ways our glorious Heavenly Father works. Only He can bring gain from loss. Only He can make us more fruitful in barrenness!

One final thought. I asked you earlier why most women want to have children. As I posed the question, I thought of my own answers. Undoubtedly one of the reasons why I wanted children was to bear offspring who were the image of my husband. I wanted little Keiths and Keithettes! I didn't want them to look like me. I've always thought Keith was far more beautiful than I. You see, the same is true of our spiritual offspring. Once we fall in love with Christ, we are so taken with His beauty, we want children who look just like Him. That's spiritual motherhood in a nutshell: raising spiritual sons and daughters who look just like their Father. What could be more important?

How does God want you to respond to what He showed you today?

Day 5
To Live Happily Ever After

Today's Treasure

"Come and share your master's happiness!"
MATTHEW 25:21

Every little girl has dreams, and if she trusts Christ with all her heart, nothing can disable God from surpassing a childhood reach with a divine reality. The suicide of her husband could not keep God from surpassing Kay Arthur's dreams. Her sudden paralysis could not keep God from surpassing Joni Eareckson Tada's dreams. Her horrifying stay in a Nazi concentration camp could not keep God from surpassing Corrie Ten Boom's dreams. Her world of poverty and suffering could not keep God from surpassing Mother Teresa's dreams.

God surpasses our dreams when we reach past our personal plans and agendas to grab the hand of Christ and walk the path He chose for us. He is obligated to keep us dissatisfied until we come to Him and His plan for complete satisfaction. At this point in our study, could you say that you have experienced some realm of 1 Corinthians 2:9 in your life?

What has God done in your life that has exceeded anything you had seen, heard, or imagined? Respond in the margin.

If our experience on the scorching pavement of earth can occasionally be extraordinary, can you imagine what heaven will be like? You see, life, at its best, for believers on this planet is only a crude shadow of a far greater reality to come. Those occasional grand moments we share with Christ when two wills converge as one are glimpses of glory. Our thoughts today will center on the fourth dream of almost every little girl—the stuff of fairy tales—to live happily ever after.

Living happily ever after wasn't original with Cinderella. It began with God. What's more, there's no such thing as fairies, but angels are a different story. No yellow brick road but streets of gold. No cottages in the forest—just mansions in glory. No crowns on our heads—just crowns at His feet. You may be thinking I'm imagining things, but actually you or I couldn't imagine it in our wildest dreams. When God fulfills 1 Corinthians 2:9 in a willing person's life on this earth, it's just a crude shadow of a greater reality.

Let's begin our treasure hunt with our theme text, Isaiah 61. Read verses 1-3 again and fill in the blanks:

"The Spirit of the Sovereign Lord is on me ... He has sent me ... to comfort all who mourn, and provide for those who grieve in Zion—to bestow on them a crown of beauty instead of ashes, the oil of gladness instead of _____, and a garment of _____ instead of _____."

Christ's ministry was to trade the willing party's mourning for gladness and give praise instead of despair. I like all these "insteads," don't you? The verse doesn't mean we'll never mourn or feel despair. But Christ will joyfully minister His gladness to us once again. He will give us a heart of praise if we let Him—then one day all mourning and despair will be behind us. Meditate on the word *gladness* for a moment. Can you think of a time when you were convinced you would never experience gladness again—but because of Christ you did?

If so, in the margin describe how he began to minister gladness to you.

Certainly, if any group of people in the world should experience gladness, it should be Christians! But what if we pressed the concept a tad further? I'd like to suggest that God also enjoys occasionally seeing us—dare I say—happy? Believe it or not, *happy* really is a biblical word, but we are indeed wise to distinguish it from two closely associated words in Scripture. Let's do a little research.

 Read John 13:3-17. What result did Christ guarantee if His followers put into practice what He demonstrated to them (v. 17)?

Both the NIV and the NASB employ the word *blessed* for the Greek *makarios*. This term means possessing the favor of God, that state of being marked by the fullness of God. I have discovered the difference between blessed and happy experientially as well as scripturally. A few of the times when I've been most aware of the fullness and favor of God, I was totally broken. Certainly, blessedness and happiness don't always coincide. When they do, however, they make a terrific pair.

How about you? Can you think of a time when you sensed the fullness and favor of God but would not characterize the time as happy? Explain in the margin.

Blessing and happiness are wonderful words, but they are not interchangeable by any stretch of the imagination. Let's look at another closely associated term.

Read John 15:1-11. What result did Christ assure His disciples if they obeyed Him and continued to abide in His love (v. 11)? _____

All the major translations use the word *joy*. The Greek word *chara* reflects rejoicing and experiencing a depth of joy. Read James 1:2-4.

What is the difference between happiness and joy?

Are you beginning to see the differences between *blessed, joy,* and *happy*? We can be blessed by God and filled with His favor at some of the most difficult moments

I am walking on the water with God.

of our lives. We can think of times when we were not necessarily happy to obey, but we knew God was having favor on us. Similarly, we can rejoice in times of tribulation because we can either see the progress God is making in us or believe by faith that progress will take place. One of the things I like best about the word *chara* is its sister word *charis,* which means "grace." Biblical joy can come from the sheer awareness of the grace of God.

Blessing, joy, happiness. All three of these terms are wonderful biblical words. The obvious difference is that blessing and joy are not circumstantial while happiness clearly is. Please understand, however, this difference doesn't make happiness lesser, just rarer. The word *happy* is getting a bad rap, so let's have the joy and blessing of clearing it up! Allow me to get this off my chest once and for all: Sometimes God just plain makes me HAPPY! There. I said it.

Sure I know that people are starving on the other side of the world. I'm deeply concerned for hurting people and I pray for other nations every single day, but I also enjoy a happy moment in Christ when it comes. Happiness is inappropriate when it's our goal, but it's not inappropriate when it's God's momentary gift. Open it. Enjoy it. And remember it when times get tough. Come on. Admit it! I imagine Christ has been known to make you purely happy sometimes too.

In the margin share a recent example of a moment of happiness.

So, what are we to do when we feel happy according to James 5:13?
☐ Don't tell anyone who is deeply spiritual.
☐ Don't show it or people will get suspicious.
☐ Get over it quickly. You might try thinking of something morbid.
☐ Sing songs of praise!

We've been talking about childhood dreams God desires to sow in us, then surpass. We talked about our dreams of being brides, being beautiful, and being fruitful. But how realistic is the dream of living happily ever after? See for yourself.

What is the invitation in Matthew 25:21?

There you have it. Christ is happy. He wants you to share His happiness—to live happily ever after. Until then He gives us a sudden splash of happiness here and there so we can wet our toes in what we'll be swimming in for all of eternity! As we conclude our sixth week of study, I ask you to meditate on all we've considered. Glance through days 1-4 and ask the Holy Spirit to help you isolate and express a meaningful moment you spent with God in this week's study.

I'd like to conclude with a moment I personally experienced with God through this subject matter. Before I do, let me share with you that I have always been a dreamer. I have no idea why. I had a few childhood moments that were far more like nightmares, but somehow God kept my hope intact. One of the things I love best about God is that He does not frown on our dreams. He simply longs to surpass them. I dreamed of romance and I am still a romantic, but not a hopeless romantic. My hope is built on nothing less than Jesus, my everlasting Groom, the Lover of my soul and yours.

The dearest Scriptures this unit engraved on my heart are Song of Songs 2:10-11. Read these two verses and allow me to share some thoughts God gave me as I visualized the Scriptures. I deeply appreciate the vulnerability our study this week demanded. Keep letting the truth set you free!

It was her 90th birthday. She didn't plan to live this long. She couldn't help it. She just kept waking up. Her youngest son's spacious home bulged with extended family. She acted as surprised by her party as a 90-year-old can act. She cackled to herself. They obviously thought her growing lack of conversation was evidence of a growing lack of sense. Why would she be surprised? They had thrown her a surprise party for the past 5 years. She guessed they figured she'd forget. What the party really meant was they were surprised she was still alive. Oh, she did love them, though. Every one of them. Pretty bags and bows crowded the coffee table. Now what in heaven's name was she going to do with a bunch of gifts? And how many pairs of socks does a woman need? But that cake was looking mighty tasty. The great-grandkids had insisted on putting all 90 candles on the cake.

The youngest great-grandchild grabbed her by the hand. "Come on, Mammie! It's time to blow the candles out." She grinned and asked God to help her keep her teeth in. Time suddenly seemed to freeze. She looked around the room and studied the faces. Life had been good—painful at times, but God had always been faithful. She had been a widow for 23 years. Her last years had been pleasant. Her family made sure of that. But she grew less and less able to participate. She found herself mostly just watching life.

The muffled insistence of the impatient five-year-old finally grew clear, "Mammie, COME ON!" Before she could draw a breath, all the little ones blew out the candles. Only blood relatives would have eaten that cake after the spraying it took. Later she sat at her old vanity as her daughter-in-law tenderly took the pins from her wispy, white hair. She stared in the yellowed mirror. When had she gotten so old? Where had the years gone? Her daughter-in-law brushed the strands gently, chattering incessantly about the evening. As she helped her with her gown and tucked her in, the old woman felt so weary. Her body hurt just to lie down.

The soft mattress seemed to swallow her frame. She rested her slight weight and stared at the stars out the window. She heard the familiar sound of the 10:00 train going over the bridge and nearly shivered as she remembered her baptism in those cold waters underneath. She smiled and voiced a good-night prayer to the Savior she had loved since childhood. She didn't say much. "Thank You, Jesus. Thank You." Almost before she could close her eyes, deep sleep overtook her. Suddenly, her slumber was startled by the most beautiful voice she had ever heard, coming from a man standing over her. "Arise, My darling, My beautiful one, and come with Me. See! 'The winter is past; the rains are over and gone … the season of singing has come.'"

Beauty instead of ashes.

How does God want you to respond to what He showed you today?

BREAKING *Free*

session seven viewer guide

Our entire lesson will build upon this important premise:

God never _____ or _____ a fire unless He can bring _____
_____ _____ _____.

First Peter 1:3-9

1. We _____ _____ fiery trials.

    a. God is much more iterested in our _____ than our
      _____.

    b. Even faithful people have tremendous _____.

2. The purpose of the refinement is always to make us:

    a. _____ of _____.

    b. _____ _____ _____. Compare 1 Peter 1:4 to
    Isaiah 61:7.

Allotting a double portion was sometimes a _____ ____ _____
(Deut. 21:17). Sometimes it was a _____ _____ _____
(Ex. 22:4,7,9)." (*Word Biblical Commentary*)

3. One primary purpose of fiery trials is to _____ the _____.

4. We cannot often refuse the fire, but we can refuse ____ ____ _____
   by it.

5. Sometimes our fiery trials are absolutely _____ to fulfill our callings.

The Potter and the Clay

Sometimes I find myself doubting it all. I learned to change my mindset from "I can't" to "God can". I must trust Him day by day, hour by hour, minute by minute. I am learning to lean on Him for everything and have begun to change through the power of the Holy Spirit. I look forward to what God has in store for me.

Day 1
Upside Down

Everything we've learned hinges on how we respond to the subject this week. We want to be free to know God and believe Him, glorify God, find satisfaction in God, experience His peace, and enjoy His presence. We want generational yokes shattered and Christ to bind up our broken hearts, bring beauty from ashes, restore our virtue, and surpass our dreams. So, how does liberty in Christ become a reality? In a word: Obedience! Obedience to God's Word.

Describe the relationship between God's Word and freedom (Jas. 1:22-25).

Rightly responding to the Word of God is our ticket on the freedom train. God's Word is the perfect law that gives freedom. I've addressed other issues first because sometimes we are in too much bondage to imagine living an obedient life. Often when I introduce this pivotal part of the journey to freedom, I see downcast expressions that show our natural desire. We want God to somehow wave a wand over us and magically remove every hindrance without requiring anything of us.

If God simply waved a wand over us and broke every yoke without our cooperation, we would probably soon pick up another. God desires to change us from the inside out—renewing our minds, starving our self-destructive tendencies, and teaching us to form new habits. These results come only to those who learn to walk all over again, this time with their Deliverer. This week the rich Book of Isaiah is going to offer us several crucial motivations toward obedience.

Isaiah addresses the dual theme of captivity and liberty more than any other Old Testament book. God didn't leave His nation wondering why they had gone into captivity. Their folly echoes through much of the first 40 chapters of Isaiah.

In Isaiah 29:16 God displayed their problem like a marred piece of pottery on a wheel. What was God's point? Respond in the margin.

Not coincidentally, Isaiah also has more to say about the authority, rule, and uniqueness of God than virtually any book of the Bible. Allow God to engrave this truth on your heart: Liberty and authority will always go hand in hand. During the ministry of Isaiah, captivity was imminent for the children of Israel because they had a serious authority problem. In essence, God was saying, "You've got things turned around. Let's get this straight: Me, God. You, human. Me, Creator. You, creature. Me, Potter. You, clay. You obey … not for My good but for yours."

My adorable youngest daughter came into the world to take over. By the time she was only two years old, she liked to walk ahead of the rest of us so she could appear to have come by herself. She was born authoritative and seemed

Liberty and authority will always go hand in hand.

to assume that she, Keith, and I were all three on the same level. Keith and I expended no small amount of energy underscoring our authority over her, the penalty for rebellion, and the safety and blessing of obedience. We haven't always done it right, but we've done it often! At this particular season, we are reaping a delightful harvest. Melissa is a wonderful young woman. But if I had a dime for every time I said, "Me, parent! You, child!," she would inherit a fortune! Over and over in the Book of Isaiah, God perfectly underscores the same three principles:

- He has the right to rule.
- He sets a high price for rebellion.
- He pours out safety and blessing for obedience.

In the margin write a one-sentence synopsis of Isaiah 30:8-21.

Pretty confrontational, isn't it? Think about your own human nature as I consider mine. Without the Holy Spirit controlling your life, do any of these verses sound familiar? I think so too. On day 3 we'll consider how rebelling is not just foolish, it is an affront to Almighty God, our Creator and King. Today and tomorrow, however, let's consider rebellion from a strictly selfish point of view.

 How did God's children cheat themselves through rebellion (Isa. 30:8-21)?

The word *rebellion* means what you'd probably expect. Words like *defiant* and *disobedient* are accurate synonyms. The Hebrew definition also uses the English synonym *refractory*. I chuckled when I checked my thesaurus for the meaning of *refractory*. It gave *pigheaded*. *Webster's* defines *pigheaded* as "obstinate, stubborn." This hits me—stubborn, resisting authority.

Can you recall a situation in which you acted pigheaded toward God? ☐ Yes ☐ No If so, in the margin describe it briefly.

Bossing ourselves is a ticket to slavery.

Without God's intervention we all tend to be pigheaded. We want to boss ourselves. A primary purpose of this week is to prove that bossing ourselves is a ticket to slavery. The vivid portrait of a rebel in Isaiah 30:8-21 helps us recognize rebellion when it wells up in us. Each of the following phrases characterizes rebellion. Several of the characteristics signal impending disaster! A rebellious child of God: (1) doesn't act like a child of God, (2) isn't willing to listen to the Lord's instruction, (3) prefers pleasant illusions over truth, and (4) relies on oppression.

1. A rebellious child of God doesn't act like a child of God (Isa. 30:9).

Take another look at verse 9. Scripture characterizes rebellious people as "_____ children."

The original word for *deceitful* in this verse is *kechash*. It means "not acting like sons … giving a false impression of who you are." If you are in covenant relationship with God but not acting like His child, you are living a lie. The only time you are true to who you are is when you are walking like one of His children.

Think about the last week or two. Identify a way you believe you gave a true impression of who you are by acting as if you belonged to God:

Now, for private introspection not group discussion, identify a way you have given a false impression by not acting as if you belonged to God.

The world preaches the "be-true-to-yourself" philosophy. Christians can only be true to self when demonstrating that they belong to God.

2. A rebellious child of God isn't willing to listen to the Lord's instruction (Isa. 30:9). The Hebrew word for *listen* is *shama*, meaning "to give undivided listening attention." Are you like me at times? Do you have difficulty giving anyone your undivided attention? Isaiah 30:9, however, doesn't describe the accidentally inattentive. Rebellious people don't want to listen. Sometimes we're unwilling to listen to God because we're resistant to being corrected, redirected, or challenged to change. That's rebellion. The tragedy is that God would never tell us anything to defeat us. He has a one-track mind as far as we are concerned. He wants us to live like the overcomers we are.

> Rebellious people don't want to listen.

Read Exodus 23:20-22 and Psalm 81:10-14. In the margin describe the relationship between listening to God and prevailing over your enemy.

3. A rebellious child prefers pleasant illusions over truth (Isa. 30:10-11). In Houston alone I could not begin to count the number of preachers and teachers termed "Christian." With so many choices, however, comes the risk of choosing teachers on the basis of what we want to hear. We crave messages that make us feel good. When living in rebellion, the last thing we want is to confront the Holy One of Israel. Notice the demand of the people of God in verse 10: "Tell us pleasant things." The KJV uses: "Speak unto us smooth things."

One of the following words reflects the Hebrew meaning for pleasant and smooth. Choose the one you assume to be the synonym.
☐ flattering ☐ caring ☐ simple ☐ kind ☐ personal ☐ partial

If enjoying flattery puts a noose around our necks, then seeking flattery hangs us! Satan could have written the book *Flattery Can Get You Anywhere*. God did not write His Word to condemn or flatter. Paul wrote that Scripture "is useful for teaching, rebuking, correcting and training in righteousness, so that the man of God may be thoroughly equipped for every good work" (2 Tim. 3:16-17).

> *God stands by my side, holds my hand, and keeps me safe.*

What charge did Paul give Timothy in 2 Timothy 4:1-2?

Now read 2 Timothy 4:3-4. Carefully compare these two Scriptures to Isaiah 30:10-11. In the margin list all the parallels between the passages.

If we strongly prefer certain teachers and preachers over others, we are wise to ask why. If our basis is anything other than balanced biblical teaching, we could be in rebellion while occupying pews every Sunday. Let's make sure we are not looking for people to scratch our itching ears and hide us from the truth.

4. A rebellious child of God relies on oppression (v. 12). Here's a shocker. Not only can God's children be oppressed, but we also can become reliant on the oppression. The word *relied* in verse 12 is the Hebrew word *batach,* meaning "to attach oneself, to trust, confide in, feel safe." The Hebrew word for *oppression (osheq)* indicates oppression by means of fraud or extortion … a thing "deceitfully gotten."

We might say this: People who detach themselves from truth inadvertently attach themselves to lies that defraud and extort. God created us to be attached to Him; therefore, He made us with a very real need to be attached. Satan knows he cannot entice us to simply detach from God and His Word and be independent. In reality, there is no such thing as a completely independent human psyche.

We were created to attach and depend so that we would migrate toward God and find safety. To entice us, Satan offers us alternate attachments masquerading as fulfillments to our inner needs. Any attachment other than God is a fraud. Please understand that the word *attachment* in this context differs from healthy relationships with things or people. The key word is *reliance.* Wrong attachment means growing dependent on something other than God.

Can you think of an unhealthy attachment you made in your life that was finally exposed as a fraud? Explain.

> We could be in rebellion while occupying pews every Sunday.

How does God want you to respond to what He showed you today?

I grew up in a stronghold of fear. I longed to find a safe place to hide. I desperately wanted someone to take care of me. From the realm of my own painful experience, let me alert you to a toxic emotional cocktail: a relationship made up of someone who has an unhealthy need to be taken care of and someone who has an unhealthy need to care-take. The relationship ended up extorting God-given liberties and proved fraudulent.

Beloved, any place we have to hide is not safe. In Christ we find the freedom to be safely exposed! If only we could begin to understand that God's authority does not imprison, it sets free! On day 2 we will continue our look at rebellion and the wisdom of obedience.

Day 2
Broken Pottery

Today's lesson is an important continuation. Take a moment to reread our focal passage for both lessons: Isaiah 30:8-21. As we learned from James 1:22-25, we don't just want to glance in the mirror of Scripture, walk away and forget what we saw. We need God's Word to become the perfect law of liberty in our lives!

Based on our previous lesson, how can God's Word become our glorious liberation? Choose one. ☐ obeying it ☐ claiming it ☐ studying it

If we study and claim God's Word but do not obey it, we will not experience liberty the Holy Spirit can bring. We must live an obedient—not perfect—lifestyle to maintain our freedom in Christ. Reflect on day 1. We began a compilation of the common characteristics of rebellion.

Complete the following sentences with the first four characteristics.

1. A rebellious child of God doesn't

2. A rebellious child of God isn't willing to

3. A rebellious child of God prefers

4. A rebellious child of God relies

Draw a star beside the characteristic of rebellion that most stirred your thinking. In the margin describe why.

The fourth characteristic most penetrated my heart. Who wants to be attached to or feel safe with a fraud? I certainly don't! Yet how often have we cast our dependency on something or someone incapable of taking care of us? I pray God will expose all fraudulent attachments in our lives and draw us to the light of healthy relationships with both things and people. Now for the fifth characteristic.

5. A rebellious child of God depends on deceit (Isa. 30:12). The Hebrew word for *depended* is *sha'an*, "to support oneself, lean against." Any time you've seen someone walk with a cane or a crutch, you've witnessed the word picture drawn in this phrase. Reread Isaiah 30:12 and note the paired phrases: "relied on oppression" and "depended on deceit." They are interdependent.

Any time we attach ourselves or seek safety in a fraudulent savior we have to depend on lies to support the habit. The following story contains a picture tragically experienced as a reality by many:

Today's Treasure
"This sin will become for you like a high wall, cracked and bulging, that collapses suddenly, in an instant. It will break in pieces like pottery."
ISAIAH 30:13-14

I reached up, clasped God's hand, and let Him pull me out.

A young Christian girl has a harsh, abusive father. She grows up with a fear and distaste for men. Satan supplies a slightly older woman who seems tender and very caring. The comforting relationship turns into a physical relationship, so the young woman assumes she must be homosexual. In her heart she knows what she is doing is wrong, but she feels helpless without her new comforter. Soon she starts socializing with other women who are practicing homosexuality because they will support her new habit with the lies she needs to continue. She avoids the Bible and chooses books that advocate homosexuality. She drops all relationships except those that support the fraudulent attachment with lies.

Scary, isn't it? I used an obvious scenario to make my point, but Satan uses countless unhealthy attachments to things or people. Interestingly, the lost world enjoys characterizing Christians as needy people who use faith as a crutch. How wrong they are. In John 5:8 Jesus encountered a man who was lame. Christ didn't hand the man a cane or a crutch. He healed him so he could walk on both feet! The biggest crutch of all is deceit. Satan's lies keep us walking in our chains.

Describe how these verses apply to depending on deceit:

Jeremiah 8:5-6

Proverbs 15:4

6. A rebellious child of God runs from the real answers (Isa. 30:15-17). Have you ever experienced a season when you knew what would rescue you but you ran from it? Perhaps, like me, you may rank these memories among your greatest regrets. You may be surprised that virtually everyone has run from the real answers at one time or another.

In the margin describe why you think we are sometimes resistant to what is best for us.

In Isaiah 30:15 the word *salvation* is not used in a strictly eternal sense. The word represents being saved or delivered from any kind of calamity or attack.

Fill in the following equation according to Isaiah 30:15:
In _____ + _____ = your salvation.

Eternal salvation requires that we repent of our sins and depend on the work of Christ. Our need of deliverance does not end, however, once we become Christians. We've been eternally saved, but we need lots of help avoiding snares and pitfalls in our earthly journeys. The same equation applies: "In repentance and rest is your salvation!"

We've been eternally saved, but we need lots of help avoiding snares and pitfalls in our earthly journeys.

The word *returning* more accurately translates the Hebrew *shuwbah*. The word *repentance* used elsewhere in God's Word usually means "turning from sin," but often we omit the next step! The next step is what helps keep us from going back to the same sin again after we've repented! We see this important twofold process in Acts 3:19: "Repent, then, and turn to God, so that your sins may be wiped out, that times of refreshing may come from the Lord."

If we only turn from our sins but do not turn to God, we lack the power to overcome the temptation the next time it arises! The word *returning* in Isaiah 30:15 encompasses both repenting and returning to God!

Now let's look at the second variable in the equation: "In returning (or repentance, NIV) and _____ is your salvation."

The word *rest* means what you think it does. The Hebrew word is *nachath*. *Strong's* dictionary gives a definition that tickles me. It says the word means "lighting down." I can picture my grandmother in our kitchen in Arkansas with a fly swatter in her hand and a most serious expression on her face. "Whatcha doin', Nanny?" I'd ask. "I'm waiting for that filthy fly to light down somewhere so I can smack it." In just a moment I'd hear, "ka-WHACK!"

We often believe we're like that fly. If we light down for a second, God's going to whack us. Untrue. We're not flies and Nanny wasn't God! God desires for us to rest in Him, to light down on His truth, and be set on who He is.

Isaiah 30:15 is telling us that in returning to God and resting confidently in His promises and power, we will continually find salvation. I love the Hebrew meaning of the word *salvation*. *Yasha* means "to be open, wide, or free … It is the opposite of *tsarar*, to cramp." *Yasha* draws the picture of a spacious place in which to move. I have personally experienced the wide-open freedom of obedience to Christ! I've also known the miserable pinned-in feeling of rebellion. We all know that God wants us to return and rest, but what kind of equation would tend to more readily reflect the practices of your past? I'll give you mine so you can get the idea: In repenting plus being determined to do better on my own strength has often been my downfall. A different equation can be found in Isaiah 30:15.

Fill in the blanks. "In _____ + _____ = your strength."

I want you to know what *strength* means in this verse. The Hebrew word implies victory. I deeply desire to be a victor, don't you?

Two primary elements are involved in victory: quietness and trust. The original word for quietness is *shaqat* meaning "to lie quietly, be undisturbed … to calm." Notice the disturbing phrase concluding Isaiah 30:15: "But you would have none of it." Can you relate to that statement? I unfortunately can!

Have you sometimes experienced defeat because you refused to calm yourself in the presence of God and trust Him? ☐ Yes ☐ No If so, in the margin share an example.

The exact Hebrew word translated *trust* in this verse appears only once in the Old Testament. The word *bitchah* means "nothing more that one can do." Once we've obeyed God, we can do nothing more. We then wait on Him to bring the victory, knowing that the consequences of our obedience are His problem and not ours.

Our human nature is to run when we're in trouble, but we've learned two very important precepts from Isaiah 30:15:

1.

    • To flee from God's salvation is rebellion.

    • To flee from God's strength is to flee from victory.

2.

As we approach our conclusion, please write all six characteristics of rebellion in the margin: A rebellious child of God ...

3.

Now let's do a little necessary introspection. Remember, I'm doing this too!

4.

Place a star by any of the characteristics that have been your tendencies in your history with God. Then draw an unhappy face by any of the characteristics that are present struggles for you.

5.

In the margin write a brief prayer, confessing any tendencies toward rebellion or areas of rebellion based on the six characteristics.

6.

God wants to respond to you. His response is already recorded in Isaiah 30:18. He "longs to be gracious to you; he rises to show you compassion." We can picture God being merciful and forgiving when we accidentally get ourselves into a mess, but we almost cannot imagine how God can be compassionate when we're outright rebellious.

Oh, what a disservice we do when we try to humanize God by imagining Him as the best of humanity rather than all-together God! God's compassion demands that He reach out to us even in our rebellion, but His righteousness demands that He bring painful chastisement if we don't grab His reaching hand and return to Him wholeheartedly.

As we end today's lesson, read Isaiah 30:12-14. What happens if we continue in rebellion, rejecting God's Word, relying on oppression, and depending on deceit? Explain the outcome in your own words.

How does God want you to respond to what He showed you today?

The figurative walls of protection around our lives will crumble like pottery broken to pieces. Those who are Christians will not lose salvation, but we stand to lose a significant amount of protection. The bottom line of lessons 1 and 2 this week is this: Clay that insists on acting like the Potter will inevitably end up in pieces. Thank goodness, God still loves cracked pots! Let's not wait until we're in pieces to return and trust.

Day 3
God's Right to Rule

This week we are focusing on obedience. Liberty was ours the moment we received Christ as our Savior; but if our internal gift is not released externally through obedience, we may never experience it. Let's see how this concept works.

What does 2 Corinthians 3:17 tell you about freedom?

Today's Treasure
"I am God, and there is no other; I am God, and there is none like me." ISAIAH 46:9

1. The Lord is the one and only possessor of true liberty. He is spirit; therefore, freedom can only be transferred through the Spirit.

Now compare John 1:12; Romans 8:15; and 1 Corinthians 2:12. What common denominator ties each of them together?

How did Christ explain this idea in John 14:15-18? Respond in margin.

I hope you noted the important word *received* in the first three verses, then saw the clear teaching of this divine reception in John 14:15-18. When we receive Christ as our Savior, we literally receive Christ! His Spirit takes up actual residence inside of us. Romans 8:9 tells the necessity of this reception: "If anyone does not have the Spirit of Christ, he does not belong to Christ."

2. The second step toward freedom is receiving Christ as Savior, thereby receiving His liberating Spirit. We received freedom in Christ, but we must understand that the freedom never leaves the bounds of His Spirit. Therefore, our liberation is expressed as a reality only in the places of our lives where the free Spirit of God is released. We are free when, and only when, He is in control.

Reflect again on the words of 2 Corinthians 3:17. Fill in the blanks.
"Now the _____ is the Spirit, and where the Spirit of the _____ is, there is freedom."

Freedom and lordship are inseparable partners in the believer's life. When we read that freedom can be found anywhere the Spirit of the Lord is, we can take it literally.

Which of the following words do you think reflects the meaning of *kurios*, the original Greek word for Lord?
☐ possessor   ☐ owner   ☐ master
☐ absolute authority   ☐ supreme   ☐ sovereign

Freedom flows
where the Spirit
of the Lord floods.

3. The third step toward freedom is yielding to the authority of God. We are to be filled with the Spirit (Eph. 5:18). We are filled with the Spirit as we yield to His lordship. Although the Spirit of the Lord is always in us, He floods only the parts of our lives where He is in authority. Freedom flows where the Spirit of the Lord floods. This point brings up an interesting question.

Have you noticed that you can experience freedom in part of your life while you are still in bondage in another? ☐ Yes ☐ No If so, describe a time when you were free in one area while bound in another.

Based on our third step to freedom, how could you have been free in one area while being bound in the other? Respond in the margin.

If your answer reflected the fact that we sometimes allow God to have full authority in one area while refusing Him another, you are biblically correct.

How, then, can we be fully liberated? Choose one correct response.
☐ study God's Word more frequently
☐ withhold no part of our lives from His authority
☐ spend more time with God in prayer
☐ rebuke the enemy on a daily basis

Actually the first, third, and fourth responses are each contained in the second as we will continue to discover. The answer to liberty is withholding no part of our lives from His authority. Again, allow me to stress that obedient lives are not perfect lives. I believe the apostle Paul reflects the mind-set of the obedient life.

How can we apply Philippians 3:12 to the obedient life?

Obedience does not mean sinlessness but confession and repentance when we sin. Obedience is not arriving at a perpetual state of godliness but perpetually following hard after God. Obedience is not living miserably by a set of laws but inviting the Spirit of God to flow freely through us so the power to be victorious comes from God and not from us. Obedience is learning to love and treasure God's Word and see it as our safety.

"The Spirit of the Sovereign Lord is on me, because the Lord has anointed me to preach good news to the poor."
Isaiah 61:1
(See also Luke 4:18.)

How did Christ refer to His Father in Isaiah 61:1? _____

Consider this question and the choices that follow, but don't mark an answer yet. What was Christ's ultimate purpose in His earthly life?
☐ to receive the punishment for sin   ☐ to set the captives free
☐ to bind up the brokenhearted   ☐ to save the lost
☐ to do the will of His Father   ☐ to show God's love

Though we know Christ came for all of these blessed reasons, He continually proclaimed His utmost purpose. Read each of the following Scriptures and record Christ's attitude toward His Father's desires.

Matthew 26:42

John 4:34

John 6:38

 What is God's will according to John 6:39-40? Respond in the margin.

Now go back to the multiple choices. What was Christ's ultimate purpose in His earthly life?

Christ, the only Son of the Father, respects God as the one and only Sovereign Lord. He came to do the will of His Father. His Father's will is for every person to know God intimately and have fellowship with Him. Christ's responsibility on earth was to obey to the point of death so that God's goal would be accomplished.

Even the Father and the Son had a Potter-Clay relationship. Christ obeyed the Potter. As an earthen vessel, Jesus had to completely trust His Father's will. Although rejection, suffering, and shame were part of His experience, Christ accepted His God-given ministry at every difficult turn because He trusted His Father's heart and poured out His life for His Father's goal.

I believe Christ's unrelenting obedience to the Father came not only out of love but from two additional motivations as well. He was committed to God's right to rule and was convinced that God's rule is right. Let's consider God's right to rule, and in our next lesson we will research the rightness of God's rule.

We've already determined that one of the clearest messages of the Book of Isaiah is that obedience is a ticket to freedom, and rebellion is a ticket to slavery. Not coincidentally, the Book of Isaiah also has as much to say about God's right to rule and the rightness of His rule. In chapters 40, 45, and 46, Isaiah powerfully addresses God's supremacy over creation, idols, and humanity. The chapters also contain personal proclamations of God's absolute uniqueness.

In the following exercise write phrases and references in four categories from Isaiah 40:12-28; 45:5-25; 46:1-13. I've supplied examples. Don't stress over the categories! The purpose is to develop a greater respect for God's rule. No one is being graded for precisely categorized phrases. Enjoy researching the One you get to call Father!

Creation: Example—He measures the waters in His hand (Isa. 40:12).

> HE CREATED ME, AND HE LOVES ME!

> Christ was committed to God's right to rule and was convinced that God's rule is right.

Idols: Example—Idols themselves are man-made (Isa. 40:19).

Humanity: Example—No human can understand or instruct Him (Isa. 40:13).

God's Absolute Uniqueness: Example—Who is my equal (Isa. 40:25)?

As I read over these passages, I am sobered and humbled once again. Sometimes what we need to cure our fat egos is a strong dose of God. Long before a certain visionary "discovered" the earth was round, God sat enthroned above the circle of the earth. Long before men were so "enlightened," God formed the light and the darkness. Long before the first billion dollars was invested in exploring space, God's own hands stretched out the heavens. Long before there was a "beginning," God had already planned the end. Like Peter on the mount of transfiguration, we're so caught up in the tabernacles we want to build that we sometimes miss a fresh revelation of God's glory right before our eyes.

If only we could realize that we make life so much more complicated when our approach to life is "all about me." Do you know why? Because the rest of the world never cooperates. No one else appears to have gotten the memo. When we see ourselves as the center of the universe, we live in constant frustration because the rest of creation refuses to revolve around us.

Life vastly simplifies and satisfaction greatly amplifies when we begin to realize our awesome roles. God is God. Frankly, it's all about Him. Thank goodness, He is the center of the universe. So how can we live with such a God-centered mentality? Freely! Because with God, it's all about us. We seek to please Him. He seeks to perfect us—and life works. Not without pain, but with purpose.

Without the Potter, clay is just dirt. "The Lord God formed the man from the dust of the ground and breathed into his nostrils the breath of life, and the man became a living being" (Gen. 2:7).

> "I am God, and there is no other;
> I am God, and there is none like me" (Isa. 46:9).

How does God want you to respond to what He showed you today?

Day 4
God's Rule Is Right

Today's Treasure
"But my salvation will last forever, my righteousness will never fail." **ISAIAH 51:6**

I have a worst nightmare—having to obey an unrighteous authority. In case you think obedience comes easy for me, let me clear up a few things. Submission and subservience are to me as easy as cuddling a litter of baby porcupines. A child who has been forced into things she didn't want to do usually grows up never wanting to be told what to do again—by anyone.

Until my mother's dying day, every time I asserted myself about anything, she reminded me of the time our family doctor told me I couldn't go swimming because I had an ear infection. Mom said I squinted my eyes, looked as mean as I could, and said, "Oh, yeah? Well, you're not the boss of me!" Unfortunately, the doctor was the president of our small-town country club. He retorted, "No, but I'm the boss of that swimming pool, and I'd better not catch you in it." I promptly began to ask for us to build a pool in our own backyard so I could boss myself.

The problem is, God did not design us to boss ourselves. Our psyches were formed to require authority for our own sakes so we'd live in the safety of God's careful rule. Satan tries to draw us away from God's authority by making us think we can be our own producer and director. The apostle Paul addressed the impossibility of mastering our own lives and destinies in Romans 6:16.

What are our options according to Romans 6:16? Respond in the margin.

We need not be distressed at being called slaves. As creatures, we will be mastered; the question is, Who will be our master? As important as our previous lesson was to me, God's right to rule is not my primary motivation for pursuing the obedient life. I'm resistant to obeying someone strictly on the basis of his or her position. Often I must, but I never like it. I am far more a rebel at heart than you could know. This will probably shock you, but I probably would have chanced eternity in hell rather than bend my knee to any ruler just because he was in charge.

My primary motivation for pursuing the obedient life is an absolute belief that the One who has a right to rule is also the One whose rule is right. I try to obey God because with all my heart I believe that He is always good, always right, and loves me in ways I cannot comprehend. God has proved His trustworthiness to me over and over again.

You can't fully appreciate the emotion washing over me as I prepare to write these next three words: I trust God. After a lifetime of trust problems, I can't even understand how such a miracle of grace has come to me, but it has. This may seem silly, but I love Him so much that sometimes I can't wait for Him to ask me to do something a little difficult, because I want to obey Him. I not only love God and trust Him but I love trusting Him. It is a constant reminder of a perpetual miracle in my life.

He was committed to God's right to rule and convinced that God's rule is right.

What about those others who lack His character? I've slowly come to trust God's sovereignty enough to believe that anyone I must obey on this earth better be careful with me or they have God to answer to! The same is true for you!

I was raised on a wonderful hymn that says, "Trust and obey for there's no other way to be happy in Jesus, than to trust and obey." The obedient life flows most beautifully from trust; however, if we do not take the first step of pure faith and obey, we'll never realize we can trust. We might write an extra verse to this marvelous old hymn that says, "Obey and learn to trust, a step of faith is a must, to earn confidence in Jesus, obey and learn to trust." Corny but true.

Now that I've been transparent with you, it's your turn. Do you also have authority problems? ☐ Yes ☐ No If so, how have you become aware of them? Respond in the margin.

Trust Him with Everything

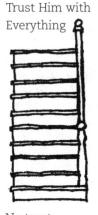

No trust

How about God's authority? How convinced are you that you can trust Him? Estimate your level of trust by drawing yourself on the staircase appearing in the margin.

Explain briefly why you think you're on this particular step right now.

Our text encourages us to trust and obey. If you're on the bottom of the staircase, possibly you will take a step of faith and obey so you can learn to build trust. Read Isaiah 51:1-16. The chapter begins with the command "Listen to me."

In your Bible, search the other 15 verses and mark each time God appears to be trying to get His reader's full attention.

Why do verses 1-2 apply to Gentile Christians as well as Jews (Gal. 3:29)?

Based on Scripture about Abraham and Sarah, which of the following do you think we could learn if we agreed to look to the rock from which we were cut? Check as many as you believe apply. We can ...
☐ believe God can do the impossible (Gen. 18:14)
☐ admit the futility of taking matters into our own hands (Gen. 16)
☐ believe God still loves and can use us even when we detour—if we agree to return to His path (Gen. 17)
☐ believe God could still call us righteous based on our faith in Him, even if our righteous acts are like filthy rags (Gen. 15:6; Isa. 64:6)
☐ believe that blessing ultimately follows obedience (Gen. 22:18)

I hope you marked each of the lessons we could learn looking to the rock from which we were cut.

✳ Because the Lord is so compassionate, what can He do with the ruins, deserts, and wastelands of His children's lives (Isa. 51:3)?

Ever felt like the waves of the sea were pounding against you and you were drowning in a relentless tide? What can God do for you (Isa. 51:10)?

How is the sovereignty of God revealed as you compare Isaiah 51:15 to Isaiah 51:10?

Reread Isaiah 51:12-14. Why do we not need to fear the wrath of our oppressor even though he is far more powerful than we are?

Have you ever felt like a cowering prisoner? I sure have! Have you ever felt like you would never be released? I love the words of verse 14: "The cowering prisoners will soon be set free." Dear friend, believe it and claim it! Obey and see that you can trust! Do not allow the enemy, our accuser, another success at using your past record against you.

What does God say He is doing in Isaiah 43:18-19? Fill in the blank: "See, I am doing a _____ thing!"

I just want to shout hallelujah! Yes, fellow sojourner, God has the right to rule. But better yet for all us creatures cast at His mercy, God's rule is right! His righteousness will never fail, nor will we fail when we choose to obey Him (Isa. 51:6). His righteousness will last forever and so will we, because He credits our belief with eternal righteousness (v. 8).

God cannot ask anything wrong of us nor can He mislead us. The Lord who is our Maker is also our Defender. Our oppressor will one day cower at His feet. The God who churns up the sea can also make a road in its depths so we may cross over. The One who set the heavens in place and laid the foundations of the earth covers us with the shadow of His hand. The Lord Almighty is His name! And we are His people.

God knows our struggles. He knows every authority problem we have. He knows the times our trust has been betrayed. Like a father cupping his rebellious child's face in his strong hands, He says, "Listen to me … Hear me … I, even I, am he who comforts you … I am the LORD your God" (Isa. 51:1,7,12,15).

I am for you, Child! Not against You! When will you cease resisting Me?

As you conclude today's lesson, reflect on the rightness of God's rule in your life. In the margin write a prayer to God recounting several specific times He has proved Himself as One you can trust and obey.

Day 5
God's Daily Rule

Today's Treasure

"O LORD, be gracious to us; we long for you. Be our strength every morning, our salvation in time of distress." **ISAIAH 33:2**

One of the things I enjoy most about God is His daily-ness. Pure appreciation for God's presence emerges from the daily walk—perhaps in the mundane more than the miraculous. When my sweet daddy had a stroke, I rode with him in the ambulance. The paramedics were wonderful, and although I appreciate them, we didn't trade phone numbers or plan to have lunch! Sometimes we tend to approach God in the same way. He gets us through an emergency, and although we appreciate Him, we do not necessarily stay in close touch once the crisis passes.

Not only will our enjoyment of God remain lacking if our walk with Him isn't daily but our willingness and readiness to obey Him will remain lacking. Much of obedience is based on trust, and trust grows from a day-to-day relationship. For years I asked God to walk with me. Then I realized God wanted me to walk with Him. For years I asked God to bless what I did. Talk about the clay trying to spin the Potter! I wanted to walk where my heart led and count on the Potter to bless my sweet-if-selfish little heart. My clay feet got scorched walking through some terrible fires sparked by the misguided passion of my own heart.

Suddenly I realized God's blessing would come when I did what He said. I have learned that I can only trust my heart when it is fully surrendered to obey God's truth. On its own, my "heart is deceitful above all things" (Jer. 17:9). For our safety and the pure enjoyment of God, we are wise to learn to walk with God instead of begging Him to walk with us. Meditate on Jeremiah 29:11-13.

 In the margin explain why Jeremiah said walking with God is so much wiser and personally fulfilling than asking God to walk with us.

I hope you noted that God is the One with the good plan! We don't have a clue where the paths we choose will ultimately lead. Walking with God in the pursuit of daily obedience is the sure means of fulfilling each of His wonderful plans. Imagine in heaven God lovingly shows you His plan for your earthly life. You see footprints walking through each day. On many of the days, two sets of footprints appear. You inquire: "Father, are those my footprints every day, and is the second set of prints when You joined me?"

He answers, "No, My precious child. The consistent footprints are Mine. The second set of footprints are when you joined Me."

"Where were You going, Father?"

"To the destiny I planned for you, hoping you'd follow."

"But, Father, where are my footprints all those times?"

"Sometimes you went back to look at old resentments and habits. Sometimes, you departed from My path and chose your own instead. Other times, your footprints can even be seen on another person's path because you liked their plan better. At other times, you simply stopped because you would not let go of something you could not take with you."

"But even if I didn't walk with You every day, we ended up OK, didn't we?"

He holds you close and smiles, "Yes, child, we ended up OK. But, you see, OK was never what I had in mind for you."

"Father, what are those golden treasure boxes on certain days?"

"Blessings, My child, I had for you along the way. Those that are open are those you received. Those still closed were days you did not walk with Me."

Does the scenario seem farfetched? Actually, it's quite biblical. Read Genesis 3:8-9. What was God doing in the garden and what do you think He wanted Adam and Eve to do? Did you note the question He asked?

Assuming He already knew where they were and why they were hiding, why do you think God asked the question? Respond in the margin.

Read 2 Corinthians 2:14. Why should we walk God's way instead of ours?

Review your last week. Ask God to help you remember as much about your week as possible. You might glance back at your calendar or your prayer journal. Which days reflect that you walked with God? If you did not walk with God on any days, try to remember where you "were" on those days. Rejoice over any opened treasure box you received from God. Do you suppose your way might also be littered with unopened treasure boxes and days with wandering footprints?

I am asking you these questions for three reasons. I want you to see how deliberate God desires us to become in seeking to walk with Him. I want you to think about where we tend to go when we leave His path, and I want you to identify the undeniable link between blessing and daily walking with God.

Remember, walking consistently does not mean walking perfectly. It means we may stumble, but we will not fall! Now let's see what God has to say to us through the prophet Isaiah about the daily-ness of God. Read Isaiah 33:2-6. We will see five benefits of a daily walk with God.

***1. God offers us the daily treasure of His strength** (v. 2)*. Read one of my favorite psalms, Psalm 84:5-7.

What do you think setting our "hearts on pilgrimage" means?

We're on a pilgrimage to heaven if we believe in Christ. One of the greatest comforts in our day-to-day struggles is remembering that this earth is not our home.

How often do you remind yourself that we're on a journey to a glorious heavenly city? ☐ frequently ☐ occasionally ☐ almost never

We may go from trial to trial, but according to Psalm 84:7, we also go from _____ to _____!

Now, think back to your calendar. If we're not walking with God when trials come, we miss the full measure of strength He had for us along the way.

2. God offers us the daily treasure of His sure foundation (v. 6).
All "constructive" life is built on one foundation: Jesus Christ. Today, however, we are learning that obedient lives flow from obedient days and victorious lives flow from victorious days. Likewise, constructive lives flow from constructive days built on the sure foundation of God's Son. The King James Version uses the English word *stability* rather than *sure foundation* in Isaiah 33:6. I love the thought of God being our stability through so many unstable times, don't you?

> "For no one can lay any foundation other than the one already laid, which is Jesus Christ."
> **1 Corinthians 3:11**

When was the last time you felt that everything in your life was quaking except the stability you had in Christ? Respond in the margin.

Once again, words to a familiar hymn ring out in my soul: "On Christ the Solid Rock I stand. All other ground is sinking sand. All other ground is sinking sand."

3. God offers us the daily treasure of wisdom and knowledge (v. 6). One of the most wonderful blessings God can give us throughout any given week on our "calendar" is the treasure of wisdom and knowledge. The wonder of God is that every day you walk with Him is a treasure! When we rub shoulders with Christ day-to-day, His wisdom and knowledge rub off on us little by little. We often think of blessings in tangible terms, but wisdom is an intangible blessing of infinite worth. Wisdom is the application of knowledge. Wisdom is knowing what to do with what you know. The world would tell us that a person doesn't have to know God to be wise and knowledgeable.

What does Isaiah 47:10 tell us about human wisdom and knowledge?

On the days we don't walk with God, we are easily misled based on human logic. God wants to guide us daily in His own wisdom and knowledge. Remember, He's the One with the plan. Psalm 119:105 paints a beautiful picture for us. His Word is a lamp to my feet, meaning a guide for the steps I'm immediately taking. His Word is also a light unto my path, meaning a guide for my immediate future.

Picture yourself on a path at night with a lamp to shed light on your next step. God chooses a similar course for His Word and your path. He doesn't want you to be worried about next year and the next. God graciously tells us what awaits us at the end of our earthly journeys, but He desires for us to come to Him consistently in the meantime. His Word sheds light on our present path and on our immediate future so we'll know what steps to take, but for further instruction we'll have to walk today and check again! If you're like me, you might not keep checking with Him if you knew the whole plan. Let's continue with benefits 4 and 5 from another text. Read Isaiah 50:4-11.

4. God offers us the daily treasure of a fresh morning word (v. 4). Based on this wonderful verse, though we can hear from Him at any time, I believe God awakens us in the morning with a supernatural capacity to hear from Him. Can you think of any reasons why we might have an increased capacity to hear from God in the very beginning of the day?

What did Christ say in Matthew 6:33? Respond in the margin.

Every day God wants to sustain someone who is weary. Sometimes I'm that person. Sometimes you are. God always has a word to speak to us and through us. Oh, that we would not be rebellious and draw back (Isa. 50:5).

5. God offers us the daily treasure of victory (vv. 7-8). We cannot escape the warfare of the Christian life. Unfortunately, Satan doesn't take time off for good behavior. He is on the prowl daily.

What did Christ say about "each day" in Matthew 6:34?

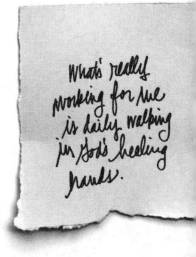

What's really working for me is daily walking in God's healing hands.

Every day can bring trouble, but every day we have a blessed Troubleshooter. Satan seeks to disgrace us, accuse us, and condemn us. We must daily set our faces like flint on the face of Christ and follow Him step by step to victory.

Let's conclude with a look at Isaiah 50:10-11. Read it now.

No matter how long we've walked with God, we will still have days that seem dark and circumstances in which His way seems terribly obscured. In those times, God tells us to trust in His name and rely on who He is.

Job 23:10 continues to be a blessing to me when I don't know what to do: "But he knows the way that I take." Whenever you feel like you've lost your way or you don't know where to go from here, my Friend, take heart! He knows the way that you take. Stand still, cry out, and bid Him to come to you! He'll lead you on from there and miraculously, when once again you see the light, you'll be able to see the footprints you made in the dark. Never will He hold your hand more tightly than when He is leading you through the dark.

What is your biggest temptation when you don't feel that God is illuminating your way clearly? Respond in the margin.

Mine is described perfectly in Isaiah 50:11. I tend to want to light my own fire and walk by the illumination of my own torch. In the past, my own paths have indeed led to torment when I walked by the light of my own feelings or logic. Thank goodness, God has never left me there when I've acknowledged my departure and cried out for rescue. Yes, you and I will still veer periodically from the path, no matter how obediently we want to walk, because we're pilgrims with feet of clay. The beauty of God's light is this: It will always lead us right back to the path. No matter how long the detour has been, the return is only a shortcut away. "Save me, for I am yours!" (Ps. 119:94).

BREAKING *Free*

session eight viewer guide

Freedom is not found in casting off a _____, but in trading a _____ _____ _____ for a _____ _____ _____.

In Matthew 11:28, the lexical Greek word *anapauo* means "to _____, be exempt; by implication to _____, take ease ... rest." *(Strong's Exhaustive Concordance)*

1. We are not _____. We are _____.

2. We _____ ___ _____ with _____ _____.

One commentary's translation of the wording based is on the Greek: "I, I _____, will give you pause or rest." (Lenski)

"For my yoke _____ _____" (Matt. 11:30, NLT).

3. We have the freedom to _____ from Christ as we simply _____ with Him.

   Genesis 5:21-23. The name *Enoch* (Hebrew transliteration *Hanok*) comes from the Hebrew word *hanak*, which means "to _____, discipline, dedicate, to _____ _____." *(Strong's Exhaustive Concordance)*

4. We share a yoke with someone who is _____ and _____.

   • Gentle: the Greek word *chrestotes* means _____.

   • Humble: "His path of humble service is the pattern for us to follow. So much of our fatigue and burdensome _____ stems from _____."

     "If we are successful, our _____ are _____ and we try for more."

     "If we falter, the _____ of others and our self-condemnation weigh us down in guilt and self-doubt."

     "It is much more freeing to take Christ's attitude of _____ others." *(Life Application Bible Commentary)*

Week 8

God's Unfailing Love

I'M FREE! Free from the thoughts that have held me captive most of my life. God tells me I'm worthy. Worthy of His Love. Worthy of His coming to Earth to die for me. He broke the chains for me. I feel a weight has been lifted off my shoulders. He loves me, and He is enough.

Day 1
Finding Unfailing Love

Today's Treasure

"'Though the mountains be shaken and the hills be removed, yet my unfailing love for you will not be shaken nor my covenant of peace be removed,' says the LORD, who has compassion on you." ISAIAH 54:10

I'm coming out of a year of unparalleled transition. Nothing seems untouched. Relationships, circumstances, surroundings—everything changed. I held on for dear life to anything standing still. One morning I stopped at my favorite little coffee shop, pranced in, and made my usual order: "a banana nut bagel with plain cream cheese, please." The server looked at me cheerfully and said, "We're not carrying that kind anymore. Is there something else I can get you today?"

I stood stunned with my eyebrows pinned like two barrettes to my hairline. I must have been in shock for some time because the person behind me finally bumped me out of the way providing all I needed to burst into tears. As I walked out to the car, I looked up and inquired, "Could I have one thing around this place I can count on?!" As I got in the car, I sensed the Father speak His Word to my heart. "Beth, I will never leave you nor will I ever forsake you."

This week we study the life-saving love of God. The word *compassion* in Isaiah 54:10 comes from the Hebrew word *racham,* meaning "to soothe; to cherish; to love deeply like parents; to be compassionate, be tender … This verb usually refers to a strong love that is rooted in some kind of natural bond, often from a superior one to an inferior." Now for my favorite part of the definition: "Small babies evoke this feeling."

I've never experienced a more overwhelming feeling than the one my two infants birthed in me. My babies brought out a capacity to love I had never experienced before, and yet I'd also never been so totally vulnerable. I once heard a child psychologist explain the necessity of some conflict with teenagers. He explained that a certain amount of difficulty must naturally arise as children become young adults or parents would never be able to "help them" out of the nest and on to independence. He said, "If the bond we had with them as infants did not change, we would never be able to let them go."

Now look back at the definition of *compassion*. All our lives God retains the strong feelings toward us that infants evoke in their parents. Do you realize why? Because He never has to let us go! God is not rearing us to be independent of Him. He's not rearing us to leave home! God is rearing us to come home! What joy floods the soul of a mom who has watched her precious girls move from my nest to building their own!

Read Psalm 136. What is the obvious point of the chapter? (margin)

Now view the chapter without the refrain "His love endures forever." On the next page I want to ask you to group the remaining Scriptures according to the three themes I've provided.

1. God the Creator

In the margin write a phrase and reference from each of the 26 verses of Psalm 136. For example, verse 1, "He is good," shows His compassion.

Psalm 136 offers many points but of utmost importance is this: God's works change, but His love stays simple, steady, and strong. The display of His power spans the gamut from the deliverance of His children to the death of His enemies. His mighty outstretched arm both saves and destroys. He works in countless ways. The moment we think we've grasped His ways and figured out His methods, they will change. Read Isaiah 55:8-11, then consider the following statements.

Write *true* or *false* based on information or inferences from the passage.
____ The point of studying God's Word is to figure out God's ways.
____ We will never grow in the Word so much that faith is unnecessary.

2. God the Conqueror

____ We can know God so well that we will begin to think His thoughts.
____ No rhyme or reason exists for the ways of God.
____ God's thoughts and ways always have purpose, but many of them are beyond our understanding.

Only in the light of God's unfathomable ways and infinitely high thoughts can we fully appreciate the bedrock of God's love. Kings will rise and fall, but His love endures forever. At times, the mountains God has created will quake into the sea. But His love endures forever. Riches will come and riches will go. But His love endures forever. Sometimes we'll be healed from physical afflictions and sometimes we won't. But His love endures forever. The heavens and earth will pass away. But His love endures forever. Think about the variables in your own life.

3. God the Compassionate One

Write four statements reflecting variables in your life.

They may be loved "variables," but each is a missing guarantee. You've just written a very personal and simple psalm embodying a great truth. Read all four statements aloud, repeating the "chorus" from Psalm 136 ("but His love endures forever") after each one. Let's drive the peg of God's truth in a little deeper.

What things do you fear most? Rewrite Romans 8:38-39, exchanging some of Paul's examples for some of your own.
"For I am convinced that neither ...

will separate me from the love of God that is in Christ Jesus our Lord."

Do you realize, Beloved, you have just penned the answer to your greatest psychological need? If we don't allow God's truth to take up full residence in our hearts, we may learn just enough to move out of one prison into another. We'll probably echo the words of Psalm 51:6 many times before our study concludes.

The inmost places or inner parts are our hearts and our minds. Next week we will center our study on the mind, but this week is a complete matter of the heart. I'd like you to see one of the most important facts recorded in the Word of God regarding the emotional needs of all human beings.

What does Proverbs 19:22 say we desire? _____ _____.

The Hebrew word *desire* comes from the word *'avah*, meaning "to covet, greatly desire." This verse puts that which we long for most into a capsule phrase for us. Every human being strongly desires, covets in others, and longs for unfailing love. Lavish love. Focused love. Love we can count on. The taxicab driver, plumber, stockbroker, runway model, actress, streetwalker, drug pusher, school teacher, computer programmer, rocket scientist, doctor, lawyer, president, and custodian all yearn for the same thing—unfailing love.

 What does Proverbs 20:6 suggest about unfailing love?

In the margin describe what the adjective *unfailing* means to you as it describes love. Try to be as specific and descriptive as you can.

Turn to 1 Corinthians 13:4-8. Does your idea of unfailing love sound anything like Paul's description of unfailing love? ☐ Yes ☐ No

Paul described *agape* love as a supernatural love that only God fully possesses and only God can give. It's the New Testament word for *God-love* just like *chesed* is the Old Testament word for *God-love*. The only way we can love with *agape* is to pour everything else from our hearts and ask God to make them pitchers of His *agape*. Before we can even begin to give God-love away, we've got to fully accept it. God loves you with perfect love.

According to 1 John 4:18, what does perfect love accomplish when we're willing to accept it?

Have you ever feared that someone would cease loving you? ☐ Yes ☐ No

Not only have I feared it, I've experienced it! God has carefully and graciously allowed some of my fears to come true so that I would discover that I would not disintegrate. I've experienced a few things I was sure would destroy me. But guess what? They didn't. Not because I'm so strong, but because God taught me to survive on His unfailing love. It wasn't fun, but it was transforming! I'm slowly

> *"Surely you desire truth in the inner parts; you teach me wisdom in the inmost place."*
> **PSALM 51:6**

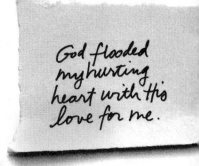

God flooded my hurting heart with His love for me.

coming to accept that the only thing I absolutely cannot survive is the loss of God's love. That is a loss I will never have to try. His love endures forever. That's what He means by perfect love driving out fear.

I am loved by many people and so are you. I am confident of my husband's love. He shows me and tells me he loves me every day. My children also truly love me. So do the members of my extended family and several very close friends. I am blessed, but the Word of God uses the phrase *unfailing love* 32 times, and not once is it attributed to humans. Every single use of the phrase refers to God and God alone. As rich as the love others can extend, only God's love is unfailing.

How would you explain the difference between God's love and human love, even at its best? In the margin offer several examples of how God's love differs.

How does God want you to respond to what He showed you today?

In *Holiness, Truth and the Presence of God,* Francis Frangipane wrote of the many aspects to the nature of Christ. "He is the Good Shepherd, our Deliverer and our Healer. We perceive God through the filter of our need of Him. And thus He has ordained, for He Himself is our one answer to a thousand needs."[1] How gloriously true! But God is not only the answer to a thousand needs; He is the answer to a thousand wants. He is the fulfillment of our chief desire in all of life. For whether or not we've ever recognized it, what we desire is unfailing love.

Oh, God, awake our souls to see—You are what we want, not just what we need. Yes, our life's protection, but also our heart's affection. Our soul's salvation, but also our heart's exhilaration. Unfailing love. A love that will not let me go!

Day 2
The Freedom of Unfailing Love

Today's Treasure
"Let them give thanks to the LORD for his unfailing love and his wonderful deeds for men, for he breaks down gates of bronze and cuts through bars of iron."
PSALM 107:15-16

Not long ago I tried a little experiment as I spoke to a group of women on the subject of God's love. I asked them to look eye to eye with the person beside them and say, "God loves me so much." Almost instinctively they turned to one another and said, "God loves you so much." I stopped them and brought the switch in words to their attention.

We tried the exercise a second time and they were visibly uncomfortable. I asked why they were struggling with my request and many said, "I can easily tell the person next to me that God loves her, but I'm having a very hard time telling her that God loves me."

Why do you think we readily accept God's love for others but struggle with the belief that He loves us equally, radically, completely, and unfailingly? In the margin list as many reasons as you can.

One reason I struggled with this truth was that I knew my sins and weaknesses. I knew all the reasons God shouldn't love me. I was sure everyone else wasn't the mess deep inside that I was. In retrospect, I'm glad I didn't go to the other extreme. Some people can be so full of self-righteousness that they seem convinced God loves them best of all. I never was righteous enough to be that proud of myself!

Why do we have such difficulty believing God could love those we perceive as good and those we perceive as bad with the same unfailing love? Because we relentlessly insist on trying to humanize God. We tend to love people according to how they act, and we keep trying to recreate God in our image. Today our attention will turn to God's outlook on the heart of the foolishly rebellious.

Read Psalm 107:1-3,10-22. Why did some sit in darkness and the deepest gloom as prisoners suffering in iron chains?

Who subjected them to bitter labor?
☐ God   ☐ Satan   ☐ foreign rulers   ☐ religious leaders

Why do you imagine God would subject His own people to bitter labor for rebelling against His words (v. 13)? Respond in the margin.

Based on verses 13 and 14, what did God do once His people cried out to Him in their trouble?

What was God's obvious motivation for doing such wonderful deeds (vv. 15-16)?

How did the Lord heal those who were suffering affliction as a direct result of their foolish rebellion (v. 20)?

What was the obvious prerequisite of God responding with His healing Word (v. 19)?

How does God obviously feel about those who have foolishly rebelled against Him (v. 21)?

Few people have grateful hearts like freed captives and the healed of affliction (v. 22). Notice God's directive to them: "Tell of his works with songs of joy."

 Why should the rebellious who have been freed be faithful to tell of His works? Respond in the margin.

I THANK GOD FOR SETTING ME FREE.

What an appropriate psalm for our study! Our hearts will never be healthy unless we learn to accept and abide in God's unfailing love. I'd like to draw two points from the psalm to encourage us toward our goal.

1. God's unfailing love extends to the most rebellious captives and most afflicted fools. Psalm 107 is refreshingly clear: God's unfailing love motivates wonderful deeds for the worst of men and women who cry out in their troubles. The Hebrew word for wonderful deeds is *pala,* meaning "extraordinary, miraculous, marvelous, astonishing." These kinds of adjectives seem like they would be limited to God's good children, don't they? Yet God's Word tells us that He does extraordinary, miraculous, marvelous, and astonishing things for the worst of the worst who cry out to Him. Why? Because He loves them with an unfailing love.

One work I'm convinced God wants to accomplish in this study is broadening our spiritual vision of His love. You see, we don't only see God's unfailing love through broken chains and healed afflictions. His unfailing love also appears in His unwillingness to allow rebellion to go unnoticed and undisciplined. I see at least five ways God dealt with the rebellious so they would cry out:

A. He allowed them to sit "in darkness and the deepest gloom" (v. 10). Rebellion can lead to literal prisons. It can just as easily lead to emotional cells of darkness and gloom. Certainly not all depression is a result of rebellion, but it can lead to depression. I think depression is especially likely if the rebel was formerly close to God. Look at the word *despised* in verse 11. The original word *na'ats* "contains the idea of disdain for one who formerly received favorable attention and then rebelled."

Why do you think rebellion could lead to a deeper depression in the life of someone who has experienced closeness with God? (margin)

Now that I know the indescribable joy of intimacy with God, living outside His fellowship would depress me. I am thankful that God allows darkness to follow rebellion or who could say how long we would remain in rebellion? I thank God that sometimes He uses darkness to lead us to the light!

B. "He subjected them to bitter labor" (v. 12). Rebellion can begin with fun and games, but eventually it leads to hard work.

How does God allow rebellion to become a heavy burden after a while?

C. He allowed them to stumble (v. 12). No doubt each of us can think of a few ways God allows the rebellious to stumble.

Cite an example of rebellion causing you or someone you know to stumble.

When I was a teenager, I could have accepted the little truth I knew, but I didn't. I not only stumbled, I crashed and burned! And I am so thankful. Had I never fallen, I don't know that I would have cried out for help.

D. He allowed "no one to help" (v. 12). How I thank Jesus for His unfailing love to make sure others "failed" in their attempts to help me! Sound strange? Read Psalm 62:1-2,5-7. Do you think we would ever acknowledge God as God alone if we didn't experience crises when no one else could help?

Think of a time when you stumbled and no one could help you. Did this lead you to God or to a deeper darkness and gloom?

E. He allowed some to suffer affliction (v. 17).

What physical symptoms did the affliction take according to verse 18?

Once again, certainly not all physical affliction is caused by rebellion, but rebellion can result in physical affliction. I can think of a time in college when I rebelled against God; I lost my appetite and became physically ill. I wasn't the first one in history to become sin sick.

**What about you? Have you ever been sin sick? ☐ Yes ☐ No
If so, what kind of physical symptoms did you have?**

Glance back at all five of these ways God can respond to rebellion. How does Hebrews 12:5-11 support the belief that all five of these responses are evidences of God's unfailing love rather than His wrathful condemnation?

You see, God loves us enough to ultimately make us miserable in our rebellion!

2. God strives with His captive children until they are free. The worst possible result of our disobedience would be God giving up on us. Remember, Psalm 107 is about the rebellion of God's own children. Over and over He disciplined them, but He never forsook them. Hallelujah!

One of the most common occurrences in the lives of men and women sent to prison is the subsequent serving of divorce papers by the spouse. Few prisoners have people on the outside standing by them throughout lengthy incarcerations. Let's face it. Most people would just as soon forget prisoners existed. They are the unpeople of our society. The same trend appears in less tangible terms among

Christians. The best of our churches tend to welcome those captive (to alcohol, drugs, homosexuality, promiscuity, and so forth.) at first, but if they don't "fix" pretty quickly, they will probably soon be despised. We like success stories—powerful testimonies. A captive in our midst soon wears out her welcome if she doesn't get with it pretty quickly.

In gracious contrast, God stands by us until we are free. He uses various forms of discomfort to woo us to cry out to Him, but He never forsakes us. God is the only One who is not repelled by the depth and length of our needs. Although God never excuses our sin and rebellion, He is fully aware of what drives our actions. In fact, He understands things about us we cannot even understand. When I was growing up, I had no idea why I was making some poor decisions, but God knew. Even though my rebellion was still sin, God's heart was full of compassion; and through loving chastisement, He continued to strive with me and waited patiently for me to leave my prison.

What was your longest length of internment in rebellion from God? _____ In retrospect, can you see ways He was constantly wooing you back to Himself? ☐ Yes ☐ No If so, name a few ways.

Please conclude our lesson with a few of your own applications.

Read the following references and explain how each applies to our present subject matter drawn from Psalm 107:10-22.

Psalm 119:67-68

Ezekiel 33:10-11

Luke 7:47

How does God want you to respond to what He showed you today?

No matter how long any of us have struggled, God is not giving up on us. Even if we've drained all the human resources around us dry, He is our inexhaustible well of living water. He may allow the life of a captive to grow harder and harder, so she will be more desperate to do what freedom in Christ requires—but He will never divorce her. He woos and He waits. The measures God takes to woo us to liberty may be excruciating at times, but they are often more powerful evidences of His unfailing love than all the obvious blessings we could expound. When all is said and done, perhaps few truly know the unfailing love of God like the captive set free. "Let them give thanks to the Lord for his unfailing love and his wonderful deeds for men. Let them sacrifice thank offerings and tell of his works with songs of joy" (Ps. 107:21-22).

Beloved, if He has become God alone to you, you have a powerful story to tell. Start talking.

Day 3
The Fullness of Unfailing Love

Everything of any worth is a direct product of God's love. Today let's focus on one of God's most wonderful works—the love that met my cavernous needs. One of the most vital segments of this study is when we studied Christ's encounter with the woman at the well. We learned a few things that we will expound on today through different Scriptures. Allow me to refresh your memory:

- Our insatiable need or craving for too much of anything is symptomatic of unmet needs or what we called "empty places."
- Salvation does not equal satisfaction.
- Satisfaction comes when Christ fills every empty place.
- While salvation comes to us as a gift of God, we find satisfaction in Him as we deliberately surrender all parts of our lives.

The big secret is that Christians are supposed to be fully satisfied with Jesus, but many still harbor an unidentifiable emptiness or need. Their unwillingness to be truthful about their lack of satisfaction in the Christian life keeps them from asking the right questions: Why do I find the Christian life lacking? How can I be more satisfied? Remember, Satan capitalizes on secrets! Secrecy always provides fertile ground for shame to grow. We grow more and more ashamed of ourselves for not being satisfied Christians. Because we won't ask questions inside the circle of believers, the enemy tempts us to look outside for godless answers.

Remember the five benefits of our covenant relationship with Christ? In the margin, write the third benefit.

Finding satisfaction and fullness in Christ was never meant to be a secret treasure only a few could find. The enemy tries to make it seem so elusive. Satisfaction is a blessed by-product of our relationship with God! It is meant for every believer.

Look up 2 Peter 1:3 and briefly note the claims of God's Word.

Either Christ can satisfy us and meet our deepest needs, or God's Word is deceptive. In the days before I began to enjoy the fullness of Christ, I somehow knew God's Word was true and that the problem rested with me, but for the life of me I couldn't figure out what the problem was. I served Him. I even had a love for Him, however immature; but I still fought an emptiness that kept me looking for love and acceptance in all the wrong places.

Never once in my youth did I hear clear teaching about the Spirit-filled life. Perhaps this is why I refuse to shut up about it now. Satan knows the Holy Spirit is key to abundant, liberated life, so he has done everything in his power to cast confusion and fear around the subject. Let's boil a few things down to the basics.

Today's Treasure
"Satisfy us in the morning with your unfailing love, that we may sing for joy and be glad all our days." **PSALM 90:14**

Secrecy always provides fertile ground for shame to grow.

Fill in the blanks with the appropriate word.
John 4:24—God is _____   1 John 4:16—God is _____

God's essence or His state of existence is Spirit. Don't get the idea that the word *spirit* implies invisible. God definitely has a visible, however glorious and indescribable, form, but we do not presently have eyes that can behold the spirit world. Just as surely as God is Spirit, God is love. Love is not only something God does, love is something God is. God would have to stop being to stop loving. Again, our temptation is to humanize God because we are limited to love as a verb. With God, love is first a noun. It's what and who He is.

Now read 1 John 4:13-15. What happens when someone acknowledges that Jesus is the Son of God?
☐ The angels rejoice. ☐ The Holy Spirit descends like a dove.
☐ God lives in him.   ☐ Other _____

Through the Holy Spirit, God takes up residence in all who accept His Son as Savior. God can no more cease being love than He can cease being Spirit; so when the Spirit of God moves into our lives, the love of God comes too. The promise of 2 Corinthians 3:17 is, "where the Spirit of the Lord is, there is freedom."

See how it all fits together? Wherever God is welcomed, His Spirit is loosed. Wherever the Spirit is loosed, so is His love. And wherever you find His loving Spirit, you find freedom. How is the Spirit of God loosed? Through confessing or agreeing with His Word. We will focus on this last element in week 9, but I wanted you to see all the pieces fit together today.

My point is this: Only the places we allow the love of God to fully penetrate will be satisfied and, therefore, liberated. Nothing expresses this truth better than the divinely inspired words of the apostle Paul. Read Ephesians 3:14-21 aloud as if you've never read it before. Take note of each statement about God's love.

Let's look at these statements individually. God deeply desires for us:

1. To be rooted and established in love (v. 17). Whose love? His love. The Greek word for *rooted* is *rhizoo* meaning "to be rooted, strengthened with roots, firmly fixed, constant." A plant or tree is as strong as its roots are deep. The deeper you and I are rooted in the unfailing love of God, the less we sway when the winds of life blow harshly. When I am going through a difficult time, this truth becomes my anchor: God cannot make a decision for my life outside His lavish love for me. I certainly haven't always had this confidence, and I still have far deeper roots to grow; but I've made significant progress in this area in recent years. At this point in your life, how deeply rooted are you in the love of God?

In the margin draw a tree planted in soil representing how rooted you estimate your life to be right now in the assurance of God's love. Write an explanation for the depth (or lack of depth) of your roots.

I pray that by the time this chapter concludes, your roots go even deeper.

2. To have the power to grasp the colossal love of Christ (v. 18). The word for *grasp* is *katalambano* meaning "to lay hold of, seize, with eagerness, suddenness … with the idea of eager and strenuous exertion." God longs for us to eagerly lay hold of the depth, length, breadth, and height of Christ's love. This prize is one worth expending our most strenuous energies on. We do not begin to have the capacity to grasp in our own strength the first inch of Christ's love.

Where does Ephesians 3:16 say we get this power? _____ _____

See the connection? The power to grasp the love of Christ comes to us through the Holy Spirit in us. The more authority we give the Spirit, the more we grab hold of the colossal love of Christ. Look back at the definition and note the synonym *suddenness.* I love this part of the definition because I've had times when I seemed suddenly to grab hold of the enormity of Christ's love for a moment.

Keith and I usually walk together in the evening, but he wasn't home one night when I was experiencing a very deep hurt. All I felt like doing was sobbing, but I decided to throw on the headphones, play some good worship music, and walk out on the neighborhood golf course all by myself. The night was pitch black, and no one appeared to be on the course but me. The more the music rang through my soul, the more the tears of my wounds turned to tears of worship. Finally, I stopped walking, lifted both my hands in praise, and worshiped Him. Flashes of distant lightning began to burst in the sky like fireworks on the fourth of July. The more I sang, the more the Spirit of God seemed to dance through the flashes of lightning. I haven't had many experiences like this one, but I will believe all my life that God allowed me a sudden, flashing grasp of His amazing love.

Can you think of a time when you were suddenly awash with the magnitude of God's love for you personally? Describe it.

If you can't think of a time when you felt lavished in God's love, ask Him to make you more aware. God's love is demonstrative. Ask Him to widen your spiritual vision so that you can behold unexpected evidences of God's amazing love.

3. To know Christ's love that surpasses knowledge (v. 19). Look closely at the words *know* and *knowledge* in verse 19. The word *know* is *ginosko,* meaning to "come to know … in a judicial sense, to know by trial … to learn … in the sense of to perceive … it could be said that *ginosko* means to believe." *Know* differs from the word *knowledge* used at the end of the phrase. *Knowledge* in this passage comes from the Greek word *gnosis* meaning "present and fragmentary knowledge as contrasted with *epignosis,* clear and exact knowledge." Now it's your turn.

Based on the original meanings, what did Paul mean when he prayed for us to know Christ's love that surpasses knowledge? (margin)

By God's grace, I can do whatever He wills me to.

If you said something like this, you're getting it: To come to know and to learn by experience Christ's love that surpasses all present and fragmentary knowledge. Paul prayed for us as we walked with Christ in our human experience to perceive a depth of love that surpasses any kind of limited knowledge our minds could now grasp. My Fellow Sojourner, Christ longs for you to know—by trial through walking with Him daily—a love you cannot begin to comprehend."

4. To be filled to the measure of all the fullness of God (v. 19). Now let's watch this all come together. The word *filled* is the Greek word *pleroo* meaning "to make full, fill, particularly, to fill a vessel or hollow place." Remember those empty places? How, indeed, could we forget them? They probably cause us more havoc than almost anything else in our lives! They grow from hardships, injustices, losses, and unmet needs, not to mention the hand of God who carves out places only He can fill. When you received Christ, God's Spirit took up residence inside of you. Through the filling of the Holy Spirit, He desires to permeate every inch of your life and fill up every hollow place with the fullness of His love.

Remember our greatest desire according to Proverbs 19:22? God alone has unfailing love. He wants to flood your life with it. The fullness of God is not a one-time occurrence like salvation. To live victoriously, every day we must learn to pour out our hearts to God, confess sin daily, acknowledge every hollow place, and invite Him to fill us fully! Then we need to continue to fan the flame of His love by reading Scripture, listening to edifying music, and praying often. We also need to avoid things that obviously quench His Spirit. Beloved, when you make a daily practice of inviting His love to fill your hollow places and make sure you are not hindering the process, God will begin to satisfy you more than a double cheeseburger! I practice what I'm "preaching" here almost every day.

I begin the day with God's Word. Although I'm learning to discern all Scripture as words of love in one form or another, if I'm feeling especially insecure, I might look up specific Scriptures reminding me how God loves me.

Fill in the blanks from Psalm 90:14. "Satisfy us in the _____ with your _____ love, that we may sing for joy and be glad all our days."

In my morning time with God, I ask Him to satisfy all my longings and fill all my hollow places with His lavish, unfailing love. This frees me from craving the approval of others and requiring them to fill my "cup." Then, if someone takes the time to demonstrate his or her love to me, that's the overflow! I am free to appreciate it and enjoy it, but I didn't emotionally require it!

See how the love of God that permeates the life through His Holy Spirit brings freedom? Not only am I freed, I am able to free others from having to boost me up emotionally all the time. Hallelujah! Where the Spirit of the Lord's lavish love is, there is freedom! Try it and see!

If we're not experiencing satisfaction, a hindrance exists and we want to identify it and ask God to remove it. Ordinarily, the primary hindrance to satisfaction in our lives is refusing Him access to our empty places.

How does God want you to respond to what He showed you today?

Day 4
Failure to Believe God's Unfailing Love

Today's Treasure
"For God so loved the world that he gave his one and only Son, that whoever believes in him shall not perish but have eternal life." JOHN 3:16

I believe Christ's bride, the church made up of all believers, is ill. She is pale and frail. Not because of judgment. Not because of neglect. Not because she doesn't have plenty to eat and drink. The meat of God's Word and the drink of His Spirit are there for her taking. Not because of warfare. She's bruised by the enemy, but he's not the one making her sick. He's just taking advantage of the opportunity. Her malady comes from within. Christ's bride is ill with unbelief.

We don't recognize the illness because most of us have suffered with it all our lives. Several years ago, I began noticing I had less energy than usual. About the time I'd decide something was wrong, I'd have a little burst of energy and decide I was imagining things. Finally, I got a blood test. I told a friend later in the day how mad I was at myself for spending the money on the test. "I feel just fine! Occasionally I'm a little tired, that's all. I wish I hadn't gone to the expense."

That evening my doctor called. He put me to bed for two weeks with a fierce case of mononucleosis. I kept asking him if he was certain. "I don't feel that bad. I'm just tired!" A few months later, I could not believe how good I felt. I finally realized that I had been sick for so long, I had forgotten how wellness felt!

I believe that the church suffers from a strength-sapping case of unbelief, but we've had the ailment so long, we don't know how good authentic belief feels. The healthiest Christians you will ever meet are not those with perfect physiques but those who take a daily dose of God's Word and choose to believe it works!

When I began to research and pray about this study, God kept repeating a word over and over to my heart: Unbelief. Unbelief! I kept sensing Him saying, "My people are suffering from unbelief!" At the time, I felt that this word was a separate message from the material He was beginning to give me for *Breaking Free.* Finally, I got a clue! Belief is an absolute prerequisite to breaking free! In week 3 we talked about removing the boulder of overall unbelief; today I want to talk to you about a specific and completely debilitating area of unbelief. Before I do, let's reflect on the very first benefit of our covenant relationship with God.

What has God chosen you to do according to Isaiah 43:10? (margin)

True service flows automatically from knowing God, believing Him, and understanding who He is. As we begin to know Him like this, no one will have to convince us to serve Him! Now, what about the issue of believing Him? I continue to see this statement in my mail: "I have such trouble really believing and accepting how much God loves me." I began to ask Him, "Lord, why do we have so much trouble believing and accepting Your love for us?"

I offered multiple choice answers so God could choose one: "Is it our backgrounds? our childhood hurts? the unsound teachings we've received? the unloving people who surround us?" I would have gone on and on except that He seemed to interrupt me—and He had the gall not to choose one of my answers.

As clearly as a bell, God spoke to my heart through His spirit and said, "The answer to your question is the sin of unbelief." The thought never crossed my mind. Since then, it's never left my mind. Humor me for a moment. Suppose I heard God correctly. (I have certainly misread Him before!)

Why could not believing God personally and lavishly loves us be considered a sin? Respond in the margin.

Think of someone (besides God) you are absolutely positive loves you. Who is this person?

In the margin list every way you know he/she loves you. Really give this activity some thought.

I'll share my answers. I'm positive Keith loves me. I'm convinced for several reasons: He tells me several times a day. He shows me in all sorts of ways. Recently I came in from an out-of-state conference. The weather was cold and rainy. I called from the airport to tell him I was home and by the time I walked in the door, he had drawn a hot bath for me. He tells me he thinks about me often during the day. I know this is true because he calls me at least once or twice at work every day. He testifies of his love for me to others. Often someone will tell me they've seen Keith; then they'll remark, "He sure seems to love his wife."

A buddy of his said, "My wife is a great cook." Keith looked back at him, thought of me and my cooking and wasn't sure what to say! Finally, he responded, "Well, my cook is a great wife!" We've laughed about it ever since!

Keith shows his love by telling me when he thinks I'm wrong. He loves me enough to stop me from saying or doing something foolish. If you're married and your husband is not as loving, please don't despair! Remember God graciously delivered Keith and me from filing for divorce several times. Don't give up! God can work miracles! I cite all these instances to introduce several points about God's love, which is far greater than any earthly relationship could ever hope to be.

I've just stated a few reasons why we're convinced someone loves us. Let's spend the remainder of our lesson searching for evidences of God's lavish love.

1. God TELLS us He loves us. Look up the following Scriptures and record what you learn about God's love for you, His covenant child.

Deuteronomy 7:8

Psalm 86:5

Psalm 89:31-33

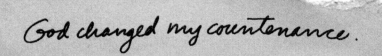
God changed my countenance.

God's Word is full of His proclamations of love for you! He made sure to inscribe His love in His Word so you would never have to wait for a phone call. You can hear God tell you He loves you every time you open the Word. When you're feeling unlovely, soak yourself in the proclamations of God's unfailing love for you!

2. God DEMONSTRATES *His love for us*. Perhaps your loved one is not very demonstrative. Many people have difficulty showing affection, but remember that God is not one of us. Innate in the nature of both *chesed* (Hebrew word for God's love) and *agape* (Greek word for God's love) is the demonstration of affection. Because God is love, He cannot keep from showing His love—even if He sometimes demonstrates it through discipline.

What is God's utmost demonstration of love (Rom. 5:8)? (margin)

Read each of the following Scriptures and record anything they have to say about God's demonstration of love.

Isaiah 52:14; 53:10-11

Matthew 27:32-54

1 John 4:10

What else could God possibly have done to prove His love for us? I might lay down my life for someone I care for, but I can assure you I don't love anyone enough to lay down my children's lives. What more could He do? And yet He does more every day to keep showing us He loves us through blessing, answered prayer, loving chastisement, constant care, intervention, and much more.

3. God THINKS *about us constantly*. In John 17:24, Jesus said, "Father, I want those you have given me to be with me where I am." I think heaven will be heaven because He will be there, but He thinks it will be heaven because you will be there. A line from a song expresses it so well, "When He was on the Cross, I was on His mind." No matter what time of night you roll over in the bed and become conscious, you will catch God in the middle of a thought about you.

4. God TESTIFIES *to others how He loves us*. Does this happen to be a new thought for you?

According to John 17:23, how much has God loved you? (margin)

Christ wants the whole world to know that God loves you and me just as God loves Him! God is proud to love you! How about you? Do you want the world knowing that you love God?

As we conclude, let's return to the question that prompted this lesson: Why do we have such trouble believing and accepting the love of God? The question hits much harder this time, doesn't it? You see, unbelief regarding the love of God is the ultimate slap in His face. God's love made the world. God nailed down His

How does God want you to respond to what He showed you today?

love on the cross. Can you imagine the grief of our unbelief after all He's done? You may say, "But I can't just make myself feel like God loves me." Beloved, belief is not a feeling. It's a choice. We may live many days when we don't feel loved or lovely; but in spite of our emotions, we can choose to take God at His Word.

You may say, "You don't know what I've been through!" Please hear my heart. I am completely compassionate, because I've also been hurt by people who were supposed to love me; but let me say this: No one has ever done more to show you that you were unloved than God has done to show you that you are loved.

If need be, make a list of ways you've become convinced no one could truly love you; then make a corresponding list of ways the God of all creation has told you differently. No list could compare to God's. Believer, let's get on our way to genuinely believing lives. Church, let's rise up from our sickbed of unbelief. How do we begin? We begin by repenting of our unbelief. Then we cry out with the man in Mark 9:24: "Help me overcome my unbelief!"

Day 5
The Fruit of Unfailing Love

Today's Treasure
"Sow for yourselves righteousness, reap the fruit of unfailing love, and break up your unplowed ground; for it is time to seek the LORD, until He comes and showers righteousness on you." **HOSEA 10:12**

This week we've warmed ourselves by the embers of God's lavish love. Though many may love us, only God possesses unfailing love. We've seen God's unfailing love extend to prisoners who rebelled against His Word. We found a love to fill our hollow places. We realized that disbelieving God's love is not only a tragedy, it is sin. Today we focus on the fruit of unfailing love. We'll discover why Satan would do anything to encourage unbelief regarding God's heart toward us.

Those who believe God loves differ significantly from other believers. Help me research several reasons why. I hope you'll find these reasons inviting enough to want to be among those who choose to take God at His loving Word. Read the Scriptures below to look into the heart of the God-inspired human writer.

Beside each reference write a couple of words to explain the effect that choosing to believe God's love appeared to have on the writer.

Exodus 15:13   Psalm 13:5

Psalm 32:10   Psalm 143:12

Lamentations 3:32   Ephesians 2:4-5

Another reference that most clearly articulates the effect of God's love on His children is Ephesians 5:1-2: "As dearly loved children … live a life of love, just as Christ loved us." God calls us to act like the dearly loved children we are. Give this admonition some thought. To gain insight, let's draw a parallel between God's children and the children of earthly parents. Virtually any expert on children will tell us that each child's perception of how much or how little she is loved will greatly affect her psyche and subsequent behavior. We don't need a degree in childhood development to imagine how differently children feel and behave based on whether or not they believe they are loved.

In the margin, give at least five endings to the incomplete sentences, offering your own thoughts contrasting two children: one who believes he or she is loved and the other who does not.

I watched firsthand the toll not believing you are loved can have on a person. Michael was our son in our home for seven years and will be in our hearts always. He suffered terribly from the traumatic changes in parental figures over his first four years. Thereafter he had a stable family environment, the best schooling money could buy, his own fully stocked room with every toy imaginable, fun vacations, and a very affectionate—albeit imperfect—family for seven years. Still, happiness seemed to elude him.

We loved Michael. Still do. But to the best of my perception, Michael never could believe it. Every attempt at discipline was misinterpreted as a lack of love. Even demonstrations of love were often interpreted as a lack of love! His inability to accept love also caused him to have great difficulty giving love. Don't think we did not have countless wonderful moments and unforgettable breakthroughs at times, but often they were the highs before the lows. I could never understand how we made so many steps forward then twice as many back.

Michael and I were very close, and I poured more energy into that little guy's life than I could ever describe. I remember telling Keith when Michael first came to live with us, "I'm just going to love him to wholeness." How terribly naïve and presumptuous I was! The truth God taught me is twofold:
1. God is the One and only One who can love anyone to wholeness.
2. Even Almighty God refuses to make anyone accept His love.

God allowed me to experience the tiniest fraction of how He feels. Watching your child drown because he won't embrace the lifesaver around him is excruciating. God has to be God to go through the rejection over and over and still love.

How about you? Have you ever loved someone wholeheartedly, but he or she would not or could not believe your love was genuine? ☐ Yes ☐ No If so, in the margin record some of your feelings.

Thank goodness, I have also had the privilege of seeing how a child who is utterly convinced she is loved grows. As you may have indicated earlier, children's

A child who believes he or she is loved …

1. _____

2. _____

3. _____

4. _____

5. _____

A child who doesn't believe he or she is loved …

1. _____

2. _____

3. _____

4. _____

5. _____

perceptions of whether they are loved affect them dramatically. We can draw a number of similarities between earthly parents and God, but we must recognize a very important difference. Sometimes earthly parents are unloving or unable to express love appropriately. Even the best of parents do not love perfectly. God, however, is not human. We cannot create His love in our image!

God loves perfectly. His love is both vocal and demonstrative. He balances blessing and discipline. God's love is unfailing, so any time we perceive He does not love us, our perceptions are wrong. Anything we perceive about God that does not match up with (1) the truth of Scripture and (2) the portrayal of His character in Scripture—is a lie.

When we realize we've been believing a lie, our bonds lose their grip. At those times we might pray something like: "I may not feel loved or lovable, but Your Word says You love me so much You gave up Your beloved Son for me. I don't know why I continue to feel unloved, but at this moment I choose to believe the truth of Your Word. I rebuke the enemy's attempts to make me doubt Your love. Satan knows the truth will set me free, and I've believed his lies over Your Word. I pray for forgiveness for the sin of unbelief. Help me overcome my unbelief."

Long-term liberation comes from accompanying God on a trek to (1) identify the problem, (2) demolish the stronghold, and (3) continue to walk in truth. The first step takes one moment. The second and third steps represent a process because getting to know the Healer is more important than finding healing.

Believing and receiving the love of God dramatically affects the child of God. Let's spend the remainder of our lesson examining the fruit of God's unfailing love by analyzing the child who knows he is dearly loved (described in Eph. 5:1-2). We will involve references you researched at the beginning of our lesson.

1. God's child who trusts His love possesses security in God's leadership. Exodus 15:13 says, "In your unfailing love you will lead the people you have redeemed." God promises the redeemed are not left to wander around aimlessly until we enter heaven. According to Jeremiah 29:11, He knows the plans He has for us. He leads those He has redeemed so they will fulfill His wonderful plan. Not only does God lead us, He leads us in His unfailing love! Oh, how my heart rejoices over the reminder. You see, I've been led a few difficult places and so have you. What a comfort to know that the places God chooses to lead us always flow out of His unfailing love. When we choose to believe God loves us, we can trust that the paths He leads us on are charted in lavish love. And, glory to God, at the end of the path, we will stand in His holy dwelling and see Him face to face!

2. God's child who trusts His love possesses security in her salvation.

Read Psalm 13. How would you describe the writer's approach to God?
☐ fearful   ☐ timid   ☐ bold   ☐ hesitant

The child who trusts in God's unfailing love does not fear that God will cease loving. We can pour out our frustration with courage as did the psalmist.

3. God's child who trusts His love possesses security in God's mercy. In Psalm 51:1 King David cried out, "Have mercy on me, O God, according to your unfailing love." How important is the link between the love of God and the mercy of God? Beloved, please receive this truth—God cannot be unbiased toward you. He cannot set His love for you aside and make an objective decision. He cannot see you through anything less than a loving Father's eyes. You and I will never be rejected when we come to God with genuine hearts of repentance, ready to fall in His forgiving arms. Remember, Christ was never resistant to sinners in the gospel accounts. He was resistant to hypocrites.

4. God's child who trusts His love possesses security in His comfort. Psalm 119:76 says, "May your unfailing love be my comfort, according to your promise." So, what is our comfort in death? The unfailing love of God. What is our comfort in life? Sometimes harder than death—the unfailing love of God.

Read Romans 8:38-39 carefully. In the margin note the greatest hardship you are facing right now. What can be your comfort at this and every time of your life?

Now read John 15:9. Since we know God loves us unfailingly at all times, what do you think "abiding" or "remaining" in God's love means?

5. God's child who trusts His love possesses security in His defense. King David said in Psalm 143:12, "In your unfailing love, silence my enemies; destroy all my foes, for I am your servant." When your heart belongs to God, those who are against you are against God. He takes wrongs done to you very personally. God upholds your cause (Lam. 3:59).

God taught me to lean wholly on Him.

Read Psalm 35:1,10,19. According to verse 19, what were the obvious circumstances? Respond in the margin.

According to Psalm 35:10, was God's covenant child arrogant or humble concerning his foe?

What rest God's unfailing love affords us when an enemy rises up against us! Do you realize that if our hearts are humble and right before God, we can hand over to Him all the conflicts and foes that rise up against us? What happens if we were also wrong? We must do everything we can to apologize and make things right, but if the foe remains against us, he or she is God's responsibility. Oh, friend, our list could go on and on. In fact, I encourage you to look up every verse in the New International Version containing the words *unfailing love,* meditate on them, and believe them!

As you conclude today's lesson, read 1 John 3:19-20; 4:16. What do these verses mean to you now after all we've studied this week? Express your heart in the margin.

1. Francis Frangipane, *Holiness, Truth & the Presence of God* (Robins, Iowa: Arrow Publications, 1986), 79.

BREAKING *Free*

session nine viewer guide

Why Does God Make Love the Priority Command?

1. Love motivates _____.

2. Love motivates _____.

3. Love provides _____.

4. Love for God empowers _____ _____ _____.

One of the biggest and least addressed obstacles to truly loving God:
_____ ___ _____ _____ when, truth be told,
___ _____ _____.

John 21:15-22. *Agapao* is "used of divine love and usually carries the connotation of _____ or _____ as well as that of _____."
(*Expositor's*)

Identifying True Love

1. Does God regularly _____ into _____ _____ (Ps.63:6)?

     Often   Sometimes   Rarely

2. Am I often _____ _____+_____ _____ with Him (Ps.27:4)?

     Often   Sometimes   Rarely

3. Does my life _____ a love for God (Rom. 5:8)?

     Often   Sometimes   Rarely

4. Do I often _____ _____ (Ps. 16:11)?

     Often   Sometimes   Rarely

5. Do I ultimately find _____ or _____ in obedience
(John 14:21)?

     Often   Sometimes   Rarely

"To love God in the way defined by the great commandment is to
seek God for his _____ _____, to have _____ in
him and to _____ _____ after him."
(New International Commentary on the New Testament)

Understanding How to Freely Love God

1. Recognize the _____ (1 John 4:7-8,19).

2. _____ it diligently through prayer (1 John 5:14,15).

The Steadfast Mind

I began to understand that Satan was after my mind, even when I was a child, and never realized how much misery this caused me both as a child and adult. But, I have started to tear down those high places and fill myself with the truth. The truth has set me free. Praise God!

Day 1
A View from the Old

Freedom from strongholds is serious business. In-depth study and deliberate application of truth is not just helpful but an absolute necessity for those who choose liberty. We win freedom on the battlefield. In this war, the battlefield is the mind.

Notice in Today's Treasure the inclusion of trust in the life of the one with a steadfast mind. Only a trusting heart will approach God honestly with the secret struggles of the mind. When we offer a trusting heart and an honest, open mind to God, renewal is on its way. Through the power of the Holy Spirit, I pray we will be able to accomplish three primary goals this week. We will seek to:

- research the concept of the steadfast mind from Scripture (days 1 and 2)
- illustrate the concept with a five-step process (days 3 through 5)
- learn to apply the five-step process to virtually any stronghold

Resist the temptation to take shortcuts or skip homework! I believe this week will be a supernatural turning point for all who take advantage of what they learn.

Pause and ask God to give you deep insight into His Word today. Now read Isaiah 26:3-6 and 2 Corinthians 10:3-5. In the margin note every concept the two passages have in common.

We will take a phrase-by-phrase approach to our two Scriptures to ensure sound interpretation. For the remainder of today's lesson we are going to dig into the Hebrew meanings in Isaiah 26:3. Tomorrow we will study 2 Corinthians 10:3-5.

In the margin note how the three passages demonstrate that Satan deals directly with the human mind.

Phrase 1: "You will keep." Satan is very cunning. Our knowledge alone will not keep us protected. What you and I need is a watchman sitting guard on the walls of our mind. Here is the good news: We have One who is willing and able—if we will also set our minds on Him. In Isaiah 26:3, the Hebrew word for *keep* is *nasar,* meaning "to guard, protect, keep; used to denote guarding a vineyard … and a fortress. Those who performed this function were called 'watchmen.'"

According to Psalm 139:1-2,23, why is God the perfect candidate for watchman over our minds?

Take a close look at the condition of the promise offered in Isaiah 26:3. Considering what you know about God and His character, why do you think He has a special commitment to guard, protect, or serve as watchman over a steadfast mind (KJV, "whose mind is stayed on thee")?

Today's Treasure
"You will keep in perfect peace him whose mind is steadfast, because he trusts in you." **ISAIAH 26:3**

Mark 4:15

Acts 5:3

2 Corinthians 11:3

195

Romans 1:28-32 shares a disturbing reality. What can happen to those who have knowledge of God but don't think it worthwhile to retain it?

Surrendering our thought lives is a safeguard.

Surrendering our thought lives to God is not just a means to more consistent victory; it is the safeguard against finally being given over to a depraved mind. We can persist so long in our willful wrong thinking that God can give us over to our desires. He can give a person over to her depraved thoughts temporarily to teach a lesson or even permanently (1 Cor. 5:5; 1 Tim. 1:20).

This is serious business. Don't become discouraged though if you want to have a steadfast mind but can't seem to get control of your thoughts. Welcome to the club! We've all been there! Keep telling God how much you want to give Him your whole heart and mind. The wayward, defeated mind and the willfully depraved mind are not the same thing; however, left unchecked, the former can certainly lead to the latter.

Phrase 2: "in perfect peace." Before we determine what this phrase means, let's set the record straight concerning what it doesn't mean. Isaiah 26:3 doesn't say God will give us perfect minds if we are steadfast in Him. He says He will give us *perfect peace* in our imperfect minds. The Hebrew term translated *perfect peace* may be familiar to you. *Shalom,* means "to be safe, be complete … As an adjective it means well, peaceful, whole, secure … friendly, healthy, sound." Though it can mean the absence of strife, "it usually signifies much more. It essentially denotes a satisfied condition, a state of peacefulness, a sense of well being. It is used of a prosperous relationship between two or more parties."

Just as surely as the kingdom of God prospers when we are steadfast in Him, so do our own hearts and minds. God will never send us into the valley and ask us to bow to His authority there without sooner or later bringing a harvest from the ground watered by our sweat and tears.

By any chance, are you still waiting to see the first signs of fruit from a previous valley? If so, can you think of ways God could use the lapse of time to bring forth an even greater harvest?

God is faithful to His Word. If you remain steadfast in Him, a twofold prosperity is inevitable. Both the kingdom of God and you will be built up.

Phrase 3: "him whose mind is steadfast." The Hebrew word for *mind* is *yetser.* Frankly, the word looks like what my siblings and I were expected to say every time our dad, the Army major, told us to do something. The mind is certainly where we decide if we're going to say "Yes, sir" or "No, sir" every time our Heavenly Father tells us to do something! *Yetser* means "frame, pattern, image; conception, imagination, thought; device … it is what is formed in the mind (i.e. plans and purposes)." Look carefully at the word *frame* in the Hebrew

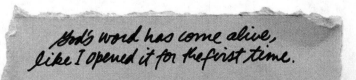
God's word has come alive, like I opened it for the first time.

definition of *yetser*. The implication of the word should be understood more in terms of a picture frame than our physical frame or body. In essence, our minds work to frame every circumstance, temptation, and experience we have.

We see events from our own perspective and context. Have you noticed how two people can look at the same experience so differently? They put the event in different frames and act accordingly. Our reaction depends on how we framed the event. Recall a crisis in your home. Perhaps a number of people were affected, but you probably noticed how different the reactions and responses were. You see, each person's mind worked differently to frame the same situation.

Let's pretend we've already won the battle over our thought lives. How could you frame that particular situation differently? (margin)

The original definition of the word *steadfast* helps determine whether we're on the right track. *Samak* means "to sustain … to be braced … to lean upon." One part of the definition draws a wonderful word picture of the steadfast life in God: to lay (one's hand on). When temptations and troubling thoughts come, the steadfast believer chooses to lay her hand on God's Word and know that it's the truth.

When I first discovered this definition, I thought of a time when I had been hurt by someone close to me. The pain in my heart felt like a searing hot iron. My thoughts were very troubled. I knew that the only way to battle the lies of the evil one was to lay a firm hold on truth. I found that during the day I could read or quote Scripture when my thoughts began to defeat me, but nighttime seemed an altogether different challenge. My worst attacks came at night. At the risk of being labeled a lunatic (I've been called worse), I'll tell you what I did during the most intense part of the battle. When I got into bed at night, I turned to Scripture that spoke truth to my circumstances. I would literally lay my head on my open Bible until I fell asleep. The Holy Spirit never failed to bring my mind comfort and relief. Had my action not been mixed with faith, it would have served little purpose, but because I believed God would spiritually accomplish what my posture simply symbolized, the enemy was not able to defeat me. Hallelujah!

How about you? Have you experienced heightened attacks on the mind when all is dark and quiet? If so, in the margin describe what you've learned through your own victories or defeats. (Don't underestimate the teaching power of defeat! Let's just make sure we're willing to learn!)

Let's conclude with a brief look at the final phrase in Isaiah 26:3.

Phrase 4: *"because he trusts in you."* The Hebrew word *trust* is *batach* "to attach oneself … to confide in, feel safe, be confident, secure." Picture a small child with her mom or dad. I want to trust God like that child trusts her parent.

Would you consider concluding with a prayer asking for a deeper trust so that you are more likely to have an open mind in which God can work this week? Remember, His plan is "not to harm you" but "to prosper you" (Jer. 29:11). Invite Him to be the watchman on the wall of your mind.

Day 2
A View from the New

Today's Treasure

"We demolish arguments and every pretension that sets itself up against the knowledge of God, and we take captive every thought to make it obedient to Christ."

2 CORINTHIANS 10:5

We researched the steadfast mind from the Old Testament perspective in Isaiah 26:3. We compared this wonderful passage with the New Testament perspective in 2 Corinthians 10:3-5. While the prophet Isaiah's words exude refreshment and security, the apostle Paul's words pack a serious punch. God inspired both men to make the same point. The latter simply made his point with a pair of boxing gloves. Today we will research 2 Corinthians 10:3-5. Read these important verses again and ask God to show you the wonders of His Word.

Phrase 1: "divine power to demolish strongholds" (v. 4). The word for *demolish* is *kathairesis*, meaning "demolition, destruction of a fortress." The original word for *stronghold* comes from the word *echo* meaning "to hold fast." The derivative, *ochuroma*, means "a stronghold, fortification, fortress. Used metaphorically of any strong points or arguments in which one trusts." You might think of the term this way: a stronghold is anything we hold onto that ends up holding us.

Now let's consider what Paul meant by demolishing strongholds. The word *demolish* implies a kind of destruction requiring tremendous power; to be exact, divine power. Much of the reason believers remain in a yoke of slavery is because we swat at our strongholds like they are mosquitoes. Strongholds are like concrete fortresses we've constructed around our lives block by block, ordinarily over the course of years. We created them, whether or not we were aware, for protection and comfort. Inevitably, however, these fortresses become prisons. At some point we realize we no longer control them. They control us.

When did you last try to break a stronghold in your own strength and end up feeling powerless and totally defeated? (margin)

Human effort is useless in demolishing strongholds. No amount of discipline or determination will do it. Satanic strongholds require divine demolition. Discipline and determination often help in opening your life to the supernatural power of God, but only He can provide the divine dynamite.

In ancient Corinth we toured the ruins of what was once a thriving city. I saw a fortress in the distance on top of the tallest mountain. I asked the guide to identify the structure. She responded, "It's an ancient stronghold. Virtually every ancient Greek city had a stronghold or a fortress on top of the highest peak in the vicinity. In times of war, it was practically impenetrable and unapproachable. It was the place of hiding for the governors of the cities in times of insecurity."

I was astonished. I was looking at the very stronghold the apostle Paul used as an analogy when he wrote these words to the people of Corinth. As I stared at the imposing fortress that still stood proudly at the top of the mountain after centuries had eroded the buildings below, I realized why the opposing army gave up. Sadly, we've too often done the same thing. My prayer is that each of us will say, "No more!" Remember, Satan's power comes from his power to bluff. Once we learn the truth and how to use it, he loses his hold. Look back at the last statement the guide made to me. She described a stronghold as the place of hiding … in times of insecurity.

Think about a stronghold you've experienced. What part did insecurity play? In the margin explain in general terms.

Insecurity played a major role in the strongholds the enemy built in my life. An important part of learning to live in victory has been discerning the heart rumblings of insecurity. I've learned to dramatically increase my prayer life and time in God's Word during times when my security is threatened. A primary example occurred with the loss of my precious mom. I knew that even during my time of mourning, I would be unwise to neglect God's Word or avoid my prayer time. Even if all I did was cry, at least I was drawing close enough to God that Satan couldn't build a wedge between us. I haven't always responded rightly at times of insecurity, but when I have, Satan has failed to gain an advantage.

Phrase 2: "We demolish arguments and every pretension" (v. 5). The Greek word for *arguments* is *logismos* meaning "a reckoning, calculation, consideration, reflection. In the Classical Greek writers, (*logismos*) was used of the consideration and reflection preceding and determining conduct." These arguments are our rationalizations for the strongholds we continue to possess in our lives. We maintain excuses for not surrendering areas of our lives to the authority of Christ. You've had them. I've had them. Never forget that Satan persists where a stronghold exists. He supplies an endless list of rationalizations for the things we do and refuse to do.

Can you think of an excuse or rationalization that no longer has power over you? If so, explain in the margin.

Never forget that the same God who came to your aid before will come to your aid again! You may feel your present obstacles are larger, but I assure you God doesn't. He is all powerful. Now, let's look at the other primary word in this phrase: *pretension*. The Greek word *hupsoma* means "something made high, elevated, a high place … figuratively of a proud adversary, a lofty tower or fortress built up proudly by the enemy. Pride." I believe we can draw three conclusions about strongholds based on this definition:
- Every stronghold is related to something we have exalted to a higher position than God in our lives.
- Every stronghold pretends to bring something we feel we must have: aid, comfort, the relief of stress, or protection.
- Every stronghold in the life of a believer is a tremendous source of pride for the enemy. Let that make you mad and determine to stop giving him satisfaction.

> Satan persists where a stronghold exists.

Often, the enemy will also stir pride in us to keep strongholds from being broken. Humility is a necessary part of the mind-set for someone ready to be free. In the body of Christ, the proud are never the free.

What role has pride played in one of your strongholds? (margin)

Phrase 3: "that sets itself up against the knowledge of God" (v. 5). The Greek for *sets itself up* is *epairo* meaning "to hoist up as a sail ... to lift up the eyes, meaning to look upon." I want to make a point that will be much further emphasized later in this week: Satan's goal is to be worshiped. This is what he's always wanted.

Read Isaiah 14:12-14. Isaiah's words referred in an immediate sense to the king of Babylon (vv. 3-4), but they ultimately refer to Satan. You can see from these verses that Satan's desire to be worshiped fuels his rebellion against God. If Satan can't get people to worship him directly, he accomplishes his goal by tempting people to worship something or someone other than God.

God created us to worship. We all worship something. According to the definition of *epairo*, the gaze of our eyes determines the focus of our worship—what or who is the object of our primary focus. Whatever we worship, we will also obey. Look at the first part of the definition: "to hoist up as a sail."

Arguments and sails serve both to propel and to determine the direction of the vessel. I hope you're seeing biblical proof of something you've already known experientially: strongholds affect behaviors! The enemy cannot enter a believer. We are sealed by the Holy Spirit of God (Eph. 1:13-14). He cannot make us do anything. He can only lead us to do things. Strongholds are the cords of the yoke by which Satan attempts to lead us.

Read Hosea 11:4. As I reflect on my history with God and how He is single-handedly responsible for my liberty, I am almost moved to tears over this verse.

How does God desire to lead His children? (margin)

What will He do if we will follow His leadership?
☐ lift the yoke from our necks ☐ take us to heaven
☐ heal us from our diseases ☐ bend down and feed us

Satan, the ultimate counterfeiter, also desires to lead us. God leads us "with cords of human kindness, with ties of love," Satan presses the yoke on our necks as he leads us with cords of falsehood and ties of lies.

Look at the last part of this phrase: "against the knowledge of God." Again we're reminded why knowing the truth is the key to liberty (John 8:32). If we don't know God's Word (His knowledge expressed to man), we can hardly recognize what is setting itself up against the knowledge of God. The more we know God's Word, the quicker we recognize Satan's attempts to cover it.

Phrase 4: "we take captive every thought" (v. 5). For now, I just want to research the meaning of the phrase. We will spend the remainder of this week on how we captivate our thoughts to Christ or, as the prophet Isaiah conceptualized

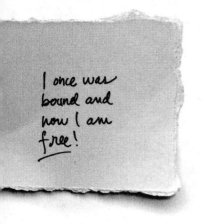

I once was bound and now I am free!

Phrase 1
"divine power to demolish strongholds" (v. 4).

Phrase 2
"We demolish arguments and every pretension" (v. 5).

Phrase 3
"that sets itself up against the knowledge of God" (v. 5).

it, how we practice the "steadfast mind." The phrase *we take captive* comes from the Greek word *aichmalotizo*, meaning "a prisoner, captive, to lead captive ... By implication, to subdue, bring into subjection." The verb tense in this phrase implies a repeated and continuous action. We're all looking for a quick fix, but God is after lasting change—lifestyle Christianity. To possess a steadfast mind is to practice a steadfast mind. You and I have been controlled and held prisoner by destructive, negative, and misleading thoughts for too long. Through the divine power of the Holy Spirit, we can take our thoughts prisoner instead!

Phrase 5: "to make it obedient to Christ" (v. 5). God wants us to be victors. We don't become victors by conquering the enemy. We become victors through surrender to Christ. We don't become victors by our independence from the enemy. We become victors by our dependence on God. Victorious lives flow from victorious thoughts. Thinking victorious thoughts comes from setting our focus on a victorious God.

How does God want you to respond to what He showed you today?

Today's complicated lesson concludes rather simply: We can be led astray by the cords of an evil yoke, or we can be led to victory by the cords of human kindness. Beloved, we have important work to do during the remainder of this week. This war is for freedom and the battlefield is the mind. Before you begin day 3, please spend a little extra time allowing God to cleanse your heart and clear your mind. Joshua's exhortation to the children of Israel applies to us beautifully today: "Consecrate yourselves, for tomorrow the Lord will do amazing things among you" (Josh. 3:5). The wonders God wants to do in all our tomorrows are prepared for in our todays. I love you, fellow sojourner, more than you know.

Day 3
Tearing Down the High Places

Our previous lesson concluded with an exhortation to be sanctified in heart and mind so God can do wonders among us. Are you prayed up and ready to go? Then let's get started. Our primary goal on days 1 and 2 was to research the Old Testament concept of the steadfast mind and the New Testament concept of the captive mind. Gathering information, however, would do us little good if we didn't learn how to apply it. For the remainder of the week, we are going to study a five-step process. The following illustrations picture the journey from captivity to our thoughts to taking our thoughts captive to Christ. Before we go through each step individually, take a moment to study the illustrations on the next page so you can begin to conceptualize the goal.

Today's Treasure
"Your enemies will cower before you, and you will trample down their high places."
DEUTERONOMY 33:29

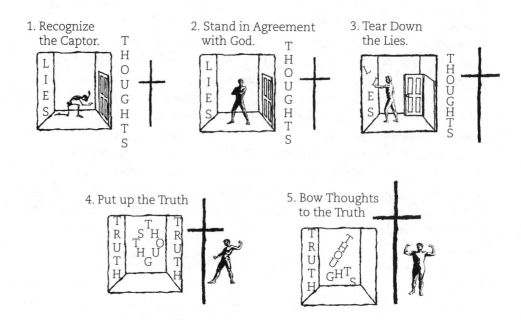

1. Recognize the Captor.

2. Stand in Agreement with God.

3. Tear Down the Lies.

4. Put up the Truth

5. Bow Thoughts to the Truth

The process we will study can apply to absolutely anything or anyone who is captivating our thoughts. Obviously God does not require us to avoid every thought about anything or anyone other than Him. He desires to keep us liberated by helping us deal victoriously with those things that capture our minds.

What do you see as the difference between casual thoughts and captivating thoughts? Respond in the margin.

Mind you, casual thoughts can easily turn into captivating thoughts. I think of it this way: Most captivating thoughts were once casual thoughts not surrendered to the knowledge of Christ.

So we can begin to think in applications from the start, in the margin describe two situations that could easily lead to captivating thoughts, for example, being betrayed or becoming attracted to someone.

Imagine how being the victim of rape could captivate your mind and nearly destroy you. Deep compassion floods my heart as I realize that someone reading this statement now knows from personal experience. If we don't surrender our minds to Christ, the loss of a loved one can also take us from appropriate grief to a lifetime of agonizing captivity. Remember, Satan fights dirty. He jumps on anything that could keep you from centering your thoughts on Christ.

Not all captivating thoughts come from painful experiences. Satan is far more cunning than that! Remember the enticing fruit he used to snare Eve? Our thoughts can be held captive to someone or something that builds up our egos or satisfies our fleshly appetites. Simply put, captivating thoughts are controlling thoughts—things you find yourself meditating on too often. Focusing thoughts.

Simply put, captivating thoughts are controlling thoughts.

Taking thoughts captive to Christ doesn't mean we never have the thought again. It means we learn to "think the thought" as it relates to Christ and who we are in Him. I will always have thoughts of my precious mother; but when I relate the thoughts to Christ, they will cause me less and less despair. They will not control me. With the power of the Holy Spirit, I will control them.

Seems impossible or too hard to attain? Don't give in, Beloved. Stay with me through this process and believe God will do a miraculous work in your heart and mind. What we need this moment before the competition gets fierce is a pep rally. Let's get Moses to lead the cheer. Read Deuteronomy 33:26-29 aloud, inserting your name in the place of Israel or Jacob. Allow God to engrave these Scriptures on your heart, my friend. "In all these things we are more than conquerors through him who loved us" (Rom. 8:37). Now let's begin to study each illustration that will teach us how to go from overcome to overcomer.

1. Recognize the Captor.

Study Illustration 1: Recognize the Captor. This drawing illustrates the imprisoned believer held captive by controlling thoughts. The cross shows she knows Christ, but that something has grown between her and her Lord. That something has grown so large, in fact, that it has become the captor; and the believer has become the prisoner. Many of our mammoth captors began as seeds in the thought life, but we watered and cultivated them by continued meditation until they grew to the size of Sequoias!

Can you think of any examples? List them in the margin.

Other times, sudden unwelcome or overwhelming circumstances cause full-grown trees to appear. A sudden death in the family or a diagnosis of a terminal illness can be examples of overwhelming thoughts that sprout quickly into full-grown trees. A sudden inheritance might seem a more welcome tree that could also end up controlling a believer. Whether the captor began as a seed or a tree, its destructive force assumes the size it occupies in your mind.

Again, I can't stress enough that the steadfast mind is not a matter of denial. Quite the contrary, it begins with admitting the truth. With our cooperation, Christ begins to strip the power from the controlling thoughts, so they no longer hold destructive power over us. We will see the important role of admission versus denial in Illustration 2. Refer once again to Deuteronomy 33:29. Compare the last sentence of this Scripture to 2 Corinthians 10:5.

Refresh your memory from day 2 with the definition of *sets itself up* in phrase 3. The King James Version translates 2 Corinthians 10:5, "Casting down imaginations, and every high thing that exalteth itself against the knowledge of God, and bringing into captivity every thought to the obedience of Christ."

Read Numbers 33:50-53 and 1 Kings 14:22-23. What do you think the Old Testament means by the phrase "high places"? Respond in the margin.

Read 2 Kings 12:3; 14:4; 15:4,35. Please keep in mind, these were the leaders of God's chosen people. Amid many successes, each of them failed to do one thing.

The steadfast mind is not a matter of denial.

Read 2 Kings 16:2-4. Considering the description of the unimaginable reign of King Ahaz, what bad fruit did the failure to remove the high places eventually bear? Respond in margin.

High places basically were monuments of idolatry. Some of the kings who otherwise followed God's ways still failed to tear down the high places. Ultimately, the oversight took its toll. The result was a kingdom in which children of God's own people were sacrificed on the altar. What an abomination this must have been to God! Likewise, many believers who otherwise serve and have a genuine affection for God overlook and thereby fail to tear down the high places in their lives. God's Word exhorts us to cast down "imaginations, and every high thing that exalteth itself against the knowledge of God" (2 Cor. 10:5, KJV). Those "high things" are the people, things, or circumstances that outgrow our thoughts of God.

> "High things" are the people, things, or circumstances that outgrow our thoughts of God.

Why do you think we, like the ancient Israelites, tend to avoid dealing with the high places in our lives? What do you think could happen in our lives and possibly to generations if we also neglect casting down our high places (strongholds)? Respond in the margin.

We can compare our strongholds to the high places in ancient Israel. Anything we exalt over God in our thoughts or imaginations is an idol. Idolatry is not only a terrible affront to God but it is also an open invitation to disaster. In 2 Kings failure to remove the high places led to full-blown depravity. Idolatry was also the primary reason God allowed Israel's enemies to carry her to captivity. Never forget the ever-increasing nature of sin (Rom. 6:19). If we do not cast down the high places, they will eventually cast us down. I don't believe I'm being overly dramatic when I say that we can either tear down our strongholds with the mighty power of God, or they will eventually tear us down.

Please keep in mind that we don't have to love something or someone to idolize or exalt it in our minds. We can easily idolize something we practically hate. I've never known an anorexic who loved her body, yet the anorexic idolizes the body whether or not she realizes it. I'll never forget realizing that a person I felt I couldn't forgive had become an idol to me through my unforgiveness. Humanly speaking, I didn't even like the person, yet Satan seized my imaginations until the whole situation stole my focus and therefore became idolatrous to me. Now take a look at illustration 2.

Study Illustration 2: Stand in Agreement with God. In our second illustration the believer has come to her feet. She is not yet free from the captive, controlling thoughts, but something very important has occurred. The key that unleashed the first wave of divine strength in her battle against the stronghold is found in 1 John 1:9 "If we confess our sins, he is faithful and just and will forgive us our sins and purify us from all unrighteousness."

Oh, how I thank God for forgiveness of sin! The word *confess* means more than simply admitting our sin to God. The Greek word is *homologeo*. The first part of the word, *homo*, means the same and the second part, *lego*, means to speak.

2. Stand in Agreement with God.

Confession means coming to the point of saying the same thing God says about any specific matter. For the believer, the first step of freedom from any stronghold is agreeing with God concerning the personal sin involved. Please understand, the object of our imaginations itself is not always sin. The sin may lie solely in the exaltation of it in our own minds. For example, nothing could be more natural or reflective of the heart of God than a mother's love for her child. However, if she has passed the bounds of healthy affection to overprotection, obsession, adoration, and idolatry, she has constructed a stronghold.

Let's take the same relationship one painful step further. Nothing could be more natural than a mother grieving the loss of a child. However, if 10 years later the mother is still completely consumed with the loss and bitterness that has eclipsed all comfort and healing, she has wedged a stronghold between appropriate grief and gradual restoration. The enemy will capitalize on normal emotions of love or loss to swell them out of healthy proportion. They can consume our very lives if we're not aware of his schemes. Loving is never sin. However, obsession that flows from putting something in the place of God is sin. Likewise, grief is never sin, but disallowing God to minister comfort and healing to you over the passage of much time is.

Virtually anything that cheats you of what God has for you could be considered sin. I say this with compassion, but I must say it, because some of us may not be recognizing how Satan has taken advantage of normal, healthy emotions. We easily view adultery, robbery, or murder as sin, but we often don't realize that sin can also be anything we allow to grow between us and the glorious completing work of God. The first step in freedom is agreeing with God's Word about your personal stronghold or high place. As you can see in the illustration, the believer is still not fully liberated from captivity; but she is no longer bowing down to the enemy in her thought life. As we conclude today's lesson, read the following questions and answer the one that applies to you:

If you are aware of a stronghold or high place presently existing in your life, have you come to a place of agreeing with God's Word and confessing all sin involved? ☐ Yes ☐ No If so, when? _____

If you are aware of a stronghold presently existing in your life that you've never agreed with God about and confessed all sin involved, would you be willing right now? ☐ Yes ☐ No

If you are not aware of any stronghold in your life, can you remember a time when Christ led you to freedom through honesty and confession of the sin involved? ☐ Yes ☐ No If so, in the margin explain in general terms.

The divine power of God is available to all of us who will agree to apply it. Once you learn how to use God's Word and live in His Spirit, "Your enemies will cower before you, and you will trample down their high places" (Deut. 33:29).

I fell to my knees and surrendered everything to God.

Day 4
Deprogramming and Reprogramming

As we begin, let's recapture our focus with another look at Illustrations 1 and 2. Study both illustrations and fill in the titles. Next, label or write a phrase identifying each part of the illustration.

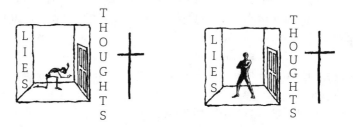

3. Tear Down the Lies.

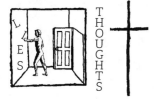

In the margin take a look at Illustration 3. It shows an important turning point. Once we see the sin involved in the stronghold, agree with God, and confess, we begin to see the lies. When we start tearing down the lies wallpapering our minds and keeping us imprisoned by our thoughts, the prison door swings open.

Satan lacks the authority to lock believers in a prison of oppression, so he works overtime to talk us into staying. Satan can presume no authority over Christians. He woos us into prison cells, but he can't make us enter nor force us to stay. Unfortunately, Satan doesn't require a written invitation. Failure to post a "keep away" sign through Bible study and prayer can be invitation by default. Do not misunderstand me to say Satan can inhabit the mind of a believer. He most definitely cannot, but the Word suggests that he can strongly encourage ideas, doubts, and thoughts in our minds (see *arguments* and *pretension* in 2 Cor. 10:5).

Meditate on 2 Corinthians 11:1-3 for a moment. Based on these three verses, what kind of person can be led astray? Respond in margin.

How does Galatians 6:1 support the fact that the immature or carnal Christian is not the only one who can be led astray?

Please hear my heart when I say this word of warning: The two most horrible seasons of warfare and bondage in my Christian life did not come in times of rebellion or carnality. They followed huge spiritual markers. Why, then, did I temporarily lose my step? Because I was doing my best to walk with God, but

I had no idea how to watch for the roaring lion seeking to devour me (1 Pet. 5:8). I thought if I ignored the devil, he would ignore me. I was deceived! Satan took advantage of what I didn't know and used my ignorance to deceive me.

Francis Frangipane explains how, because sin wears a cloak of deception, the first step to holiness involves the Holy Spirit cleansing our hearts from lies. Once the Spirit breaks the power of lies with truth, He can break the power of sin:

> The Bible warns us that sin is deceitful (Heb. 3:13). If, prior to sinning, one could display his thoughts upon a screen, the entire sequence of rationalizations and compromises—the decline into deception—would be very apparent. But the process of deception is not apparent. The enemy's lie enters our minds in whispers, not shouts; it walks in darkness, not light.[1]

3. Tear Down the Lies.

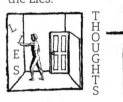

Look at Illustration 3 again. Picture the captivity of our thought life like a prison cell wallpapered in lies. The demolition of strongholds really begins when we expose and tear down the lies fueling our strongholds. We cannot repeat this fact enough: Deception is the glue that holds a stronghold together. By the time a stronghold exists, our minds are covered with lies.

Where do these lies originate? Read John 8:43-45. What do you learn about the devil from this passage? Respond in the margin.

Satan uses lies because he is a totally defeated foe. Lies are all Satan has. That's why he has to be so adept at using them. Think about a stronghold you've battled or may be battling. Picture yourself in Illustration 3. You have agreed with God about the stronghold and confessed the sin involved. You have come to your feet as in Illustration 2. God saw your willingness to be free and your faith to believe He could accomplish what you are powerless to do. He then began to open your eyes to the lies plastered like graffiti on the walls of your mind.

The illustration pictures you recognizing the lies wallpapering the prison cell and receiving the divine strength to rip them down. As you picture yourself with eyes pried open to the lies, I want you to think what several of them were. I'll share a few of my own as a springboard for yours. The most powerful stronghold of my young life came from childhood victimization. As if the experiences themselves were not traumatic enough, I also believed such lies as:

- I am worthless.
- All men will hurt you.
- When men hurt you, you can do nothing about it.
- You can't say no.
- I am not as good as my friends.
- If people knew what was happening to me, I would make them sick.
- I can never, ever, ever tell what has happened to me or I'll be destroyed.
- I am the only one this has ever happened to, and it's all my fault.

That's just one wall! I could have gone on and on with all the lies I believed.

"You, dear children, are from God and have overcome them [evil spirits], because the one who is in you is greater than the one who is in the world"
1 JOHN 4:4

Satan became far more sophisticated in my adult life. One yoke he put around my neck involved a relationship with someone who came to me for help. Satan twisted God's concepts of mercy and compassion to persuade me I was responsible for helping this person. The Holy Spirit signaled me not to get involved in the situation, but I chose my religious duty over obedience. When I suggested we go to others for help, the response would always be: "I don't want anyone else involved." It was a trap set by the enemy. The person was certainly worth helping, but I was not the one to help. The problem was out of my league.

I learned that if you don't listen to God and obey in the early stages, the longer you wait, the less discernment and strength you have. Listen! Not every person who comes to you for help has been sent by God! We must learn to discern the schemes of the evil one. God used the encounter to teach me more than a college degree could have, but the lessons were excruciating.

A stronghold could be anything from compulsive eating to paranoia. No matter what it may be, all strongholds have one thing in common: Satan is fueling the mental tank with deception to keep the stronghold running.

In the margin describe a little about your own experience with a stronghold and note a few specific lies the enemy used. As always, be general if the subject concerns a sensitive issue or something private.

Beloved, I want to say something with tenderness and much compassion. If you know a stronghold exists somewhere in your life (even if you've never admitted it to anyone), yet you cannot identify the lies, you are still a captive. That's not condemnation but truth that I hope will give you a jump start toward freedom. There is "no condemnation for those who are in Christ Jesus" (Rom. 8:1). But there can certainly be captivity. If you've not yet recognized the lies keeping you glued to the prison cell, please ask God to drop the scales from your eyes and help you see! "Then you will know the truth, and the truth will set you free" (John 8:32).

Now study Illustration 4: Put Up the Truth. Our captive has escaped the prison of her controlling thoughts and is very close to controlling them instead.

What has happened to set her free? First, she was forgiven for all sins involved in her stronghold the moment she agreed with God and confessed (illustration 2). We can be forgiven, however, and still not be free. And if we're not free, we will soon cycle back into sin. Happens all the time. The believer in our illustration didn't just ask for forgiveness of sins; she determined to be free. Because she fully cooperated with God, her eyes were opened to mind-binding lies and she sought the divine strength necessary to tear them down. Excellent progress, but thankfully she realized more needed to be done to make liberty in Christ a reality in life. She wasn't satisfied until she could walk freely from the prison cell.

How did she do it? She didn't just tear down the wallpaper of lies on her prison walls; she determined to put up the truth in their place. Give this next statement your full attention: The walls of your mind will never stay bare. Never. Let's face it. Our minds work even when we sleep. Once we tear down lies, we have to re-wallpaper with truth or the enemy will happily supply a new roll of

---

The longer you wait the less discernment and strength you have.

4. Put up the Truth

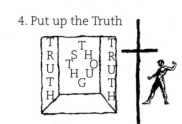

wallpaper. Different pattern maybe—a more updated look—but the same deceptive manufacturer. I cannot emphasize this step enough. Illustration 4 represents our only means of both deprogramming and reprogramming our way out of captivity. TRUTH is the only way out.

Say John 8:32 out loud until it sticks to your ribs. Take it very literally.

The question then is, how do we re-wallpaper our minds with truth? First, by understanding the goal. What does God want to accomplish in our minds? We possess the mind of Christ (1 Cor. 2:16), but we still have the full capacity to think with the mind of the flesh. We are mentally bilingual, you might say.

Amanda is almost fluent in Spanish, but she still thinks in English because she practices it more. The same concept is true of you and me. We will think with the mental language we practice most. In Romans 7 the apostle Paul portrays the struggle with the two "languages," as we're calling them.

Read Romans 7:21-23. On a scale of 1 to 10, just how much can you relate to Paul's struggle? If you relate as a 10, count me right with you! However, I've learned to think more victoriously—and so can anyone else. I've learned that God will not release us from anything that has enslaved us until we've come to the mind of Christ in the matter. Take the bondage of unforgiveness, for example. Often when we want to be free of the burden of not forgiving, we want God to wave a magic wand so we'll never think about that person again. That's not how God works. He wants to transform and renew our minds (Rom. 12:2) so we can think the thoughts of Christ about the person we are forgiving. We will not be free until we adopt the mind of Christ in the matter that has enslaved us.

For instance, if a believer has allowed Satan to build a stronghold through an adulterous relationship and she finally repents and desires to be free, her mind will not be released until she has torn down the lies and reprogrammed with the truth. She might beg God to simply remove the person from her mind. God knows that little would be accomplished, and she would be vulnerable to a similar attack in the future. Rather than drop the person from her mind, He wants her to begin to think the thoughts of Christ toward the situation and the person.

God unlocked the prison I built around myself.

Glance back at Illustration 4. Applying God's truth to the matter is what brings the cross between the former captive and her thoughts. Once the mind of Christ has taken over, the power of the stronghold is broken and the person and situation will finally begin to evacuate the premises. We'll see this reflected in the next illustration, but we have more to understand about this step first.

How does God want you to respond to what He showed you today?

Do you see the picture now? Stop and reflect on what you're learning so far. Is it making sense? On day 5 we're going to learn very specific ways to accomplish this re-wallpapering of the mind, but I'd like to conclude with your feedback.

Use the margin to respond to what you're learning. If you're thoroughly confused, write it! If you're beginning to understand, express the concepts that are becoming clearer to you.

I am so proud of you. Hang in there, my friend. Liberty in Christ is about to become a reality in life!

Day 5
Taking Thoughts Captive

Let's begin day 5 by taking another good look at Illustration 4. In the margin fill in the title for the illustration, then label each part of the picture to describe what has happened. How do we re-wallpaper our minds with truth? First, we need to understand the goal.

What is God's goal for our thought life?

☐ to think deep thoughts   ☐ to think only happy thoughts
☐ not to think at all   ☐ to think with the mind of Christ

I hope one or two of the choices made you grin, but I trust you checked the last one. God's goal for our thought lives is that we learn to think with the mind of Christ. Rarely will God release us from captivating or controlling thoughts by suddenly dropping them from our minds.

In our previous lesson, we cited a possible reason why God usually does not simply remove temptation from us. What was it?

How could we possibly learn to be overcomers otherwise? God rarely performs lobotomies. If we simply and suddenly forgot the object of our stronghold, we might also forget to praise Him and thank Him for deliverance.

 Read Psalm 107:13-16. What should always be the response of the former captive?

Even when Christ healed the leper, He didn't cause him to forget he ever had leprosy. The richest testimonies come from people Christ has made whole who still well remember what it was like to be broken.

In my travels, staggering numbers of women have confessed being involved in affairs. Often I am relieved to hear them say that they have repented and walked away in obedience to God's will. Just as often, however, they will say, "He's out of my life, but I can't seem to get him out of my mind." I can see their sincerity. God has forgiven the sin, but the mental stronghold is still overwhelming.

Just as many women come to me wanting to forgive people who hurt them. They cry, "I'll think I've forgiven so many times, but it still keeps coming up in my mind." When I began research for this book, I knew a key existed somewhere that would help us be victors on the most challenging battlefield of all: the mind. I believe the key is right there in 2 Corinthians 10:5. Before we can get controlling thoughts out of our minds, they must become Christ-controlled thoughts while still in our minds. That, my beloved, is taking every thought to make it obedient to Christ. This process begins in illustration 4 as we re-wallpaper the mind with truth—specific truth.

The Word of God was divinely inspired for all generations. I believe God's Word has encouragement and exhortation that can relate to any sin or stronghold. The Bible never says the words *anorexia nervosa,* but plenty of Scriptures speak truth to the stronghold. Likewise, the Bible doesn't specify all the phobias modern psychiatry defines, but Scripture has volumes to say about dealing with fear. If we're going to walk out of the prison of controlling thoughts, we are going to have to re-wallpaper with God's Word.

Please allow me to share a few practices God used profoundly in renewing my mind and providing subsequent freedom from some strongholds. I am willing to beg you to consider using them because I am jealous with a godly jealousy for you to be free! I'm going to give you a chance to practice some of what we've learned this week at the conclusion of our lesson. For now, I want to ask you to just absorb the information.

1. Search God's Word for Scriptures. Find Scriptures that speak the mind of God to your specific stronghold. Look up key words using a Bible concordance or a topical Bible tool. If you're new to the study of Scripture and you have no idea how to find specific Scriptures speaking to your stronghold, seek help. Whatever it takes, compile a list of Scriptures. Keep looking until you find them. Don't just look for one or two and don't just look for those Scriptures that rebuke. Also find specific Scriptures that speak God's unfailing love and forgiveness to you.

2. Write these Scriptures on note cards. The best way to keep them compiled is on spiral-bound note cards. These cards have been so useful to me that I am almost convinced God created them for this very purpose! I have a set on my desk right now because a situation recently occurred that had the potential to really stir some (unrighteous) anger in me. These are my Truth Cards. You see, now I'm learning to use appropriate Scriptures, not only defensively to tear down existing strongholds but offensively so Satan can't pitch one up when an opportunity arises.

3. Take these Truth Cards wherever you go. How long? Until the power of the stronghold is broken and you are walking out of that cell! Beloved, listen! If you're not ready to get serious about it, you'll never make liberty in Christ a reality in your life. When the enemy sees that he's about to lose a captive, he will fight as hard as he can to keep you bound. Be prepared to fight for your freedom with some radical choices.

Demolition of strongholds is radical. Expect the battle to heat up when you start tearing down the lies. Take your Truth Cards everywhere you go. In the heat of a battle to be free, I can remember a time when I took my spiral Truth Cards into the grocery store with me! I put them right in the baby seat and every aisle or two I flipped to the next card! Our cupboard was filled with the strangest concoction of stuff you've ever seen, but Beloved, I'm free today! Right this moment I'm laughing and crying at the same time as I remember it. Praise be to my God, my

Controlling thoughts must become Christ-controlled thoughts.

Deliverer, Jesus! I may find myself in that same position again someday, but I'll know what to do.

4. Avoid as many forms of deception as possible. If you have been in a stronghold, your mind has been inundated with lies. The person coming out from under the influence of lies desperately needs a season of intense deprogramming. Until you are less vulnerable, flood your mind primarily with truth and secondarily with materials that line up with truth. Many forms of media entertainment are full of deception. When we're not presently in or coming out of a stronghold, we still need to be very careful about the things we program into our minds, but we must exercise radical caution when we're escaping.

Remember, you're deprogramming and reprogramming! Coming out from under the influence of a long-term stronghold can be like coming out from under the influence of a drug. You'll often find that the magnitude of the stronghold takes a while to fathom. The more you "wake up" to truth, the more you'll realize how Satan has deceived you. It's not at all unusual to feel twice the regret several months after your release than you did when you first walked away. God's Word is your truth serum. The more you use it, the clearer your mind will become.

Now let's consider our final illustration; then we'll practice what we've preached. In the margin, look at Illustration 5: Bow Thoughts to the Truth.

Glance back to the five-part illustration on page 202. Contrast the first and last picture. For a moment, don't look at the three in between. In the space below, note every detail that has changed positions.

Now read 2 Corinthians 10:3-5. Yes, again! Do you see what has happened? The figure in our illustration has gone from captive to captor. Now glance at Illustrations 2, 3, and 4. In your own words and from your best recollection, how did the person go from captive to captor?

The final question becomes: How did the believer get her thoughts to bow to the truth? By believing, speaking, and applying truth as a lifestyle. This step is something we live, not just something we do. I promised to remind you that the verb tense of the phrase *take captive every thought* is a present active participle that expresses continuous or repeated action. Our well-trained thoughts of Illustration 4 are somewhat like a well-trained dog. We can't just shout, "Sit!" and expect

God's Word is your truth serum. The more you use it, the clearer your mind will become.

5. Bow Thoughts to the Truth

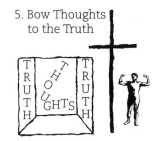

the dog to stay there for a week. We've worked a long time to get that dog to sit; but once it learns, it's still not going to sit forever. Our thought life is something we'll work on for the rest of our lives in our desire to be godly. But take heart in two important facts:

- Working on our thought lives is the only thing that will keep them from working on us. Either our thoughts have control of us through the power of the enemy or we have control of them through the power of God. Neutral doesn't exist among the mental gears. That doesn't mean rest doesn't exist. In fact, no rest compares to the relief of thoughts captive to Christ. Re-wallpapering is hard work, but rest comes as we learn to abide in what we know. Thankfully, God does force the enemy to back off intermittently, and we get a bit of a breather. When the battle heats back up, we get back to more radical measures.
- Staying at work on our thought lives is the very essence of godliness. The mind is the last frontier. By the time you're ready to invite God to take authority over your thought life, you're serious.

I've never met a soul who called herself a godly woman, but I know plenty of women I'd call godly. What is godliness, anyway? Is it perfection? No, because Scripture sets godliness as the goal for human beings occupied by the Spirit of God. It means giving our hearts, souls, minds, and bodies to God and desiring to obey Him more than anything. Until we see Christ face-to-face, surrendering the inmost places of your heart and mind to God is the essence of godliness. If you are striving daily to give God your heart and mind and are sensitive to sin in your thought life, Beloved, I'd call you godly. But, do you know what? I could never call myself that. Maybe that's how it should be.

I'd like to interject a rule of thumb regarding the thought life that will, in turn, be a catalyst to victory in all parts of the life: starve the flesh and feed the spirit. These phrases are not original with me, but I no longer remember where I first heard them. They were pivotal for me, and I hope they will be to you. The believer in Illustration 5 is practicing this rule, and every day she does, victory will be the rule in her life and defeat the exception.

Read Romans 8:5-8. List every fact given about the mind that thinks according to the Spirit and the mind that thinks according to the flesh.

According to the Spirit	According to the Flesh
_____	_____
_____	_____
_____	_____

> Working on our thought lives is the only thing that will keep them from working on us.

Even though you and I may be believers in Christ, we certainly can still think according to the flesh. When we do not make the deliberate choice to think according to the Spirit, we tend to "default" to the flesh. You've noticed we never have to wake up in the morning and choose to be self-centered. I default into self-centeredness automatically unless I deliberately submit to the authority of Christ and the fullness of His free Spirit.

Romans 8:6 tells us that "The mind of sinful man is death, but the mind controlled by the Spirit is life and peace." Even when the Holy Spirit convicts me of sin, the purpose is for life and peace. The Spirit of God edifies the believer. He does not tear us down. When we think according to the flesh, we are often anxious, unnerved, insecure, and fearful. Not to mention greedy, lustful, jealous, and all sorts of things we were never meant to be as Christians.

> We can change the way we think, and that will change the way we feel.

Pray for God to give you a heightened awareness of the way you're thinking. Become alert to times you're thinking according to the flesh. Think about the feeling it is sowing in your heart. I often hear people say, "I can't change the way I feel." No, but we can change the way we think, and that will change the way we feel. Every day and in every situation, we have the invitation to think according to the Spirit or according to the flesh. In the worst of situations—even in the midst of pain and tears—the Spirit of God can still speak life and peace into our hearts. If we want to think according to the Spirit, however, we have to learn to feed the Spirit and starve the flesh.

Underline each phrase below describing an activity that feeds the Spirit.

having lunch with a friend	taking a vacation
studying Scripture	having lunch with a godly friend
listening to Christian music	staying busy
attending a Bible study	memorizing Scripture

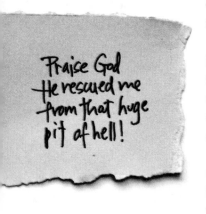

Praise God He rescued me from that huge pit of hell!

Certainly nothing is wrong with having lunch with a friend who may not be a Christian, taking a vacation, or being busy at times; but if God's presence is not invited and involved, the Spirit within us is not fed by these activities.

The less we feed the Spirit of God within us with things that energize Him to fill us, the more His presence "shrinks" within us. Praise God, the opposite is also true. The more we feed the Spirit of God within us and yield to His control, the more His presence will fill and satiate us with life and peace. Let's start catching ourselves when we're thinking destructively and anxiously and see if we're presently feeding the flesh instead of the Spirit.

Remember the dilemma concerning our desire for certain things or people to leave our minds once we've repented? Starving the flesh and feeding the Spirit is the process by which former concentrations on people or things out of God's will finally depart our thoughts. Let's use our two examples from the beginning of today's lesson.

If someone has repented of an ungodly relationship and walked away from it physically, the first thing she must do is tear down the lies and put up the truth. She must begin to meditate on truth that speaks to her specific challenge. She would purposely choose to inundate her mind with things that feed the Spirit and avoid environments or situations that feed the flesh. (If the person is at the same workplace, I would strongly suggest a change in departments or a change in employment. Yes, it's that important!) Over time, the person formerly filling her thoughts will fill them less and less until, finally, the thoughts are neglected and starved to death. This process takes perseverance! Many people give up before the old thoughts give out! I assure you, based on the authority of God's Word, this process works! Give God your complete cooperation and time to renew your mind. You will be victorious and Satan will be defeated.

I want to conclude today with a very important assignment. The second example we discussed toward the beginning of the lesson concerned forgiving someone who has hurt us badly and finally being free from thoughts exalting this hurt. I specifically want you to use this example for your practice time because all of us have been or will be badly hurt by someone. We know people who have harbored bitterness toward others for decades. Whether you are presently being challenged to forgive someone or are willing to prepare for a time when tempted not to forgive, this exercise will help!

On a sheet of paper draw each of the five illustrations vertically down the left side of the page. Write each caption above the illustrations. To the right, write what the person imprisoned by unforgiving thoughts should do to take her thoughts captive to Christ step by step.

When you get to Illustration 3, think of lies an unforgiving person might have wallpapered on her mind that need to be exposed and torn down.

On Illustration 4, do a little research and cite a few Scriptures she could put on the walls of her mind. Remember, don't just look for Scriptures that give negative commands but also positive exhortations.

Beside Illustration 5, describe the thought life of someone who has gone from forgiveness to freedom. Please give lots of effort to this exercise and take it with you to your small group.

Again, I'm not looking for right or wrong answers. My heart's desire is for you to have these illustrations and practices so embedded in your heart and mind that you will always know how to make the transition from captive to blessed captor!

How does God want you to respond to what He showed you today or this week?

1. Francis Frangipane, *Holiness, Truth & the Presence of God* (Robins, Iowa: Arrow Publications, 1986), 60-61.

BREAKING *Free*
session ten viewer guide

The Emphasis of 2 Timothy 3:1-5

- What will most remarkably define the times as "terrible" will be _____ phenomena rather than _____ or _____.

The Construction of 2 Timothy 3:1-5

- Seventeen characteristics fall between two profoundly purposeful bookends.
  "People will be _____ of _____ ... rather than _____ of _____."

Abusive—a word in Greek that especially emphasizes _____.
(*New American Commentary*)

Without love—(Greek *astorgoi*)—_____ toward _____.
(*Strong's Exhaustive Concordance*)

Unforgiving—_____ ... without _____.
(*Word Biblical Commentary*)

Slanderous—*diaboloi* means _____ (Titus 2:3).

Brutal—_____. (*Word Biblical Commentary*)

Treacherous—_____ ready to _____ _____ _____.
(*New American Commentary*)

Conceited—_____ with _____-_____. (*New English Bible*)

The Repetition of 2 Timothy 3:1-5

• Interestingly, 11 out of 18 vices begin with something in Greek called an
"_____ privation" an "a" at the beginning of a word corresponding
with our English "un."

The Warning of 2 Timothy 3:5-7

• The primary target: _____-_____ _____—"The term
is a Greek diminutive, literally suggesting '_____ _____' but
more precisely showing them as easily _____ and _____ to
_____. Their weakness was primarily _____, _____
_____." *(New American Commentary)*

Exercise tremendous caution toward ...

    A. _____: People with a _____ of godliness but
         _____ its power (2 Tim. 3:5). *Form* is the recognizable
       Greek word _____.

    B. _____ _____: "the kind who _____
         _____ _____ into homes."

    C. _____ _____: "the kind who _____ control
       over time."

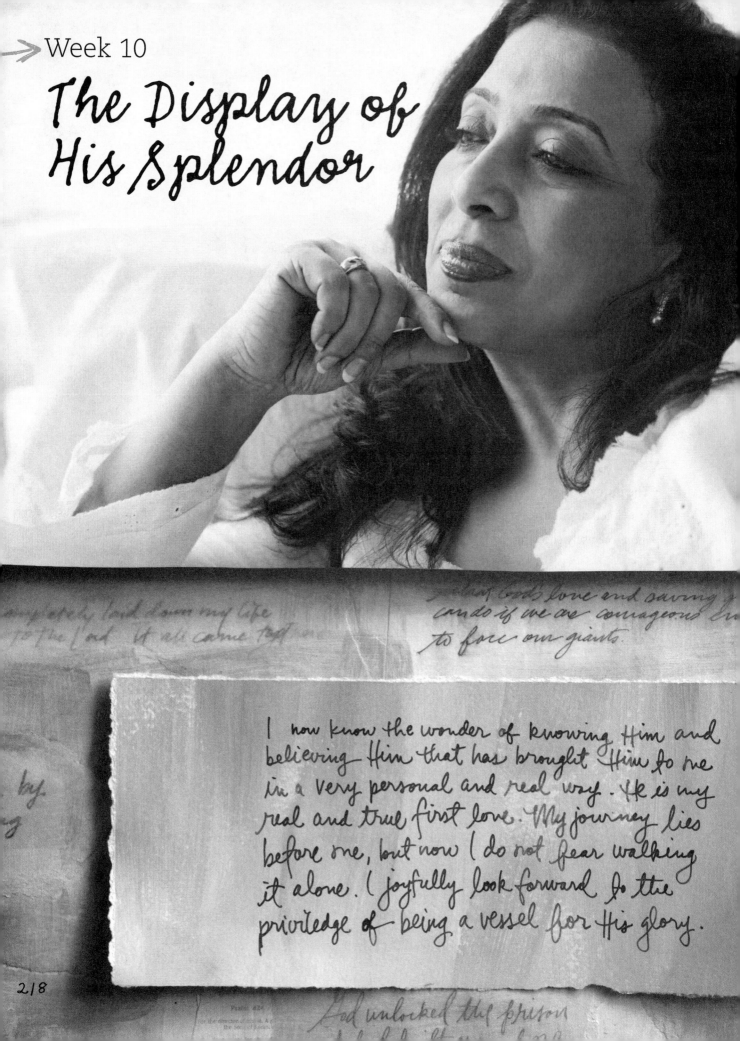

The Display of His Splendor

...ampletely laid down my life ...to the Lord. It all came ...

...plant God's love and saving ...can do if we are courageous ...to face our giants.

...by...

I now know the wonder of knowing Him and believing Him that has brought Him to me in a very personal and real way. He is my real and true first love. My journey lies before me, but now I do not fear walking it alone. I joyfully look forward to the priviledge of being a vessel for His glory.

Psalm 42:1
...the dream of ...
the Second birth

God unlocked the prison

Day 1
A Planting of the Lord

I can hardly believe we are approaching the last miles of our journey together. I pray we will conclude our joint journey with a vivid picture of what freedom looks like. During these last nine weeks we've been learning the active demonstration of the *agape* love Christ wants from us more than anything in life.

Read the familiar words of Mark 12:28-30. What is God's absolute priority commandment for you and me, and according to 1 John 3:18, what form should a genuine love for God take?

Today's Treasure

"They will be called oaks of righteousness, a planting of the LORD for the display of his splendor." **ISAIAH 61:3**

Consider the four areas Jesus named (heart, mind, soul, and strength). We can sing "I love you, Lord" with warm, fuzzy feelings, but our actions reflect the reality of our hearts. We actively love God with all our hearts when we surrender to His authority because we know and rely on the love God has for us (1 John 4:16).

Loving God with all our minds is the most difficult challenge of the four. Everything we studied last week reflects loving God with our minds. Surrendering the inmost places of our thought lives to God and asking Him daily to take control are ways we love God with all our minds. The term *soul* involves the whole person. Psalm 103:1-5 speaks of our actively loving God with all our souls.

The challenge of loving God with all our strength touches my heart right now because I so recently watched someone I love slowly diminish in all areas of physical strength. In this portion of God's priority command I believe He is saying, "Love Me from the basis of whatever physical strength you have. Offer Me your temple for my full habitation in weakness or in strength, in living or in dying."

I watched my weak and dying mother as she tried to move her lips to sing hymns with me in her last hours. In those last hours she loved God with all her strength until He finally came and lifted her burden for her. We love God with all our strength when we give Him all we have, however little, however much. Is your body physically ill or handicapped? Offer it to Him! Love Him with it! He greatly esteems your offering and He will use what you give.

Over the last nine weeks you have been actively living out Mark 12:28-30. This journey has required the full participation of your heart, soul, mind, and strength. If you have fully participated in every lesson and every exercise, you have withheld nothing from Him. This, my highly esteemed friend, has been an exercise in loving God.

Would you be willing to do something right now? In view of all the ground God has plowed on our road to freedom, would you now sing to the Lord a song of praise that means something special to you?

How I pray that all the freshly exposed portions of your heart, soul, mind, and strength have granted you a new and increased capacity to love God. Surely freedom to obey His priority command for each of us is the greatest freedom of all.

If you love Him more today than you did nine weeks ago, this difficult road has been worth traveling. I can't think of anything more appropriate than turning to Isaiah 61:1-4 again. Hopefully you know these verses well by now. Throughout our final week of study we will highlight the last sentence of Isaiah 61:3.

Write the last sentence of Isaiah 61:3 in the margin.

The goal of our journey is wrapped up in this solitary statement. Christ came to set the captives free so they could be called "a planting of the LORD for the display of his splendor." Let's research the meaning of this wonderful, earthly attainable aim. First look at the phrase, "They will be called." The Hebrew word for *called* is *qara* meaning "to cry out, call aloud, roar; to proclaim, pronounce, preach ... celebrate ... to be named; to read aloud." Probably the part of the definition truest to our context is *being named*. I've been called a lot of things in my life, and I can't think of one I wouldn't gladly trade for being called a display of God's splendor!

Perhaps most significant is who will be doing the calling or naming. Will others look on the lives of captives set free and call them displays of God's splendor? Maybe. Often, however, we will find that others won't understand our freedom and may even despise us. We can't count on others always calling us as God sees us! Will angels look on the lives of captives set free and call them displays of God's splendor? Could be. It provokes a nice thought, but the affirmation of angels has never been our goal. So, who will look on the captives set free and call us displays of His splendor? I believe God will.

Read and paraphrase Malachi 3:16-17. Then read Zephaniah 3:14-17.

Psalm 1:1-4

Isaiah 60:21

He celebrates your willingness to be victorious through His might. "He rejoices over you with singing," so put on your dancing shoes and celebrate! He who is mighty to save is delivering you! If you're like me, you may be pretty excited about being called a "display of his splendor," but you may not be all that thrilled about being called a tree. Yet captives set free will be called "oaks of righteousness, a planting of the LORD."

Jeremiah 17:7-8

Read the four references in the margin, and write any insight you gain concerning our representation as an oak, a tree planted by the Lord.

Matthew 12:33

According to Ephesians 3:17, what deeply roots us as plantings of the Lord?

I felt God's love for me.

In Isaiah 61:3 God's Word specifies that we will be called oaks of righteousness. The Hebrew word for *righteousness* is *tsedheq,* reflecting honesty, integrity, liberation. It is righteous conduct that issues from a new heart.

Honesty:

In the margin list a few antonyms (opposites) for the three words reflected by *tsedheq*:

Integrity:

Read Romans 6:20-21 carefully. Then consider these antonyms again. Each one is the bad fruit of an enslaving stronghold. Do they remind you of things you are ashamed of just as they do me? Celebrate the fruit of righteousness that reaps honesty, integrity, and liberation in us! No matter what our strongholds have been, God can plant us deeply in His love, grow us by the water of His Word, and call us "oaks of righteousness." We can be persons of honesty, integrity, and liberation.

Liberation:

As you can see from the definition, these results come only to those who have allowed God to create in each of them a new and clean heart. Take heart if your stronghold was really ugly like mine. Prettier strongholds, like self-righteousness, arrogance, and a judgmental spirit, are far uglier to God because they tend to veil the need for a new heart. See Proverbs 8:13 for a little proof.

Being a tree isn't so bad when you've been planted by the Lord for the express purpose of displaying His splendor! Let's consider what God means by "displays of his splendor." In the original language the words *display* and *splendor* in Isaiah 61:3 are the same Hebrew word. *Pa'ar* means "to embellish, beautify, adorn; to glorify, be glorified; to bring honor, give honor; to boast."[1] To display God's splendor is to radiate His beauty. Can you imagine such a high and wonderful calling? We're called to be the radiance of God's beauty on this earth.

"One thing I ask of the LORD, this is what I seek: that I may dwell in the house of the LORD all the days of my life, to gaze upon the beauty of the LORD and to seek him in his temple."

PSALM 27:4

Like Moses, whose face shone with the glory of God in Exodus 34, the life of a captive set free radiates the splendor of God. Is it any wonder? Any captive who has victoriously made freedom in Christ a reality in life has spent more than a little time in the presence of God.

Psalm 45:11 could be appropriately spoken of any captive who has been set free. Write this verse in the margin.

I served on a leadership team in India with two godly men who were also from the United States. The three of us spoke at several conferences together. Something about them really blessed me. Neither of them could speak without boasting about their wives and talking about how beautiful they were. They never acted like anything but devoted husbands very much in love with their spouses. If they showed their wives' pictures once, they showed them a hundred times! I finally teased them and said, "Gentlemen, it's time for you to go home." Their actions and words captured the essence of the phrase "the display of his splendor."

Look at the very last English synonym in the definition of *pa'ar.* To be a display of God's splendor is to be someone God can boast about! My friend, if you've stuck with God through some pretty tough stuff, let me assure you, He's bragging about you! If you've agreed to go the extra mile with Him and do what-

How does God want you to respond to what He showed you today?

ever freedom requires, God is proud of you! God always loves us lavishly, but imagine God being proud of us and having the privilege of boasting about us.

Imagine Christ, your Bridegroom, boasting about how beautiful you are because of the time you've spent gazing on "the beauty of the LORD" (Ps. 27:4). My heart is leaping at the thought! I am secure in God's love for me, even when I'm not very beautiful, but the idea of giving Him something to boast about sends me! You see, the more we gaze on the beauty of the Lord as we seek Him in His temple, the more our lives absorb and radiate His splendor. Like those two husbands serving in India, God also wants to show off our pictures. His ultimate goal is to display our portraits and say, "Doesn't she look so much like my Son? A remarkable likeness, wouldn't you say?" That's what it means to be a "display of his splendor." A living and visible portrait of the beauty of God.

For the remainder of the week, we will discuss lives God can boast about. Captive set free, this is your destiny.

Day 2
The Display of His Renown

We're exploring qualities God can boast about—elements in lives that display His splendor. Second Peter 1:3-4 tells us that His divine power has given us everything we need for life and for godliness. We fulfill the high calling to display His splendor when we reach up and fully receive the benefits He bowed low to give us.

Read Isaiah 43:1-12. What do verses 8, 10, and 12 suggest God purposes to do with your life?

Today's Treasure
"Yes, LORD, walking in the way of your laws, we wait for you; your name and renown are the desire of our hearts." **ISAIAH 26:8**

You memorized Isaiah 64:4. Paul paraphrased Isaiah's words in 1 Corinthians 2:9 "No eye has seen, no ear has heard, no mind has conceived what God has prepared for those who love him." Christ gave His life so you could be free to live the reality of 1 Corinthians 2:9. Free to become displays of God's splendor. Free to enjoy everything that is yours through the costly covenant God made with you in Christ.

In the margin, please write the five benefits of your covenant relationship with God based on the Book of Isaiah.

1.

2.

3.

4.

5.

One of the most important truths I hope we've learned is that any benefit missing in our individual lives for any length of time is an indicator of a stronghold, an area of defeat. As we approach the conclusion of our journey, we're going to look at each of the benefits one more time. This time, however, we're going to see them fully applied and actively exhibiting the display of His splendor. Let's find out what each benefit looks like at its most beautiful moment.

Take another look at Isaiah 43:10, and fill in the blanks in the margin.

The first benefit of our covenant relationship with God is to know God and believe Him. Isaiah 43:9 states the primary purpose of a witness: "Let them bring in their witnesses to prove they were right, so that others may hear and say, 'It is true.'"

We are never more beautiful portrayals of mortals who know and believe God than when others can look at our lives, hear our testimonies, and say, "It is true." Beloved, that's what it means to be living proof! If you bask in knowing God and dare to believe Him, someone close by has seen truth through your witness whether or not you are aware of the effectiveness of your testimony.

Think of someone who helped authenticate some part of God's Word as a witness to you. In the margin describe what about his or her life made you think, *It is true.*

Now let's watch the portrait of belief painted in Isaiah 43:9-10 evolve into a radiant display of God's splendor. Read Isaiah 26:8.

What is the heart desire of those "walking in the way" of His laws?

"You are my _____," declares the Lord, "and my servant whom I have chosen, so that you may _____ and _____ me and understand that I am he."
ISAIAH 43:10

Consider what Isaiah meant by God's name being the desire of their hearts. Then we will discuss the word *renown*. The Hebrew word for *name* is *shem*. "Semites" comes from this word. Deuteronomy 28:9-10 says: "If you keep the commands of the Lord your God and walk in his ways. Then all the peoples on earth will see that you are called by the name of the Lord, and they will fear you."

God chose one nation to be called by His name. This would be a blessing to all other nations. The "Semites" or Israelites were literally a people of God's name. The concept of a name is far more than a title. *Shem* means "the idea of definite and conspicuous position ... a mark or memorial of individuality. By implication, honor, authority, character" (*Strong's*). Thus the Israelites were called forth as a nation to show the definite and conspicuous position of the one true God in their lives. They were called to be a mark of His individuality and were to show His honor, authority, and character.

Based on what you've just learned, what do you think Isaiah was implying when he said, "Your name [is] ... the desire of our hearts"?

The name you and I are called most in reference to our spiritual beliefs is Christian. We are a people of Christ's name. Based on what we've learned about a name, what should this mean to us? (margin)

In addition to God's name, the writer also said God's renown was the desire of their hearts. The concept of God's renown is the swelling of the acceptance of God's name. We could restate Isaiah 26:8 accurately this way: Your name and Your fame are the desire of our hearts. Stay with me here! Read the very next verse: Isaiah 26:9. What kind of relationship would you say a person had with God if her soul yearned for Him in the night and her spirit longed for Him in the morning?

Without a doubt, the more you know God, the more you want to know God. The more time you spend with Him, the more you will yearn for Him. The opposite is also true. When we spend little time with God, we may ache and feel a loss or emptiness but not the kind of yearning reflected in Isaiah 26:9.

Compare Psalm 63:1-7. How do you know that the yearning described in verse 1 evolved from intimacy with God and not from the emptiness of hardly knowing Him?

The yearning described in Isaiah 26:8-9 and Psalm 63:1-7 comes from the heart and soul of a person who has truly known God. Why is this distinction so important? Because people who know God well want God well-known. No one has to force a person who is intimately acquainted with God to be a living witness. Those who truly know His name (and all it implies) always want His fame.

Our goal of today's lesson is to view Benefit 1. Please trust my heart toward you because I do not have a hint of judgment or condemnation: Do you presently have a yearning for the presence of God? I'm not talking about guilt feelings or even conviction of sin when He's not your priority. Do you feel a yearning for God that draws you over and over into His presence? A yearning that makes only a few days without time in prayer and His Word seem like an eternity?

Your original motivation for this study may have been to find deliverance, but I am praying you've found more of the Deliverer! I believe God can use any motivation to get us into His Word and into prayer, but He wants to refine our motivations until they become first and foremost the desire for Him.

My motivation for Bible study and prayer could still be all about me. Fix my circumstances, Lord. Use me powerfully, Lord. Direct me in obvious ways today, Lord. Make me successful, Lord. Listen carefully: Not one of those prayers is wrong. But if my motivation for my relationship with God is what He can do for me, a lust for His power may grow but a yearning for His presence will not. God deeply desires to hear our petitions, but His greatest joy is to hear them flow from the mouths of those who want Him more than anything else He could give.

The last thing I want you to feel is guilt. Creating awareness is my goal. Awareness is always the first step to freedom. In my late 20s awareness motivated me to begin asking God to give me a heart to love Him and know Him more than

Benefit 1
To know God and believe Him.

We can have a lust for His power without a yearning for His presence.

anything else in life. I don't have the words or space to explain the transformation that has come through this petition. To this day it is my most repeated request for myself. I pray for God's power and for Him to work out my circumstances. I pray for His direction and for His favor. But more than anything, I pray to know Him.

I don't very often use myself as a good example, but I want you to see that God is faithful to turn Isaiah 43:10 into 26:8 for anyone! Once you really know His name, you'll want His fame! What He has made known to you, you will want to make reknown to everyone else. That's the heart's desire of seeking God's renown! Isaiah 26:8 is Isaiah 43:10 displayed in the radiance of God's splendor.

Please allow me to ask several difficult and personal questions. If you had to estimate your present yearning to know and believe God, where would you place an x on the line below?

_____

minimum desire   *my heart's chief yearning*

How quickened is your desire to make Him known at this present time?

_____

minimum desire   *maximum desire*

Let's recap today's point: Knowing God and believing Him displays His splendor most when our soul's desire is for others to know and believe Him too. Be careful what you assume, however. You may be thinking that you lack a yearning for God because you don't have the courage to knock on the doors of strangers and evangelize. Although I have a great respect for knocking on doors and giving out tracts, these are not the only or even the most effective ways we can seek to make God known. Here are just a few of the ways we can share our love for Christ:

- Invite people to Bible study. I'll never forget the letter I received from a group who had studied *A Woman's Heart: God's Dwelling Place*. At the very last meeting the leader asked, "Does anyone have anything to say before we end our journey together?" One of the women who had finished every lesson of that study said, "Yes, I'd like to pray to receive Christ."
- Bring people to church. Let's keep the goal in mind, however. We're not seeking the renown of our denominations. We are seeking God's renown!
- Invite people to Christian concerts or plays.
- Visit with friends or neighbors over coffee or get a little exercise together to provide opportunities for casual conversation in which Christ can be seen as part of your life.
- Support home and international missions through prayer and financial giving.

Oh, God, may we allow You the joy of boasting over us with these words: "My name and My renown were the desire of their hearts."

How does God want you to respond to what He showed you today?

Day 3
The Display of His Glory

Today's Treasure
"'No weapon forged against you will prevail, and you will refute every tongue that accuses you. This is the heritage of the servants of the LORD, and this is their vindication from me,' declares the LORD."
ISAIAH 54:17

As we walk our last couple of miles together, we slow our pace and reflect on five displays of God's splendor. Let's imagine them as landscape portraits propped on easels toward the end of our journey. They help us remember what complete liberty looks like. Each represents lives God can boast about. On day 2 we viewed Benefit 1: To know God and believe Him. Today we'll examine the portrait depicting Benefit 2. On day 4 we'll see portraits of Benefits 3 and 4, and we'll end our journey with the final portrait on day 5.

Now let's consider the portrait of our second benefit. In the margin write Benefit 2 of our covenant relationship with God.

Weeks ago when we studied this benefit, we defined God's glory as the way He makes Himself known or shows Himself mighty. Therefore, when God seeks to glorify Himself through an individual, He proves who He is by causing the believer to be what is otherwise impossible and to do what is otherwise impossible.

A wonderful example of persons living beyond their human responses appears in 2 Corinthians 4:8-9. In one word, how you would characterize the kind of person these words describe?

Read 2 Corinthians 4:7 and 10, the verses that sandwich the testimony above. In the margin describe why God often insists on pushing us beyond our human limitations.

Any time we glorify God we become displays of His splendor, but today I want to paint a portrait of a life that truly withholds nothing from God. A life through which God does something only He can do. We're going to view the ultimate captive set free! I've waited to look at the first Scripture recording captives set free. Let's go back in our biblical time machine to the land of Egypt and hear the groans of the Israelites, the children of God, held fast in a cruel captivity.

Read each portion of Scripture; then give the segment a caption or title. Complete the questions or activities that follow.

1. Exodus 2:23-25; 3:7-10. Your caption:

What does Scripture mean by the words "he remembered" (2:24)?

Virtually every time you see God described as remembering someone, He moves to act in their behalf as in Exodus 3:8. He remembered, so He came to rescue.

How does this scene apply to us? God knows our suffering from the first pang, but He wants to hear us cry out specifically for His help. God never misses a groan or cry of His children. He always has a rescue planned. When the time is right, God will move in behalf of His children. God will keep His Word. We've each been in Egypt at some time, but the Israelites were enslaved for 400 years.

How long were you in your own Egypt?

2. Exodus 12:21-30. Your caption:

If you are tenderhearted as I am, this scene is hard to imagine. Keep in mind our God knew what deliverance of His children would cost. He would one day lay down the life of His own Son so that any captive, Jew or Gentile, could be free. While God set His plan in motion, He demanded preparation out of His people.

The same is true for us. God sent Christ to set the captives free, but He demands our attention and preparation. He wants us never to forget that blood was shed by the perfect Lamb of God so we could be delivered. We have no door of escape unless the doorpost has been painted with the blood of Christ.

3. Exodus 12:31-36. Your caption:

Now the application gets to be fun. The Hebrew word for *plunder* is *nasal*, meaning "to snatch away." When God delivers His children, they never have to escape by the skin of their teeth! The Israelites were impoverished slaves in Egypt, but when God delivered them, they left with the riches of the Egyptians. We can draw a wonderful parallel from this event. In the classic *Streams in the Desert*, Mrs. Charles E. Cowman expresses this wonderful phenomenon better than I can.

> The gospel is so arranged and the gift of God so great that you may take the very enemies that fight you and the forces that are arrayed against you and make them steps up to the very gates of heaven and into the presence of God … God wants of every one of His children, to be more than conqueror … You know when one army is more than conqueror it is likely to drive the other from the field, to get all the ammunition, the food and supplies, and to take possession of the whole … There are spoils to be taken!
>
> Beloved, have you got them? When you went into that terrible valley of suffering did you come out of it with spoils? When that injury struck you and you thought everything was gone, did you so trust in God that you came out richer than you went in? To be more than conqueror is to take the spoils from the enemy and appropriate them to yourself. What he had arranged for your overthrow, take and appropriate for yourself.[2]

Beloved, what about you? Did you come out of your Egypt, your time of slavery, with plunder from the enemy? Did you give the enemy an offensive blow by allowing God to bring you out of your captivity twice the person you were when you went in?

 What did God promise in His covenant in Genesis 15:14? (margin)

Don't forget! What God appropriated to the nation of Israel in a tangible sense, we can almost always see applied to New Testament believers in a spiritual sense. He wants to bring us out of our times of captivity with possessions!

Check out Exodus 12:35 one more time. Fill in the following blank: "The Israelites did as Moses instructed and asked the Egyptians for articles of _____ and _____ and for clothing."

We'll see that they also escaped with jewelry. Remember, they had nothing in slavery, but God delivered them with riches. Read 1 Corinthians 3:12-13.

God desires to accomplish works in our lives that stand up to the flames of fiery trials. The wood, hay, and straw in these verses represent works that go up in flames the moment a fire ignites. Gold, silver, and costly stones represent works that endure. Do you realize you don't have to escape from captivity with nothing to show for it? After all the enemy has put you through, take your plunder. Let God bring you forth from your time of slavery with gold, silver, and costly stones. Stronger than ever because in your weakness God was strong. More of a threat to the kingdom of darkness than Satan ever dreamed you'd be. Steal back from the thief who came against you to steal, kill, and destroy! Don't just reclaim surrendered ground. God wants to enlarge your borders and teach you to possess land you never knew existed. Make the enemy pay for scheming against you so hatefully. Snatch the plunder! Oh, how I pray that you are already aware of plunder you stole from the enemy after God delivered you from a time of slavery.

What is your plunder? Don't hold back. You are boasting in the Lord your God! By His mighty power you have escaped richer than before.

Oh, my friend, I beg you. Let God have your failures. Surrender to Him your most dreadful times of slavery. Your most humiliating defeats. God and God alone can use them to make you twice the warrior you ever dreamed you'd be. Let there be plunder! There's more! Let's see this plunder become a display of God's splendor.

4. Exodus 35:4-29. Your caption:

The Israelites had few possessions in Egypt. Where do you suppose they got the gold, silver, and the fabrics described in Exodus 35:5-6?

If you answered the plunder of the Egyptians, you are right on target. The Israelites reinvested the plunder by offering it right back to God. A God who can take a few simple fish and loaves and multiply them to feed thousands. A God of awesome returns. OK, you draw your own parallel on this point.

In the margin describe how a person can reinvest the plunder she or he brings out of captivity. Give this some thought.

Have you already had an opportunity to offer your plunder to God as a reinvestment and see Him bring greater returns? ☐ Yes ☐ No Explain.

While I was still a sinner, Christ died for me. And He heard the groans of my self-imposed slavery, and He … the God of the universe … His holiness … His majesty … looked on my ugliness and called this captive free. And was there plunder? Beloved, you are staring it in the face right this moment. This book, for whatever it's worth, is nothing but plunder. Every line of this book is what God allowed me to take from my seasons in Egypt's humiliation. I deserved to be placed on a shelf and simply live out my time patiently until the glory of heaven. Instead, God chose to use the very things Satan used to defeat me to teach me. How could I not pour my life back into God? He is the only reason I have survived—let alone thrived.

Dear friend of God, you become a display of His splendor every time you take the plunder of Egypt and offer it back to God for His magnificent glory. If you have repented and escaped from Egypt, don't hang your head another minute. God will force the enemy to give up plunder to you, but if your head is not lifted up in expectation, you might not catch it.

I want to share one final word of testimony with you. Some days I don't feel like being vulnerable or transparent, no matter who it would help. Some days I want to forget I've ever been to Egypt. Some days I just want to act like I've always done it right. Some days I don't want to give. I want to take. And some days I just want everybody out of my personal business. My times in Egypt are very painful for me to remember. Embarrassing for me to admit. Leaving nothing for others to admire. Some days I think I just can't do it. But each morning the Holy Spirit woos me once again to the place where I meet with God. The God of grace bows low and meets with me. In the simplicity of my prayer time, I am suddenly confronted by the majesty of my Redeemer. The One who is responsible for any good in me. My past sins are forgiven, and fresh mercies fall like manna from heaven. And once again, my heart is moved, and I surrender all. Morning after morning.

How does God want you to respond to what He showed you today?

Day 4
The Display of Satisfaction and Peace

Today's Treasure

"The LORD will guide you always; he will satisfy your needs in a sun-scorched land and will strengthen your frame. You will be like a well-watered garden, like a spring whose waters never fail." **ISAIAH 58:11**

Today we're going to look at Benefits 3 and 4 in full display of God's splendor. Our goal is to see these two benefits at the summit of their beauty—as displays of God's splendor. We have lots to accomplish so let's get started. First, consider:

*1. **The Display of Satisfaction Found in God.*** We simply must find satisfaction in God (Benefit 3) because dissatisfaction or emptiness waves a red flag to the enemy. The empty places in our lives become the enemy's playground. Picture a spacious, green golf course. The flags tell the golfer where the holes are. Something similar happens to us in the unseen. None of us have reached adulthood without some holes in our lives. Some have more than others due to hurts and traumas, but we all have holes. You can be sure the enemy has flagged every hole as a target. We spend untold energies in anger and bitterness over why those holes exist and who is to blame. Healing begins when we recognize how vulnerable those empty places make us, tally the cost of filling them with useless things, and seek wholeness in Christ alone. In my opinion, wholeness in Christ is that state of being when every hole has been filled by Christ.

No one can take away the holes my childhood traumas left. The damage cannot be undone. It must be healed. The holes can't be taken away, but they can be filled. As we take our last look at satisfaction in Christ, our goal is to see satisfaction at its greatest beauty. We want to see a picture of a satisfied person fully displaying God's splendor. Isaiah 58 paints the portrait perfectly. Let's step up to the easel and take a good look.

Read Isaiah 58:6-12, and in the margin write a one-sentence summary expressing the heart of this passage.

God inspired the prophet Isaiah to pen a play on words. The Holy Spirit expresses a beautiful paradox in these verses. Careful meditation brings two themes to the surface—themes that seem to be virtually opposite concepts.

Theme 1 (v. 6): The kind of _____ [God] has chosen.

Theme 2 (v. 11): [The Lord] will _____ your needs in a sun-scorched land.

While fasting speaks of emptiness, satisfaction speaks of fullness. How does God bring both concepts together? He promises that those who empty themselves of other pleasures will have themselves filled by something only He can give.

✳ Compare verses 10 and 11. What statement can you make drawing
together the themes of self-denial and satisfaction?

You may have said something like: If we pour out our lives to satisfy the needs
of the oppressed, God will be faithful to satisfy our needs. No matter how you
worded your statement, if you reflected the idea, you grasped the concept.

Reflect on the fasting God has chosen. Usually we think of fasting as avoiding
food for the purpose of prayer. Our empty stomachs remind us to pray. Although
New Testament Scripture often speaks of fasting from food for the purpose of
prayer, Isaiah 58 speaks of a fasting I believe God may honor most of all. Allow
me to offer you a bit of a brain cracker. I've spent some time on this question, and
I don't think it's an easy one to answer. Don't look for just one thing.

What is God proposing we fast from in these verses? In the margin list
as many possibilities as you can. Perhaps a leading question might help.
"What do we have to give up or fast from to reach out to the oppressed?"

God took me to the other side of the world to supply a few answers to these
questions. In India these verses came to my mind more than any others. If you're
looking for a fun little mission trip, keep India out of your travel plans. I'm not
sure any other nation is quite like India. You never get away from its suffering.
Pain follows you down the streets in the form of orphaned, filthy beggars. It penetrates your hotel room with the eerie sound of Hindu music played to appease at
least 300 million gods. Agony stings your eyes as you stare at the sea of poverty.
It wretches in your throat when you smell the rotting flesh blocks away from the
leper colony. When I returned, people asked me if I had a good time. No. Actually,
I didn't have a good time. I had a profound time. I will never be the same. I can't
forget what I saw.

What kind of fast did God require of me as He sent me to minister one-
on-one to the oppressed? A fast from comfort. A fast from my pretty little world.
A fast from rose-colored glasses. The fast I enjoy in Houston, as freeways loop
around the inner city to keep me from facing the poor. I can live days on end here,
stay in my very own neighborhood, and choose to deal only with pretty problems
that smell better. I can choose to fast from poverty and oppression. But if I do, I'll
never have a heart like God's.

One of the purposes of a fast is for the emptiness to prompt us to a spiritual
response. The emptiness in the people of India brought back vivid memories of
my own at one time. So many things tore at my heart. The faces most engraved
on my heart are those of the women. Heads covered. Meek. Many to the point of
seeming shamed. I stood in a village with raw sewage running only a few feet from
me and spoke to four women through an interpreter. I wasn't planning to. The
Spirit just came over me. I touched their faces and told them they were so beautiful. I told them that God saw them with great dignity and honor. Like princesses.
Within a few moments four women turned into many. I still can't think about it

I completely laid down my life to the Lord.

without crying. They wept, held on to me, and were willing to do anything to receive such a Savior. They knew their circumstances might never change, but one day they would lay down this life and wake up in the splendor of God's presence. Do you know what God used to provoke a bond between those women and me? A very acute memory of my own former emptiness and oppression.

Beloved, we don't have to go to the other side of the world to reach out to the oppressed. Oh, how I pray we will each discover glorious satisfaction in Christ; but when it's the real thing, we must find a place to pour the overflow of our lives. Captives truly set free are the most compassionate people in the world. They don't see others as less than themselves, because they've lived a little of their own lives in the gutter too.

Our motivations for reaching out and serving others aren't always pure. My dear friend Kathy Troccoli, who ministers full-time, asked a critical question: "Am I ministering out of my need or out of the overflow of my own relationship with God?" We would be wise to ask ourselves the same question. Do we crave the affirmation of those we serve, and do they help us feel important? Or do we serve because Jesus has so filled our hearts that we must find a place to pour the overflow? A ministry to the truly oppressed helps purify our serving motives. You see, they don't have much to give back. The satisfied soul is never a more beautiful display of God's splendor than when willing to empty self for the lives of others.

> Am I ministering out of my need or out of the overflow of my own relationship with God?

In the margin, please write your own testimony of a time when you discovered a deep filling of soul after emptying your life out for another.

2. The Display of God's Peace. The fourth benefit of our covenant relationship is to experience God's peace. What might the peace of God in the soul of a person look like at its most beautiful moment? When does peace become an eye-catching display of God's splendor?

Turn back to the beginning of our journey and quickly review week 2, day 4. Read Isaiah 48:18. Glance through the lesson until you discover where we stated the key to peace. What is it? Choose one.

☐ salvation   ☐ serving   ☐ loving God
☐ loving others   ☐ submitting to God's authority

I hope you remembered the key to peace even before you reviewed the lesson. Isaiah 48:18 infers that we have "peace ... like a river" when we pay attention to God's commands. Therefore, the key to peace in each of our lives is submitting to God's authority through obedience.

Think of the last time obedience to God was momentarily not much fun. Describe the experience in general terms.

Obedience to God's authority doesn't come easily for any of us. I heard a preacher I admire say that the life of the disciple requires a "long obedience in the same direction." Isn't that a great expression of truth? So are we saddled with nothing but sacrifices? Hardly. Let's consider peace at its most beautiful moment.

Read Isaiah 52:7-9. In the margin describe the relationship that develops between peace and joy.

You may have noticed that I tend to be a little demonstrative, so I really love the picture these verses paint of joy. Shouts for joy! Songs of joy!

Now fill in the blanks in one of my very favorite verses in the Book of Isaiah, chapter 55, verse 12:

"You will go out in _____ and be led forth in _____;
the mountains and hills will burst into _____ before you,
and all the trees of the field will _____ their hands."

Don't stop there! Take a look forward at Isaiah 58 and read verses 13 and 14. How would they find (their) joy in the Lord?
☐ fellowship with one another   ☐ obedience to God's commands

Obedience to God often entails not going our own way, not doing as we please, and not even speaking as we please. But if peace is the fruit of righteousness (Isa. 32:17), then joy is the wine from the fruit! Joy ultimately flows from obedience, and few things display God's splendor more appealingly than joy! Think I'm stretching the analogy a bit? Check out John 15. "I am the true vine, and my Father is the gardener … If a man remains in me and I in him, he will bear much fruit … This is to my Father's glory, that you bear much fruit … If you obey my commands, you will remain in my love … I have told you this so that my joy may be in you and that your joy may be complete" (John 15:1,5,8,10-11).

Slap Isaiah 32:17 next to John 15 and here's what you get: Peace is the fruit of righteousness that, in essence, is obedience to God's commands—the product of abiding in the vine. The wine that flows from the ripened fruit is joy! Close today's lesson with a celebration verse that puts it all together in a display of God's splendor.

What is the kingdom of God according to Romans 14:17-18?

How does God want you to respond to what He showed you today?

You've got it! The wine of joy will eventually flow from the fruit of peace produced by righteousness. "Weeping may endure for a night, but joy cometh in the morning" (Ps. 30:5, KJV). God will look on you in the full harvest of your obedience, and perhaps He'll say something like my grandmother used to say when I was all dressed up (buck teeth and all): "Girl, you sho is purty."

Or maybe He'll say, "Woman, you sure are a display of My splendor."

Day 5
The Display of His Presence

Today's Treasure

"The LORD is the stronghold of my life—of whom shall I be afraid?" **PSALM 27:1**

I never fail to cry as I write the final lesson of any Bible study journey, but I'm at full sob now. Each of the journeys God has allowed me to take through His Word have meant the world to me, but this one has been in a league all its own. *Breaking Free* has undoubtedly been the most difficult Bible study I've ever written. God wanted this study to come from a fresh heart with the tenderness and deep passion only true brokenness can bring. Hurts and losses occurred during this time that could not have been coincidental. I have no idea how this Bible study will be received. I don't even know if it's good. But it's real. And God is good.

I feel a little like I did returning from India. I can't say this trip has been fun, but I won't soon forget it. Never will I be able to express my gratitude to you for sticking with the demands of this journey. Oh how I pray God will engrave— not my truth—but His truth on your heart forever. Anything at all that has been accomplished has been God. We conclude our journey together with a look at the fifth benefit of our relationship with God in its full display of His splendor. Please write Benefit 5 in the margin from memory.

The Book of Isaiah is so rich. I could not imagine how I would ever be able to choose a final passage for our journey. I believe God has chosen one for us: the best possible place in Isaiah to bid one another Godspeed as we travel on alone.

Read the familiar words of Isaiah 40:28-31 and savor every word. In the margin write your favorite part of these verses.

Peace came at last.

We live in a spiritual battle. I believe God's Word indicates spiritual warfare and demonic deceptions will worsen as time goes on. In heaven we'll undoubtedly be "Free at last!" Until then, we're challenged to make our newfound freedom last!

I'm praying for three goals to be accomplished as we part: (1) that if you are not yet free, you will cooperate with God fully until you are, (2) that you will know how to maintain your freedom, and (3) that you'll always know how to get back to the freedom trail if you ever lose your way. Sometimes I get tired of fighting the good fight, don't you? How can we muster the energy to hang in there and keep fighting for our liberty? For heaven's sake, even the youth grow tired and weary and young men stumble and fall. If you're like me, you're neither young nor male! We could be in big trouble! So, what's a soul to do?

✳ I believe Isaiah 40:28-31 tells us exactly what to do when we get weary in the walk. Whose strength will the Lord renew? (margin)

What does Scripture mean by the phrase *hope in the Lord?* The Hebrew word for *hope* (KJV, "wait upon") is *qawah* meaning "to bind together (by twisting) ... to be gathered together, be joined; to meet; to lie in wait for someone; to expect … to be confident, trust; to be enduring."

Read Isaiah 40:31 once more and insert these synonyms in the place of the words *hope in*. **Based on your own conclusions, what do you think Isaiah meant by "hope in the Lord"? (margin)**

Beloved, if we want to keep a renewed strength to face our daily challenges or regain a strength that has faded, God's Word tells us to draw so close to the presence of God we're practically twisted to Him! The thought of fighting our way through life is exhausting. Can you think of anything more arduous than waking up to win every single day? I could probably do it about four days a week. The other three days I'd want to wake up, push snooze, and go back to sleep.

There's got to be a better way. I believe Isaiah 40:31 is telling us to wrap ourselves so tightly around God that we end up automatically going where He's going. And, never forget, the only way He's going is to victory (2 Cor. 2:14). God doesn't want our goal to be to win. He wants our goal to be to win Christ. Look at Philippians 3:8-9. The New International Version uses the words "that I may gain Christ" and the King James Version uses the words "that I may win Christ." No one had more to say about warfare and fighting the good fight than the apostle Paul; yet his primary goal was not to win, but to win Christ. The very next phrase explains what the apostle meant by winning Christ.

What is the first phrase in Philippians 3:9?

Being "found in Christ" is the very same idea as "hope in the Lord" in Isaiah 40:31. Both describe binding self to God. When my children were little, if I wouldn't stop to play with them, they would hold on to my waist and wrap their legs around one of mine. I'd whistle, go about my business, and say, "I wonder what Amanda (or Melissa) is doing right now?" They would laugh hysterically. My heart never failed to be overwhelmed with love because I realized that their favorite game was to hang on to me! My muscles might ache afterward, but it was worth it.

To "hope in the Lord" is to do with God what my children did with me. To wrap ourselves around Him as tightly as we can. Why does Isaiah 40:31 present the concept of binding ourselves to God in context with being weary and faint? Think about the game my children and I played. Who did most of the work? I did! What was their part in the game? Binding themselves to me and hanging on tight. Do you see the parallel? When we start feeling weary, like stepping out of the way for a while, we're probably taking on too much of the battle ourselves.

Isaiah 40:31 offers the perfect prescription for former captives who sometimes get tired in their struggle to maintain freedom: Seek the presence of God and hang on to Him. Go where He goes and let Him fight for you. Invariably when we're most exhausted, we'll find we're expending more energy fighting the enemy than we are seeking God's presence. More than you seek to win, seek Christ! More than you seek to defeat the enemy, seek his Foe! More than you seek victory, seek the Victor! As you do, you are binding yourself to His presence and trusting God to carry you on to victory. You'll never be more beautiful to God than when He can look down and see you hanging on to Him for dear life!

Can you confirm experientially the concept we're considering? Offer a little feedback in the margin concerning the relationship between weariness and self-effort or renewed strength and the presence of God.

We're approaching the last steps of our journey together. We each have a different road ahead of us, but we all have the same glorious destination. My precious friend, we have shared some awesome moments the last 10 weeks, but now it's time for us to go our separate ways with God. I'll miss you and you may miss me too, but please never confuse missing my companionship along the way with needing my companionship. You don't need me. Not in the least. I leave you in the hands of the only One you need. Cling only to Him, the One who will lead you on until He leads you home—where once and for all, you'll be free at last.

Right this moment I feel a little like I did when I left my Amanda at college for the first time. Humor me for a moment and allow me to say a few motherly things before we go. Remember, we never find freedom from bondage in independence. We find it by taking the same handcuffs that once bound us to sin and binding ourselves to the wrist of Christ. When you're imprisoned in the will of God, your cell becomes the Holy of Holies. Never forget, there is only one Stronghold that frees when it binds.

Read Today's Treasure aloud; then write 2 Samuel 22:2-4 in the margin.

How does God want you to respond to what He showed you today?

I'm so proud of you, I can hardly stand it. You've worked so hard. More importantly, God is proud of you. You are someone God wants to boast about. For just a moment, don't think about how far you have to go. Just think about how far you've come. Just rest for a few minutes. No transparency required. No vulnerability. No telling on yourself. No looking in. Just look up. For a moment, sit back and let me pray Psalm 32:7 over you: May God be your hiding place, may He protect you from trouble, and may He incline your spiritual ears to listen carefully while He surrounds you with songs of deliverance. I come down to my knees in your honor and in God's. You, my fellow sojourner, are a display of His splendor. I am humbled beyond description for the privilege of walking this road with you.

Nothing could be more appropriate than concluding with Isaiah 61:1-4. Read or quote the verses, and allow God to bring back to your memory the torrents of truth we've studied. May this prayer God wrote on my heart bring summation to our journey and provide a fitting farewell.

1. Spiros Zodhiates, ed., *The Hebrew-Greek Key Word Study Bible* (Chattanooga, TN; AMG Publishers, 1996), 1543
2. Mrs. Charles E. Cowman, *Streams in the Desert* (Los Angeles: The Oriental Missionary Society, 1933), 362.

A Healing Captive

O, God, Who frees the captive

Do not liberate this carnal slave for freedom's sake
For I will surely wing my flight to another thorny land.
Break, instead, each evil bond
And rub my swollen wrists,
Then take me prisoner to Your will
Enslaved in Your safekeeping.
O, God, Who ushers light into the darkness,
Do not release me to the light
To only see myself.
Cast the light of my liberation upon Your face
And be Thou my vision.
Do not hand me over
To the quest of greater knowledge.
Make Your Word a lamp unto my feet
And a light unto my path
And lead me to Your dwelling.

O, God, Who lifts the grieving head,

Blow away the ashes
But let Your gentle hand upon my brow
Be my only crown of beauty.
Comfort me so deeply,
My Healer,
That I seek no other comfort.

O, God, Who loves the human soul

Too much to let it go,
So thoroughly impose Yourself
Into the heaps and depths of my life
That nothing remains undisturbed.
Plow this life, Lord,
Until everything You overturn
Becomes a fertile soil,
Then plant me, O God
In the vast plain of Your love.
Grow me, strengthen me,
And do not lift Your pressing hand
Until it can boastfully unveil
A display of Your splendor.

This is my life story.
Praise God for writing it!

I love you, Sister.

BREAKING *Free*

session eleven viewer guide

Identifying ourselves *daily* by God's own descriptions will profoundly impact our sustained success.

1. We are _____ (Isa. 43:10-12).

2. We are _____ (Isa. 54:12-17).

   Never forget …

   • The tie between _____ and _____.
     "Be far from _____, because you need _____ _____, and from terror, because it will not come near you." (*New International Commentary on the New Testament*)

   • The tendency to expend energy on the _____ _____.
     "Direct my _____ according to your word; let no sin _____ _____ _____" (Ps. 119:133).

3. We are _____(Isa. 61:10).

Hephzibah: "My-_____-Is-in-_____" *(New International Commentary on the New Testament)*

Beulah: "_____. The basic sense of the word is 'to possess.'"
(New International Commentary on the New Testament)

"When circumstances and _____ and blighted _____ combine to convince us that our name is '_____,' that is the hour to hear the _____ of the Bridegroom to his Bride, with the name that it is his _____ ____ _____ and hers _____ ____ _____."
(New International Commentary on the New Testament)

How do we conclude our journey?

Nehemiah 9:36-38

- "making"—*karat*—to cut ... to make a _____."
  (Old Testament Lexical Aids)

- "binding agreement"—*amanah*—from *aman*—"to believe, trust." *Amanah*
  means "covenant, _____ _____, _____ provision."

BETH MOORE

a Bible study library

ASK A QUESTION, GRAB A FRIEND, START A STUDY, CHANGE YOUR LIFE.

How can I ... become a woman of integrity?

Develop integrity in our modern-day culture. Explore prophecies from the Books of Daniel to Revelation in **Daniel: Lives of Integrity, Words of Prophecy**.

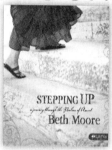

How do I ... talk to God?

Learn to voice your own petitions and praises to our God, who is always available and ready hear us. **Stepping Up: A Journey Through the Psalms of Ascent** leads you to find unit joy, gratitude, redemption, repentance, the power of blessings, and more.

What do I really know about ... the God of history?

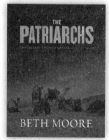

Plunge into **The Patriarchs: Encountering the God of Abraham, Isaac, and Jacob** to discover the heart of Genesis and the unfolding of His earthly plan: that through one nation—and ultimately, one man—all people on earth will be blessed.

Who ... was Jesus really?

Get to know Jesus intimately, as though you had walked with Him during His days of ministry on earth, through the careful examination of the life of Christ in **Jesus the One and Only**.

What does God want ... to do through me?

God desires to dwell among His people and in our hearts. Discover the parallels of the tabernacle's building and your life as a chosen vessel of God with **A Woman's Heart: God's Dwelling Place**.

Why is God's love ... hard to feel sometimes?

Do you want to understand the depths of God's amazing love? Study the life of David and his relationship with God in **A Heart Like His: Seeking the Heart of God Through a Study of David**.

LIFEWAY.COM/WOMEN | 1.800.458.2772

LifeWay | Wome

Week 2

"You are my witnesses," declares the Lord,
"and my servant whom I have chosen,
so that you may know and believe me
and understand that I am he.
Before me no god was formed,
nor will there be one after me."

ISAIAH 43:10

Week 1

The Spirit of the Sovereign Lord is on me,
because the Lord has anointed me
to preach good news to the poor.
He has sent me to bind up the brokenhearted,
to proclaim freedom for the captives
and release from darkness for the prisoners ...

ISAIAH 61:1

Week 4

They will rebuild the ancient ruins
and restore the places long devastated;
they will renew the ruined cities
that have been devastated for generations.

ISAIAH 61:4

Week 3

Since ancient times no one has heard,
no ear has perceived,
no eye has seen any God besides you,
who acts on behalf of those who
wait for him.

ISAIAH 64:4

Week 6

... and provide for those who grieve in Zion
to bestow on them a crown of beauty instead of ashes,
the oil of gladness instead of mourning,
and a garment of praise instead of a spirit of despair.
They will be called oaks of righteousness,
a planting of the Lord for the display of his splendor.

ISAIAH 61:3

Week 5

... to proclaim the year of the Lord's favor
and the day of vengeance of our God,
to comfort all who mourn

ISAIAH 61:2

Week 8

"Though the mountains be shaken
and the hills be removed,
yet my unfailing love for you will not be shaken
nor my covenant of peace be removed,"
says the Lord, who has compassion on you.

ISAIAH 54:10

Week 7

"Remember the former things, those of long ago;
I am God, and there is no other;
I am God, and there is none like me."

ISAIAH 46:9

Week 10

"No weapon forged against
you will prevail."

ISAIAH 54:17

Week 9

You will keep in perfect peace
him whose mind is steadfast,
because he trusts in you.

ISAIAH 26:3